COLONIAL WILLIAMSBURG

Revised Edition

COLONIAL WILLIAMSBURG

By Philip Kopper ∼ *Original Photography by Langdon Clay*

HARRY N. ABRAMS, INC., PUBLISHERS, *in association with* THE COLONIAL WILLIAMSBURG FOUNDATION

In words borrowed from a marble stone in Bruton Parish Church, the first edition of this book was dedicated to "a gentleman of the most amiable disposition, generous, just and mild, and possessed in an eminent degree of all the social virtues," to wit my beloved brother, Wm. Bruce Kopper, Esq.

~

Likewise this second edition is inscribed to him and dedicated also to our younger kinsman, who as a toddler made that selfsame Bruton Parish churchyard his playground and Duke of Gloucester Street his first highroad, to wit my brother's nephew and namesake, my own pride, my joy, my hero and hope, my perpetual surprise, my beloved son, Timothy Dana Bruce Kopper.

For the Revised Edition:
PROJECT MANAGER: Margaret Rennolds Chace
EDITOR: Elaine Stainton
DESIGNER: Brankica Kovrlija

Library of Congress Cataloging-in-Publication Data

Kopper, Philip.
   Colonial Williamsburg / by Philip Kopper ; original photography by Langdon Clay.–2nd ed.
      p. cm.
   Includes index.
      ISBN 0-8109-0609-0
      1. Williamsburg (Va.)–History. I. Clay, Langdon, 1949- II. Colonial Williamsburg Foundation. III. Title.
      F234.W7 K67 2001
      976.5'4252–dc21

                                     2001002277

Printed and bound in Hong Kong
10 9 8 7 6 5 4 3 2 1

Harry N. Abrams, Inc
100 Fifth Avenue
New York, N.Y. 10011
www.abramsbooks.com

HALF-TITLE PAGE: Molded and rubbed bricks adorn the Governor's Palace, one of the crown jewels of Williamsburg architecture.

TITLE PAGE: The cupola and upper stories of the Governor's Palace, a building reconstructed as faithfully to the 1722 original as research and historical technology allowed in the 1930s.

CONTENTS

FOREWORD

The purpose of Colonial Williamsburg is to recreate, accurately, the environment of the men and women of eighteenth-century Williamsburg, and to bring about such an understanding of their lives and times that present and future generations may more vividly appreciate the contribution of these early Americans to the ideals and culture of our country.

John D. Rockefeller, Jr.

A telegrapher dispatched the message from New York in twenty-three cryptic words, a single unpunctuated sentence written in what amounted to a code: "AUTHORIZE PURCHASE OF ANTIQUE REFERRED TO IN YOUR LONG LETTER OF DECEMBER FOURTH AT EIGHT ON BASIS OUTLINED IN SHORTER LETTER SAME DATE." Thirty-seven minutes and one relay later, the wire cleared the Western Union desk in Williamsburg. The teletype keys rattled off a secret signature: "DAVIDS FATHER." It was 11:28 A.M. Tuesday, December 7, 1926, the instant when time divided what Williamsburg had been from what Williamsburg would be; or perhaps more accurately, the instant when it was ordained that Williamsburg would become once again what it had been more than a century earlier.

The reprinting of Philip Kopper's revised *Colonial Williamsburg* commemorates the seventy-fifth anniversary of that moment. It helps us understand just what that telegram meant to America. It tells a story of inspiration, preservation, and restoration. From the time of the wire, John D. Rockefeller, Jr., and the Reverend Dr. W. A. R. Goodwin began to assemble the homes and shops, the gardens and greens of the only American capital capable of re-creation in its eighteenth-century form. Kopper's account of what made the town worth the time, the trouble, and the considerable expense is as readable as the tale of how it was done, and as thoughtful as his examination of what has become of this bold initiative.

Why it matters is a question just as interesting. What if there had been no telegram?

Colonial Williamsburg is a place fashioned not only of bricks and of lumber but of time and of ideas. A million or more visitors come to the Historic Area each year to gain a deeper understanding of how the eighteenth-century residents of Williamsburg became Americans. They come to learn about America as it became a nation, about another moment in time on the boundary between what was and what would be. They come to experience and understand the past.

Understanding.

That was important to Mr. Rockefeller—that Americans have this opportunity not only to understand the past but also to understand why what happened in Williamsburg remains so relevant to their lives today.

Rich in colonial homes, rare livestock, fine museums, working trades sites, uncommon artifacts, and careful reconstructions, Colonial Williamsburg embodies another of his goals: "That the future may learn from the past." Peopled with interpreters, researchers, tradespeople, and visitors, this is an educational institution that teaches an appreciation of what the eighteenth-century Americans bequeathed to the nation they helped to create. The lessons come down to us from men and women, black and white, who strode Williamsburg's streets on the eve of our Revolution. Not just Thomas Jefferson but his body servant Jupiter; not merely George Washington but his Martha; not only Patrick Henry but Clementina Rind.

Walking where they walked, seeing what they saw, hearing what they heard, doing what they did, we come to the readiest understanding of their lives and their times, far closer than we might in a textbook or a classroom. Understanding through experience is what the eighteenth century's Doctor Samuel Johnson thought of as the difference "between a man who knew how a watch was made and a man who could tell the hour by looking at the dial plate." Any Colonial Williamsburg visitor who has helped a carpenter plane a weatherboard, chatted with Peyton Randolph, sat on a courthouse jury, or marched up Duke of Gloucester Street with the Fife and Drum Corps knows what Johnson had in mind.

Doctor Goodwin probably said it as well as anyone could seventy-five years ago as he sought a philanthropist to share his restoration dream. "You can talk about history in lecture rooms, and in books, but it all seems very far away," he said. "When, however, people are brought face to face with the very houses in which historic personages lived, and with the buildings where historic events took place, and where history was actually made, the past becomes real to the present, and if these places can be preserved, the past will be made real to the future. If this town could be secured as a whole, it could be converted into a visible school of history and of historical associations."

Think for a moment of the Declaration of Independence. Its ideas are not original—nor were they intended to be—and the document itself is only a transcription of a spoiled and soon discarded original. What makes the Declaration dear is its power to evoke the ideals of justice and liberty. To sit and read Jefferson's words is to be inspired.

But to stand in Duke of Gloucester Street on the Fourth of July and hear an interpreter representing the colonial mayor read the Declaration from the courthouse steps is to understand them anew. It is to experience how, in 1776, the moment must have been, on that very spot, for the people of Williamsburg. It is to grasp more deeply why those antique words and phrases remain so central to the shared experience our multicultural society treasures, the American experience.

You could call that experience magic and not miss the mark by much, but the word Colonial Williamsburg uses to describe the interplay between presentation and visitor in its historic setting is "interpretation." It is the unplanned and spontaneous experience that awakens the spirit of inquiry and expands knowledge. My colleague Cary Carson calls it "the invisible life of ideas that interpretive exhibitions bring into being."

Short of having the experience of Colonial Williamsburg at first hand, I commend to you the pages that follow. The vitality of Philip Kopper's descriptions, insights, and observations reveal the power of Mr. Rockefeller's purpose.

Preserved in masonry and weatherboard, and in time, ideas, and experience, Colonial Williamsburg gives special definition and meaning to the history that made us a country, the understanding of which should inform our lives, the lives of our children, and the lives of future generations. That's why Colonial Williamsburg, that telegram, and this book, matter—"That the future may learn from the past."

COLIN G. CAMPBELL, Chairman and President,
The Colonial Williamsburg Foundation

A misty sun glows behind the Capitol as first it did nearly three hundred summers past, and over the brick colonnade the colony's seal proclaims EN DAT VIRGINIA QUINTAM, "Virginia makes the fifth" [realm of Britain's growing empire]. On the staff above the cupola—the only one on earth that flies this banner now—Queen Anne's *Great* Union flag hangs limp. At the Magazine, militiamen salute newer colors—the *Grand* Union, first banner to bear America's storied stripes. On a morning such as this, the windless air lets every flag lie loose along its staff. It is as if time itself fell still and waits upon the breeze.

~

A chestnut gelding stands still in the lea beyond the Gaol. A ewe still sleeps beneath a wagon on a meadow lot in town. The birds awake: crimson cardinals flit from bush to bush, white pigeons float from George Wythe's cote to the churchyard wall, a great blue heron weaves its heavy way toward the marsh at College Landing. Mark Catesby, friend of John Custis whose son's widow married the planter and surveyor George Washington, painted these. They fly through time and back again.

~

At the Governor's Palace a gardener weeds terraced beds in the acres that the governor himself, Alexander Spotswood, planned. At midcentury, this garden grew vegetables and herbs to season the hundred dishes served to celebrate the victory at Culloden. A few hours hence, young Alexander Spotswood Clark, blond hair tied back in a queue, will study the King's English before starting his day's work guiding visitors through the Palace his ancestor saw built.

~

Behind Raleigh Tavern now an apprentice stokes the fires, fueling the brick oven for the daily bread. In a new barn the stable grooms harness a pair of bays for the blue phaeton, a noble carriage ready to perform its gracious work around the town. Across the meadowed hill, James Sampson talks his slow brace of oxen toward the cart for the ten thousandth time or more, commanding the lumbering beasts with his gentle voice alone. A maid, a cloth tied round her head, hitches an old mare to the dray; it's time to think about collecting eggs.

~

A few folk pursue their errands soon after dawn, rippling the calm with talk along Duke of Gloucester Street. You can tell it is morning by the noise: the caws and calls and voices. At half past eight a shepherd girl drives her flock along the street from the sheepfold by Prentis Store to pasture near the Capitol. Her skirt swirls around her ankles as she runs behind the ewes and lambs, wielding a crook half again her height. Listen close for the gentle tack of lambs' feet on the cobbled verge. Then come sounds that carry far: fifes shrill enough to pierce the tat-ata-ta-tat-at-ata-tat rattle of musket fire, and rolling drums that reach beneath the boom of cannon. A fife and drum corps, whether two boys with another carrying the colors or a company of twoscore behind their major, come up the street that bears Lord Botetourt's name. They wheel westward toward the Magazine to

OPPOSITE: The royal purple of globe amaranth flowers, the precious yellow of marigolds and a slim hawthorn tree grace a garden nook behind the Governor's Palace, one of Colonial Williamsburg's 400-odd buildings that were rebuilt on the footprints of 18th-century originals. Did this very spot await the pleasure of King George III's royal governor in the erstwhile colony, or feel the pacing of some restless revolutionary, a founding father of these United States? Venue of a million visitors today, Williamsburg is a place of past and present, a capital reborn and restored, a village revived from vestiges of yore. Thomas Jefferson called the city "the finest school of manners and morals in America" and here Virginians first came to see themselves as Americans, citizens of a new nation. Once Britain's "Seat of Empire," Williamsburg welcomes modern visitors to join the drama of historical discovery by the simple act of being here.

the bright shrill tunes of "British Grenadiers" and "Roast Beef." Some lads look proud, some sleepy as they pace off ninety-six steps a minute, thirty inches in each pace. All sweat, none smile. In winter they will shiver stone-faced and still walk the frozen street at ninety-six steps a minute, to march the measured rate of two and three-quarter English miles each English hour just as His Majesty's regiments progressed three hundred years ago.

～

Spring rains so soak the earth that every gale fells trees, like the big and ancient oak in the ravine near the Gaol where Blackbeard's crew were penned, its roots tearing up china shards and black bottles from the soft-soaked earth. Perhaps its acorn fell when Patrick Henry rent the air with fighting words.

～

Then the shadbush bursts out in clouds of white throughout the town to mark the days when those river fish come up to spawn. The fruit trees bloom: cherries sour and sweet, plums, peaches, lady apples, green apples, cider apples. Men ply the fields with wooden tools, planting corn, cotton and tobacco. Flax ripens in a field glowing periwinkle blue at dawn, then fading before noon as the tiny flowers close. By full summer crepe myrtles blaze in every shade of red the rainbow knows and promise to last the season. One day a new flowered shrub appears in a garden where Sir John Randolph walked: tiny purple petals with a crimson hue lie upon a bush of dark and shiny boxwood green. A second look reveals just boxwood leaves sprinkled with myrtle blooms from the tree above after the brief rain that blew through here an hour since. This beauty cannot last a day.

～

In the General Court, a wizened judge lays the black patch upon his wig to pronounce death by hanging for the mob-capped maid who stole a silver spoon from her tavern-keeper master. In the Apollo Room, a stately couple steps the minuet to begin an evening's gaiety. The House of Burgesses hears its members weigh angry words again—of loyalty to king and distant country versus the natural rights of free men here—in stern and well-rehearsed debates that once had revolutionary consequence. A company of players presents *Hob in the Well* and Congreve comedies again before a mob that drinks and cheers. But these are only actors after all, echoing their antecedents.

～

The carpenter lays wooden sills, hews posts by hand and raises beams at James Anderson Blacksmith Shop, which again will see blacksmiths smite glowing rods into cold nails for clenching oaken boards to roofs and walls, as Anderson himself did before he factored other iron stuff to supply a rabble army, then followed in its train. Painters renew the white, ocher and red colors of walls and roof that St. George Tucker once ordered from a merchant whose record of the purchase has survived the centuries. Just down Nicholson Street, named by and for another governor, Andrew Edwards systematically digs in Peyton Randolph's yard to unearth whatever lies therein: bits of broken china, a button, a buckle. These shards and shreds will prove this gentleman owned the most elegant urban household in these parts circa 1775, on the eve of the Revolution he did not live to see— death by apoplexy, or by love of his dinner and his glass. At Greenhill nearby an unmarked grave turns out to have been twice filled, the first occupant's bones rewrapped and reinterred above the second, who was laid here to rest in imperfect peace. At noon the diggers stop to seek the shade, among them dirty-fingered persons with Ph.D.s who read clear messages in the dim lines and folds of earth as arcanely as any gypsy in a palm—scientific archaeologists.

～

Soldiers smudge the air on Courthouse green with the smoke of cooking fires, and the market rings with cries of farmers and factors gathered for the autumn fair. The bell peals evensong in

ABOVE: Carriages, wagons and other horse-drawn vehicles again ply Duke of Gloucester Street, which carried its first traffic in the early 1700s. Restored by Colonial Williamsburg, it was surfaced with paving that resembles a dirt or gravel road. Today it serves all comers, including visitors and students from the College of William and Mary who jog its length of one English mile.

OPPOSITE: A rain-soaked garden behind the home of Thomas Jefferson's teacher George Wythe displays a hallmark of Georgian design in the symmetry of its hedges, boxwood and flower beds.

Bruton Parish Church, where Thomas Jefferson knelt to pray from time to time, as did Washington and Patrick Henry too, perhaps together on "the day of fasting and humiliation" when they and other soon-to-be-called rebels rose in protest against a distant and ever more alien authority.

~

The miller's girl flails her master's wheat. Springtime's flax, now broken and carded into stuff called tow, is spun into thread, which the weavers shuttle into linen cloth. The wind that winnows chaff away also turns the windmill's sails, grinding grain to flour for the flaxen sacks. The wool shorn from last spring's bleating sheep comes out again—as capes of crimson and forest green worn by the workers of this town. Reflecting from the Capitol's curved crown-glass windows, which gleam like insect eyes, the sun sets lower in the west.

~

Now the moon lights frosted roofs, and suddenly each fig tree has dropped its leaves. The maple by the Courthouse turns flame red tonight.

~

Cooks in George Wythe's warm kitchen set their iron pots on coals and heap more embers on the lids to bake sweet or savory pies, a method as sure today as long ago. They scrub and salt new pork, pack it in wooden tubs to cure, then smoke hams and bacon sides in the fume of slow oak fires. Thus was cured the meat for General Washington's plate the day he woke in George Wythe's house, and breakfasted, and led his force to Yorktown—at ninety-six steps a minute, if you please, as disciplined troops were wont in 1781—and laid siege to the host commanded by Lord Cornwallis, who, his back to the sea, surrendered his sword and lost for his king the first colony that became a nation.

~

The crops are in, the shops shuttered. When folks in polyester garb pass an evening in Chowning's rooms, they play the ancient games of goose and nine-man-morris, drinking toddies or mulled wine against the chill. The catalpa trees along Palace green have shed their leaves; their seedpods shake like rattles in the wind. The streets incline toward emptiness until the throngs return for December's Grand Illumination.

~

Water freezes in the trough at Market Square and James Sampson must break it for his oxen. But there is mirth at Christmas all about, a Yule log in the Inn, and bowls of punch and Handel's tunes plucked upon the harpsichord in the blue-walled Palace ballroom. In Mistress Powell's parlor the young tutor who so pleasingly plays the viola da gamba chides guests in modern dress for failing to return the favor of his music with their song.

~

The year winds down. What year was this? A year like any other in this resurrected place. What men and maids are these? Living, breathing folk of course, as quick as you and me, some of them playing the dead you know: Washington and Patrick Henry; young Jefferson and good George Wythe who taught him law, the sojourning naturalist Mark Catesby whose name adorns a marble Bruton slab, ambitious Annabelle Powell, whose husband raised Bruton's steeple, and great Governor Alexander Spotswood. They are dead, of course. But aging William Penny opens the silver shop called the Golden Ball again each dawn, even as my infant son sleeps in a house called the Unicorn's Horn next door. James Sampson has driven oxen around this town for thirty years or more, while the young man who digs in Peyton Randolph's yard plies a profession not known two centuries ago, archaeology, and will dig from the yard a thousand secrets of its master's life before I come this way again. Alexander Spotswood Clark, known as Alex and wearing Botetourt's livery, welcomes

OPPOSITE: Similar symmetry reigns in many aspects of the ballroom of the Governor's Palace, decorated as it would have been in the 1770s. Beneath balanced portraits of Queen Charlotte and King George III, the governor and his lady, portrayed by costumed interpreters of today's Colonial Williamsburg, open a ball with the minuet in which the dancers show off their grace, ease, knowledge of the dance, clothing and social status. Country dances followed the minuet and the longways dances anticipated legacies found in the later Virginia reels and other line dances of modern "folk" traditions.

guests to the halls his ancestor designed. James Geddy wrought silver in his shop two hundred years before my neighbor James Curtis began to ply the sterling trade nearby. William Parks printed the first newspaper in Virginia; Willie Parker sets the type today and beats the wooden chase of hand-set type with inking balls.

~

Think on this: The town was planned in 1699, and settled soon after, and thrived about threescore years and ten (a good man's lifetime like enough) then faded, like the myrtle, when its purpose—to govern all Virginia—was transplanted west in Richmond. Then it languished at least two human lives long, and rose again when it was rebuilt on its own foundations and in its own older image with new purposes: no longer to govern but to teach, not to rule but to remind, not to lead a body politic but to inspire the people of a nation and visitors from every part of Earth. The place that had been the "crown jewel" of an empire in older days, capital of the Virginia colony, Williamsburg, became most clearly capitalized: Colonial Williamsburg.

~

And now permit your faithful author to add new words to those foregoing, revealing that my selfsame son who learned to walk on Duke of Gloucester Street is now about to march himself to college. Sixteen years have passed since your obedient servant resided here and penned the first edition of this tome. The time is ripe for an update.

~

Some aforementioned denizens of the reconstructed town have gone—to their reward or simply elsewhere, though their spirit and the fruits of their labors and the images of their work abide. Some, like Sampson, died, may they rest in peace; the carpenter of the Anderson Blacksmith Shop became a television star (of minor magnitude). Alex Clark moved on to the Yorktown Victory Center. Others have stayed and grown in stature: George Cloyed, barely a journeyman silversmith in James Craig's Golden Ball when I and mine lived just next door, is the supervisor now, and the apprentice of yore, Preston Jones, a journeyman himself. Gentle Gayle Clark still saws the bowls of silver spoons in minute runcible designs delicate as lace, yet also leads a guild of craftswomen, a group that had not even been imagined when I was here before. That was three presidents ago on two accounts—before Bill Clinton and George Bush *père,* Ronald Reagan held the White House; and in Colonial Williamsburg, before Presidents Colin Campbell and Robert C. Wilburn there was Charles Longsworth—*seriatim* three commanders-in-chief of the company that revived this place threescore and fifteen years ago.

~

In fact, Colonial Williamsburg saw a sea change, one that was caused by and celebrates changes in our land itself. One long-lived participant described the collective changes best by quoting the godfather of this place's resurrection, John D. Rockefeller, Jr., the man whose money made the new old city. Cary Carson wrote:

> Rockefeller himself understood the essential difference between libraries and collections on the one hand and the newfangled whatever-it-was that he was creating at Williamsburg. Early in 1932 he selected a motto for the corporation's official seal [after his subordinates submitted two lists that included some real zingers]. . . . The motto he selected—"That the future may learn from the past"—has served Colonial Williamsburg ever since. It makes a promise to future generations that educators will take the organization's basic mission back to the drawing board as often as necessary. Rockefeller understood that changing times always demand something new and different even from the past. So, Colonial Williamsburg embraced a perpetual obligation to keep its interpretation of history "trained on the future"—and, I might add, the present as best it can.

ABOVE: The sheepfold near the Magazine holds a flock of Leicester Longwools, descendants of one of the first varieties of livestock to be called a breed. Livestock breeds were creatures of the Enlightenment, the era that saw great innovations in agriculture and industry as well as the strides in political thought that gave rise to our Revolution. George Washington, for one, kept Leicester Longwools at his plantation, Mount Vernon.

OPPOSITE: A young visitor wearing a historically correct colonial dress (rented from stalls near Market Square) makes a woolly friend.

The ageless face of time
marches on in a table clock
with animated figures painted by
John Zoffany in London circa
1760, whence it could have
found its way to Williamsburg
in colonial times. In fact the
timepiece with an eight-day
movement once belonged to
the newspaper magnate William
Randolph Hearst and only
arrived here in 1938. The figures
above the dial represent an
18th-century music ensemble.

Another thing: Back when this volume first appeared, the Cold War raged, and this patriotic shrine had the obvious *raison d'être* to quietly proclaim the merit of our original hard-won liberties in a kind of iconic litany against dangers threatened by "the evil empire," as the USSR was called by some. But when the seemingly monolithic "Red Menace" (as it was called by others) fell into pieces as struggling independent states, and even "the Russian bear" became an ambitious capitalist, it happened that the new Williamsburg would change its focus. It must have done. I beg to overstate so subtle a change in course and attitude that its makers may not have named or noticed it: The absence of the old *bête noire* made Americans less responsive to the old shibboleths and more likely to visit amusement parks in their leisure time. As Colonial Williamsburg itself lives in a capitalistic world, and so must earn its keep, the governors of this historical town were forced to find new reasons for red-blooded visitors to come (with their greenbacks)—new assets in patriotism, new messages to teach. In a way it was pie-simple, for although the politically bipolar world "is history," and as this nation no more has one single foreign foe of consequence, we have reasons still to honor our beginnings, and withal, to study them, to learn of and from our forebears' lives.

Since I lived here, a gross oversight has been mended. From the start, the complexion of the town was quite lily-white, as its first managers congenitally overlooked a simple truth: that over half the folk in colonial Williamsburg by 1775 were of African origin or descent. That fact started to be noticed a score of years ago, and in the manner of institutions per se, some who noticed set about to change the policy that begat the error—given that policies can change about as fast as oak trees grow. Blacks were hired in greater numbers, they served in higher posts and in due course played more complex roles, whether in the reconstructed streets and craft shops or the administrators' offices. No single change in the growth of eighteenth-century Williamsburg, nor the contemporary legitimacy of Colonial Williamsburg, would be so apt, and not just because it corrected an injustice to people of darker skin; it also signaled a shift in focus from Great Americans of the Nation's birth to all our forebears.

Many names and faces have changed since my home was here and still the place abides, however differently today. Altered too are the lessons this reborn city has to teach—and its visitors have to learn as part of their recreation in the city's re-creation—for the very world beyond our modern shores has changed. So too the nation herself and the reasons people come to see and love this cradle of democracy, as if the cradle rocks as a pendulum swings, to the end of an arc and back again. So be it.

Thus as my prologue closed in 1984, I ask again: "What year is this?" And again I answer: Does it matter? Since this place was resurrected, each day can seem a time returning.

Between two ancient rivers an eddy twists the stream of time. It deepens as it swirls, a slowly drifting whirlpool. It widens, almost vanishing, only to deepen again and alter the course of all within its invisible reach.

This eddy recalls a conundrum as old as any human epic: In every river the same water flows today as yesterday; yet different water must be that river now. So be it here. This eddy remains the same yet ever changing as time, its river, flows on toward an unseen abyssal sea. It is constant yet constantly new, a locus in time's current, a vortex in the course of human events.

The eddy is Williamsburg.

~

From the beginning this was a realm of water, a land shaped by rains, tides, the ebb and flow of oceans as sea level fluctuated hundreds of vertical feet. When the first human inhabitants found this country, they were sustained by the abundance that rivers, bays, inlets and marshes held for their taking. When alien newcomers arrived millennia later, they gained access via the vast estuary, at once a treasure trove and branching avenue for their transport and commerce—but first a lifeline for vital provisions shipped from home an ocean away. They came in search of gold but the land itself between the water and westward mountains barely yielded even useful iron let alone any precious metal. Still these colonists grew rich from the earth that contained the metallic elements that in minuscule amounts nourish a most demanding plant and its golden leaf. The evolution of these people's society and "tobacco culture," the pattern of their towns and settlements, were all dictated by the land, which lay in extended peninsulas; and the lay of the land was defined by the lay of water, the great bay once called "mother of waters," or *Chesapoek,* in the tongue heard here a civilization before our own. In time the area would be known as the Tidewater, and, ambiguously, as "tidewater country" to this day. What it would become in human terms was determined by its bounding water.

The first people to find this place—once an ancient river drowned by a rising ocean—fished the broadening bay's tributaries. They settled on its peninsulas, the remains of much older hills that divided the arms of tidal inlets and still-widening rivers. These people foraged the ravines, gathering a wild bounty of roots, nuts and herbs. They planted beans, maize, gourds and tobacco. They waded the warm water to gather clams and snare innumerable fish with wicker weirs. In spring they gathered shoals of horseshoe crabs for food and fashioned the straight, sharp tails into ready spearheads. In winter they tracked the canny deer where mastodons had lately ranged, and hunted shaggy bison that would outlive their own culture hereabouts. They collected oysters with each falling tide and struck down waterfowl from flocks so dense they blotted out the sun.

Departing from the wandering ways of their ancestors—who walked all the way from Asia, after all—the Indians built long-lived towns around the Chesapoek. Here they forged a confederation of tribes numbering twelve thousand strong, making war with neighbors and love among themselves.

OPPOSITE: Seen through the doorway of the manor house at the plantation called Carter's Grove, the sun sets behind the James River at the figurative dawn of the third millennium just as it did during the waning days of the colonial era in America.

"Heaven & earth never agreed better to frame a place for man's habitation" than the Chesapeake Bay region, wrote Captain John Smith in one of his New World advertisements. More Englishmen may have responded to John White's 1580s painting of Indians fishing rich tidal waters in dugout canoes. However idyllic they appear, such paintings were crucial "media" in the period—key sources of information such as the ways that natives fished, and the appearance of exotic creatures like the great blue heron (upper left) and horseshoe crab and blue crab (lower right). Lured by such claims and images, about a hundred English adventurers set forth in three ships to found Jamestown in 1607.

The manner of their fishing.

Canoe

They practiced complex diplomacy and commerce, trading their sea's shells for native copper from beyond the Great Lakes. Led by priestly castes, they worshiped a vengeful god and buried their dead with ritual ceremony. Then the strangers of an alien race came from across the even broader water beyond the "mother of waters." Spanish missionaries, meaning to possess the inland sea they called Bahia de Santa Maria, camped beside a tidewater river (later named York) in 1570 and were all slain within the year.

A decade later another light-skinned tribe of seafarers began to probe the coast, soon to leave settlers on Roanoke Island to the south in 1584. The first who stayed simply vanished from the realm they'd named Virginia for their virgin queen, Elizabeth I, who died herself before this place was truly England's. Then came three ships: the *Godspeed, Susan Constant* and *Discovery.* The little fleet sailed up the river named James for the new king, whose subjects staked out an armed camp, a "permanent" settlement. It became a city of sorts, and the first rude capital of a colony presumed to stretch as far west as the next ocean. Thus the English found a footing in North America and founded Jamestown on May 13, 1607.

The company of five score men and boys nearly met the fate of their vanished predecessors at Roanoke and the Spanish *padres* before them. Having thrown up the fort, they repulsed an Indian attack twelve days after landing. But the fort stood near a swamp alive with mosquitoes that carried killing malaria. During their first years, as many as four out of five settlers died—of hunger, disease and battle. Warring was inevitable because, in the wry words of an English archaeologist who would excavate this region centuries later, the first adventurers did not announce "the rather provocative idea that the Indians' land no longer belonged to them." Ivor Noël Hume continued, "In the manner of most colonial enterprises, the tiresome details needed only to be understood by the new management."

But before the old tenants fully realized the drift of things to come, they'd made brief peace with the immigrants. Powhatan, chief of the native confederation that bore his name, sought new allies against his old adversaries to the north—though the alliance cost him dearly in James River lands. He welcomed the blandishments of one English captain in particular and adopted him as a member of his tribe. The winning diplomat, John Smith, also provided sound leadership for his own people. Where other bands of New World adventurers had wasted energies on ill-aimed treasure hunts and petty conquests, he demanded productive discipline. "He that will not work, shall not eate," Smith declared, though notably the settlers' toil was not for bread alone.

John Rolfe, who married Powhatan's newly Christian daughter Pocahontas, set a few acres in tobacco as early as 1612. Avoiding the strong-smoking native species that gave Indians dizzy delight, he imported a milder, kindred Caribbean plant. It thrived in Virginia, and by 1615 Rolfe reaped enough to fill two hogsheads for the voyage home in one of the ships that brought new settlers and vital provisions. By 1618 Virginia exported fifty thousand pounds of leaf and England became a land of smokers, though King James had long since called their habit a "custome lothsome to the eye, hatefull to the Nose, harmefull to the braine, dangerous to the Lungs, and in the blacke stinking fume thereof, neerest resembling the horrible Stigian smoke of the pit that is bottomelesse."[1] The king proposed to ban the addicting weed from his realm, but customs duties on it lined his purse,

Chief Powhatan adorns the cartouche of a contemporary English map. The leader of a confederacy of Indian tribes, he won support against native rivals by befriending early colonists and trading land with them, his new allies. He is also remembered as the father of the celebrated princess Pocahontas.

---

[1] The Gentle Reader of this modern text may be addled by odd capitalizations and spellings in old quotations. The Author has the honor to remind You that Pecksniffian orthography and rules of spelling came into fashion only in the nineteenth century. He has endeavored to preserve eighteenth-century words as they were written, save only in two respects. First, the "long s" (as in *Princefs*) was never read as an "f" but simply as another shape of "s." Second, the letter "y" was used like a more ancient character, the thorn, to represent a "th" sound. These letters will be transcribed according to modern usage while eccentric spellings will remain as they appear in the original quotations. Ergo, "Ye Olde Tea Houfe" becomes "The Olde Tea House."

and the stock company that sponsored settlement needed something to sell back home. The king held his royal tongue (and nose perhaps), the Privy Council insisted that all Virginia tobacco go to England, and the colony's economic future seemed assured. But other problems remained.

There was the simple matter of survival. When promised goods didn't arrive in 1609, most colonists perished during the winter called "starving time." Those few that saw spring come then rigged a ship as best they could and meant to flee for home. But before they could leave, Sir Thomas Gates sailed up the James with new supplies; he had been delayed, accidentally discovering Bermuda, where he was shipwrecked in a storm. There was also the matter of population. At Eastertide, 1619, for example, one thousand English settlers were living here, but one would die almost every other day throughout the year. The next twelve months saw ten ships arrive with more than another thousand new immigrants, yet by the next Easter only 843 remained, the rest having perished or sailed back to England in ships carrying tobacco.

That new colonists kept coming by the boatload was at least in part due to Smith, who proved as able a huckster as he had been ambassador and autocrat. Back home he published memoirs— biased advertisements for the Virginia Company, in which he held stock. Of the Chesapeake region in particular, he enthused, "Heaven & earth never agreed better to frame a place for man's habitation." If he overlooked the ravages of malaria, dysentery, hunger, and friction with the neighbors, there were in fact some splendid things to sing about. For one, the land was fertile; for another, he had promised in England: "No man will go from hence to have lesse freedome there than here" and thus transplanted the seed of British legal custom. His company's de facto government formally established "the rule of law—the common law of England . . . and orderly process to change the law," as historian Samuel Eliot Morison summarized it. "A legislative Assembly, the very first in America," convened at Jamestown in 1619.

In short order that body solemnized a principle of remarkable ramifications: "That the Governor shall not lay any Taxes or Impositions upon the Colony . . . [through any means other] than by the Authority of the General Assembly, to be levyed and ymployed as the said Assembly shall appoint." Thus the matter of local taxes in principle became the prerogative of the colonists' elected representatives, a nicety that gained astonishing political importance a century and a half later.

The colonists imported not only their native law but private enterprise as well, which other proprietary colonies had not enjoyed. The immigrants were mostly men who owed seven years' service to those who had paid their passage. When substantial numbers of these indentures were fulfilled, the decision was made to let individuals work tracts of land as their own property. This brought about a manifold increase in garden crops. The community had depended for its bare subsistence on provisions from home (and on food bartered from Indians or sometimes robbed from Indian graves). Now it developed a market economy boasting surpluses, especially in edibles. Furthermore, women in England had been encouraged to emigrate; while Virginia bachelors were required to live in common barracks, couples could live apart in dwellings of their own. In private terms these habitations, however humble, offered undescribed delights; in practical terms they contributed to the spread of farmsteads and the colony's territorial growth. In Morison's expert opinion, Virginia gained a firmer footing thanks to the unusual triad of democracy, capitalism and sex.

Each piecemeal step that strengthened the English presence undermined the Indians' dominion. When Powhatan died in 1618, his lands and influence reduced, he was succeeded by a brother or half brother, one of the Pamunkey tribe. Opechancanough secretly strengthened the confederation, promising his allies to rid the land of the intruders who now ranged far along the James. With blitzkrieg effect the Indians arose on March 22, 1622, to attack every settlement, farmstead and

An English man-at-arms lost this "closed helmet" early one morning in 1622 when Powhatan's heirs attacked every British settlement and massacred hundreds of colonists. In 1977 it was unearthed by Colonial Williamsburg archaeologists along with another like it, the first examples of such armor ever found *in situ* in English North America. They lay buried at the place called Carter's Grove, a plantation built in the 1750s on the site of the lost hamlet of Wolstenholme Towne overlooking the James River.

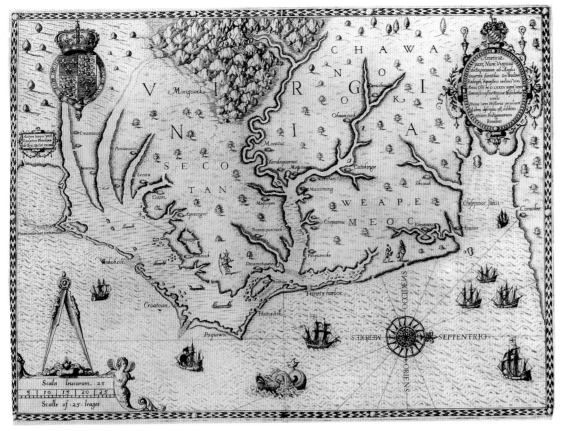

This 1585 map of Virginia's coast—north is right—was the work of the artist and later governor John White. He drew it two years before his granddaughter Virginia Dare was born in Sir Walter Raleigh's ill-fated colony on Roanoke Island and three years before the stormy destruction of the Spanish Armada gave England freedom of the seas.

outpost, killing 347 settlers by Smith's later account, or nearly one-third of the 1,240 colonists counted in the latest "muster rowle." Only Jamestown itself, a little hamlet that had begun to spread beyond its wooden walls, escaped torch and tomahawk, thanks to a friendly native's warning.

News of this disaster reached London, where it prompted new debate about the wisdom of a proprietary settlement, and the king revoked the Virginia Company's charter. Established by entrepreneurs and stockholders, the place became a royal colony ruled by a governor and Council with the Assembly's advice. Wary of new Indian attacks, the colonists secured the peninsula with palisades extending from the James to the York. They divided the unmarked ground into units imported from home: hundreds, plantations, counties and parishes. Thanks to their now growing numbers and always superior weapons, they continued to expand their territory despite persistent unpleasantness with the neighbors.

In its 1632–1633 session the General Assembly passed "an Act for the Seatinge of the Middle Plantation," a place whose name remains subject to speculation though its significance is undeniable. The bill stipulated "that every fortyeth Man . . . be imployed in buildings of Houses, and securing that Tract of Land" between Queen's Creek and Archer's Hope (later College) Creek. "And Yf any free Men shall . . . voluntarilie goe and seate uppon the sayd Place of the Middle Plantation, they shall have fifty Acres of Land Inheritance, and be free from all Taxes and publique Chardges."

"Staked out and paled in" in 1633, the place was already inhabited by one Dr. John Potts, whose fortunes waxed and waned like those of the city that would rise here. Once physician general of the colony, he was a respected healer whose skills varied with the supply of "his good Liquor." Governor in 1629, he was a convicted cattle thief by 1630, then five years later a member of the Council that helped unseat another governor. While Potts's name does not exactly echo down through history, those of his neighbors would be heard for generations. Among others there was a Tyler whose line begat a presi-

Bruton Parish's "new" church, finished in 1715, was the third built on the site where Palace green meets Duke of Gloucester Street. Though it gained a longer chancel, tower, steeple and spire before the Revolution, its appearance changed little more before 1836 when Thomas Millington, son of a William and Mary professor, captured it in watercolors (top). A century later this "document" and others like it proved invaluable to restorers as they began returning the town to its antique mien (bottom).

dent, and a Ludwell whose family home won fame both here and in Samuel Johnson's London.

As a later scholar (Rutherfoord Goodwin) would surmise in the eighteenth-century manner,

> The Reader . . . should not be misled to picture Middle Plantation in his mind, as some have done, as a Town to be compared with the Towns of this present Day, nor even as a Town in the Sense that Jamestown was a Town in that early Day. More Truth will be found in looking upon it as a wide-scattered Settlement in which no Man had Need to be disturbed by the Wailing of his Neighbor's Offspring; yet which, with the Years converged upon a middle Point until, of a Sudden, it became a City.

Before that occurred, however, the mother country was rocked by civil war in the 1640s. James I's successor, Charles I, neglected the colony, then for unrelated reasons lost both his throne and head. Parliament seized power and Oliver Cromwell rose as Lord Protector of the Commonwealth, but Virginia Governor Sir William Berkeley and the Assembly remained loyal to the crown. Faced with a show of force in ships from England, Berkeley negotiated a bloodless truce: Royalists retained their property in the colony; the established church remained intact (with fewer references to royalty in the Book of Common Prayer) and the Assembly increased its power. The governor had less luck dealing with the local challenge of Bacon's Rebellion, the first armed uprising against royal authority—albeit in pursuit of Indian genocide, not English liberty.

Through a series of parish mergers, Bruton Parish was established at Middle Plantation in 1674 and named for the English town on the River Brue in Somerset, whence the Ludwell and Berkeley families came to Virginia. The high ground of the peninsula's spine, soon boasting a brick church, became a likely site for a college founded (in part) to convert heathen natives to the faith of Protestant England. This college, successor to one planned in more remote Henrico County before the 1622 massacre, was championed by the Reverend James Blair, a Scottish cleric named by the bishop of London as his Virginia representative. Blair was commissary, the agent of the distant diocese of which the colony was an ecclesiastical part. He sailed home and won a royal charter in 1693 for the College of William and Mary, named for Britain's newly crowned monarchs. The second college in English America, it was the first one founded under royal patronage.

The college was also the catalyst for relocating the colony's capital. Again quoting Rutherfoord Goodwin, the modern antiquary who sublimed in archaic style:

> While the College was yet building at *Middle Plantation* in the year 1698, a final Calamity fell upon *Jamestown* in the Burning of the new State House at that Place. And, now, the Desire to establish the Seat of Government in a more central and healthful Spot having gained great Strength and the Plan having the strong Support of the Governor, the Hon. *Francis Nicholson*, Esq., *Middle Plantation* was brought forward in this Wise: "and forasmuch as the Place commonly called and known by the Name of the *Middleplantation* hath been found by const[an]t experience to be healthy and agreeable to the Constitutions of the Inhabitants of the His Majestyes Colony and Dominion haveing the naturall Advantage of a serene and temperate Aire [,] dry and champaign Land and plentifully stored with wholesome Springs and the Conveniency of two navigable and pleas[an]t Creeks that run out of *James* and *York* Rivers necessary for the Supplying of the Place. . . :" The Thought of rebuilding the State House at *Jamestown* could not stand in the face of so handsome a Reputation; and in the Year 1699 the Assembly was prevailed upon to pass an Act entitled *An Acte directing the Building of the Capitoll and the City of Williamsburgh*, which among other Things in its great Length, directed that the city . . . "in Honour of our most gracious & glorious King *William*, shall be ever hereafter called and known by the Name of the City of *Williamsburgh*."

The legislature thus moved its seat to the hamlet on the high ground that by mid-century boasted nearly one thousand inhabitants. During its first few decades, the city's population would swell twice

King James I occupied the throne when the first British colony after Roanoke Island—and the first one actually to succeed—was planted on the James River and named for him in 1607.

a year during "Publick Times" when the elected House of Burgesses met, the appointed Council sat as the General Court, and folks flocked to the capital as if for a fair. For reasons involving tobacco culture and peninsular geography, the city did not grow large in physical size or permanent population. Since tobacco plantations had their own wharfs, Virginia did not greatly need a shipping center here. Rather it was the political hub and center for society.

The colony's ruling class—its gentlemen planters who also served as vestrymen, judges and legislators—frequented Williamsburg seasonally. Building town houses or lodging in the taverns, they flocked to this epicenter of Virginia, the crown's most populous colony. They built an ideal community, at least one planned according to new ideals imported from the mother country. As Daniel J. Boorstin explained in *The Americans: The Colonial Experience,* "If other colonies sought escape from English vices, Virginians wished to fulfill English virtues. . . . If Virginia was to be in any way better than England, it was not because Virginians pursued ideas which Englishmen did not have [at first]; rather that here were novel opportunities to realize the English ideals."

When courts and Assembly met, Williamsburg seemed a crowded and sophisticated metropolis as befitted the seat of a government that claimed dominion as far west as the Mississippi, nay the Pacific, on parchment if not in practical fact. In 1716 the governor himself tested the frontier, leading an expedition across the Blue Ridge Mountains. With a company of scouts and a dozen gentlemen, Alexander Spotswood crossed the head of the Rapidan River (mistaking it for the James), then found a pass to the Shenandoah ("River of Stars"), which his troop dubbed the Euphrates before celebrating. A diarist recorded "We drank the King's health in champagne, and fired a volley; the Princess's health in burgundy, and fired a volley; and all the rest of the Royal Family in claret, and a volley. We drank the Governor's health and fired another volley. . . ." They sported for four weeks, living off the land and covering four hundred miles before reaching Williamsburg again. There the convivial leader gave each companion a little gold horseshoe as a souvenir and dubbed them all Knights of the Golden Horseshoe. This expedition notwithstanding, for the next few decades one governor after another vainly tried to bar land-hungry settlers from crossing the mountains.

The Indians were less tractable there, and France had claimed the territory. Yet because land meant wealth, there was no stopping the westward movement by both penniless loners and well-connected colonists who took absentee titles to tracts larger than some European principalities. Defense of this growing realm—and the spreading empire elsewhere—cost England dearly during the first half of the century. The crown sought repayment from its far-flung subjects for successfully waging a series of wars in the Old World and the New, wars that in the end served the interests of both king and colony alike, though colonists would soon object to having to help pay their costs.

The transplanted Englishmen of Virginia still pledged their loyalty to the crown, which had passed from King William to Queen Anne, then to the first of the Georges by 1714. During the reign of George II, the colonists had grown accustomed to questioning royal authority over many things, from who had the power of appointing clergy to matters of trade. When George III's minions imposed new taxes from distant London to pay old war debts, still-loyal colonists argued that their traditionally English toes were being trod upon. In the 1760s and '70s, the transatlantic argument grew hotter, and when the burgesses voiced notions that verged on treason, the royal governor dissolved their House around their ears. But no English fiat could erase this colonial community nor mute its band of leaders in Williamsburg. Though disenfranchised, Virginia's burgesses resumed deliberations in the Raleigh Tavern, empowering themselves to speak for Virginia's people without royal permission! Then they joined the emissaries of twelve kindred colonies in Philadelphia. Led at first by Williamsburg's preeminent citizen, the fated Peyton Randolph, Virginians became part of the

The young Virginia colony's best ambassador to King James's England was Pocahontas, the fabled Indian princess who captivated the royal court when she went to London as tobacco planter John Rolfe's bride in 1616.

THE OLD RALEIGH TAVERN.

Like a Phoenix, Raleigh Tavern has gone and come again. Built about 1717, it served as a hub of colonial life and politics for more than six decades: Jefferson danced and Washington dined here; Virginia leaders defied the crown by meeting without royal permission in its Apollo Room and took a giant step toward Independence, resolving that "an attack made on one of our sister Colonies, to compel arbitrary taxes, is an attack made on all British America." In 1859 the building burned and a century after the tavern's heyday *Scribner's Monthly* published this woodcut (above). Rebuilt, the Raleigh opened again in 1932, the first exhibition building in the town dubbed the "birthplace of the Republic."

inner circle of the Continental Congress, which was thus led by men who had cut their governmental teeth in Williamsburg as burgesses. (Did they then represent the perfect democracy? Not by later lights. To qualify to vote, a person had first to be male, free, white and possessed of land. Further, most leaders rose to local prominence as parish vestrymen and justices of the peace, virtually hereditary positions that devolved through ownership of vast plantations.)

In short order an elder son of the Old Dominion, George Mason, would draft the Virginia Declaration of Rights in 1776; a younger son, Thomas Jefferson, who had read law in Williamsburg, would write the Declaration of Independence; an erstwhile surveyor, George Washington, who had charted the hinterlands and led militia bands, would become commander in chief of the Continental Army. From Williamsburg, Washington planned the siege of a royal army encamped at Yorktown a half-day's march away, and there fought the battle that won the war called Revolution. But a year earlier the seat of Virginia's government had moved again, west to Richmond, a more central site and thus more efficient and effective as more and more settlers moved westward. (Also, this location upriver was thought safer from enemy attack, though Redcoats soon and Yankees a century later would prove that notion false.) In part the capital was moved because no less a light than Jefferson, the second elected governor, disliked the Tidewater town and perhaps believed the new Commonwealth deserved a capital whose design would more truly reflect the new political order.

Williamsburg might have gone back to woods scarped by eroding ravines and sunk with little swamps except that it boasted the provincial college and the first public insane asylum in America. Grander cities than this have given up their ghosts when History's course flowed elsewhere. Yet this hamlet, once capital of the British Empire's premier possession, would cling to shreds and shards of its past. In one particular it was nearly unique: Other colonial capitals became seats of states or hubs of industry and commerce in nineteenth-century America. Boston, Providence, New Haven, New York, Trenton, Philadelphia would all be transformed by new forms of manufacture and business while the Civil War would see Richmond burned, its edifices razed, and precious records turned to ash. But this former colonial capital eluded the cataracts of modern history; Williamsburg escaped because it was a backwater.

Then in 1902 a young minister came to Bruton Parish and the cruciform brick church raised in 1715 with the help of King George I's governor, Alexander Spotswood. Bruton Church, said to be America's oldest Episcopal church in continuous use, had changed over the centuries, notably when its Victorian stewards—with the best of intentions, no doubt—transformed the interior bric by brac. A visionary of boundless energy, the new rector was inspired by plans to celebrate vanished Jamestown's tercentenary in 1907 and he persuaded his congregation to restore the sanctuary in time to rededicate it during the gala celebration that drew people of every station to the region.

But then the minister left Williamsburg for a spell, and the town lapsed into its old malaise. Suffering a relapse of parsimony, the city fathers decided that the annual appropriation of $50 was too much to pay the man who wound the clock in Bruton's tower. So they canceled his contract, the clock stopped, and Williamsburg became known as the place where time stood still. Another year, the sleepy authorities simply forgot to print ballots and open the polls on Election Day, so a nearby newspaper dubbed the backwater "Lotusland" and its denizens "Lotusburgers."

In 1923 the minister returned to teach at the college while building its endowment fund, and ultimately to fill Bruton's elevated pulpit again. He resumed his earlier work of returning the building to its grander simplicity, removing partitions from the interior and a coal bin from the tower and reconstructing high-backed pews like those where Washington and Jefferson had prayed. It was not enough. The Reverend William Archer Rutherford Goodwin could no longer confine his

A wharf scene brightens the cartouche on a 1768 edition of a map first made by Joshua Fry and Peter Jefferson, Thomas's father. This nice bit of propaganda implies the geographic merit of the Tidewater, where planters could ship tobacco from their own docks.

vision within the old brick churchyard wall. After adapting as his parish house the home where Jefferson read law, he set his sights on the entire town, the nexus between Jamestown and Yorktown, the "cradle of liberty." Through Phi Beta Kappa, which had been founded at William and Mary at the beginning of the Revolution, he met one of that honor society's most famous members, one whose stature transcended scholarship per se.

John D. Rockefeller, Jr., one of the world's richest men, was also a quiet revolutionary of sorts. Scion of a fortune earned in the industrial century that had passed this city by, he brought into full flower a new estate among men: the business of philanthropy. Rockefeller believed that great wealth—even his father's and thus his own—must be used for the benefit of great numbers of people. He was a pioneer in the causes of charity, a crusader in the force of alms.

A conservationist in the broadest sense, he had already given fortunes to preserve Europe's war-torn churches, created a sanctuary for medieval art in upper Manhattan and dedicated Maine's Acadia National Park to public enjoyment. He had endowed universities, social service agencies and medical institutions around the world. Guided through Williamsburg by the Reverend Dr. Goodwin, he glimpsed the village parson's patriotic vision and gently seized it as his own. The Williamsburg "Restoration," as it would soon be familiarly called, became his personal cause, hobby and benevolent preoccupation. The colonial capital also became another home, a retreat from his New York headquarters and rambling Hudson River estate.

When Bruton Parish Church was reconsecrated in 1907, President Theodore Roosevelt sent a brass lectern in the shape of an angel standing on a globe to commemorate "the three hundredth anniversary of the permanent establishment of English Civilization in America." The angel's rampant wings support a Bible given by King Edward VII, a book bearing a seal conferred to the Virginia colony by his predecessor Charles II.

Applying pure wealth to the re-creation of the place that Williamsburg had been, he bought brick, mortar and talent in fabled amounts. At the outset he wrote to the trusted associate who would handle the details: *"The purpose of this undertaking is to restore Williamsburg, so far as it may be possible, to what it was in the old colonial days and to make it a great center for historical study and inspiration"* (italics added). His successors have never coined a more elegantly succinct expression of the Restoration's goals, though they would benignly give the lie to Rockefeller's next sentence: "The purpose of this letter is to authorize my office to finance this entire program whether it costs three or four, or even five millions of dollars." By the time of his death, he alone had spent more than $68 million here and his heirs would continue to give millions more.

At first the aim was physical: to restore and replicate antique buildings, to frame a town so that modern folk could visit its halls and walk the streets of history. Generations of Rockefeller successors would expand the dream and modify the work; in the process they would pursue the donor's original goal more closely than he had. Not content with rebuilding in brick and weather alone, they would probe both earth and history to understand what *life* had been like in eighteenth-century Virginia. Cultural historians, political scientists and archaeologists would join the army of architects, decorators and laborers. Artisans would come to practice forgotten crafts, rediscovering ancient ways to make beautiful and useful things. Sociologists and the grandchildren of slaves would surmise the forgotten particulars of African-American beginnings, for blacks had been nearly half the colonial town's population (a fact the first restorers overlooked, in concert with the genteel biases of the time). Music teachers, students and performers would rehearse the minuets that the Founding Fathers danced, and sing the songs with which they wooed the Founding Brides.

In all their efforts, these researchers discovered an awful fact of historical life and then learned to live with it as they coped with the essential nature of history. Williamsburg's scholars, antiquaries, architectural restorers, archaeologists, antique craftsmen, et al. would learn perhaps better than any other community of students in their diverse disciplines that historical examination is the study of the incomplete. It is the reconstruction of lost worlds, of puzzles that inevitably lack more pieces than those at hand. These diverse historians (for lack of a better general term) learned of these

Reconstructing the past means more than palaces, pulpits and the trappings of antique splendor. Thus the slave quarter at Carter's Grove plantation recalls the rough-hewn cabins and African lifeways of slaves in colonial Virginia.

frustrations because this place offered singular shortcomings along with its unique opportunities. They also learned that historical truth changes with the time, as even does historical "fact" on occasion.

To seek the truth about the past the investigator in any one of these disciplines must of course contend with his own bias and a vast body of accepted but unproved suppositions. Even more frustrating is the inevitable fact of voids in data and proof that will never be filled. Consider:

The account books of a tradesman, the blacksmith James Anderson, survive, and so enable an economic historian to reconstruct his ways of doing business. But only two objects proven to be made by Anderson, two hinges, have ever been found for the modern smith to examine in his effort to rediscover lost techniques.

If the colonists modeled their society on the English example—as has long been assumed—music must have been a central part of social life, but proof of that was scant. Thankfully a physician's wife, Ann Blaws Barraud, played the harpsichord, and Bruton Parish's organist James S. Darling discovered a folder of her sheet music (including pieces attributed to that Italian master "Vi-Vally") in the archives at the college. Recording it on an eighteenth-century instrument, Darling advanced knowledge of specific doings in colonial Williamsburg. It bears mention that Darling's original predecessor, Peter Pelham, the first organist at Bruton, had to wear a second hat to make ends meet in Williamsburg; he was the keeper of the Gaol, and an advocate of humane treatment for his prisoners. A lately discovered music book shows him to have been a gifted composer as well. Influential in the colonies, an admired music teacher and au courant about music being played in London—he knew pieces by Handel within years of their debut—Pelham also proves to have been well connected; his father's second wife was the mother of the painter John Singleton Copley.

The legislative act that established the city survives in an English archive, along with the original survey map of the town's boundaries. Yet despite years of dedicated searching, no trace can be found of the first town plan. Thus it must be surmised from the scraps of evidence recompiled from later maps, land records, chance details gleaned from diaries and published histories.

This unique city itself escaped the ravages of progress through historical accident: Its reason for being—the government establishment—was removed to Richmond. But half the city lay within the original boundaries of James City County, which sent its land and court records to the capital "for safekeeping" during the Civil War. Thus half of Williamsburg's records were destroyed when Richmond burned. In sum, more of the "fabric" of a colonial city remains here for practical study than for many other eighteenth-century cities of comparable importance, but fully half the documents are missing, while the papers of some other cities remain more complete, though the cities themselves are transformed beyond recognition.

~

Scholarship aside, this place raised a manifold institution eventually attracting a million visitors a year. (As it changed, so did its overseeing corporations, first organized as Colonial Williamsburg, Inc., and the Williamsburg Holding Company, which in 1934 was renamed Williamsburg Restoration, Inc. In 1970 Williamsburg Restoration, Inc., and Colonial Williamsburg, Inc., were merged into the nonprofit Colonial Williamsburg Foundation, which in turn adapted to changing tax codes and spawned a wholly owned subsidiary to run its hotels and restaurants for profit in 1984. Corporate identities notwithstanding, the protean institution has been known among friends first as "the Restoration" then as "CW.") In its commercial guise it became a hamlet of hotels—the flagship Williamsburg Inn, the Lodge and Motor House—and a village of antique guesthouses along with taverns that offer colonial-style food and drink. It also licensed the manufacture of everything from soap to furniture, offering what is arguably America's widest array of home furnishings

Nor were all whites aristocrats in colonial times (of course). In the James Anderson Blacksmith Shop (another cluster of buildings raised with rediscovered tools and techniques), journeymen and apprentice blacksmiths practice their laborious trade in conditions close to those of the 18th century—if not with its back-breaking twelve-hour workdays.

bearing a single trademark. (Mr. Rockefeller insisted on the trademark to protect Colonial Williamsburg's reputation when vendors started plastering similar names on vulgar wares.) Purveying copies and adaptations of colonial fabrics, furniture, potpourris, porcelains and more, the Restoration inspired the national interest in period reproductions and changed American tastes—in balance for the better.

Williamsburg became a destination for families in search of interesting relaxation, flocks of children instructed to see history, and corporations seeking amiable conference surroundings. It became an academy of sorts, as scholars came to study its collections of antique porcelain, furniture and folk art, to gather in seminars, to publish learned works bearing the institution's colophon. It became a diplomatic way station as foreign heads of state used its finest accommodations to recover from jet lag on their globe-girdling flights to Washington, a chopper-hop to the north. Coming the other way, President Franklin D. Roosevelt and eight of his first ten successors visited on official business or private pleasure. Most spectacularly, in 1983 Ronald Reagan hosted the Economic Summit of Industrialized Nations here, a meeting of eight heads of state attended by three thousand members of the world's press. The Tidewater had hardly seen the likes since Washington marched on Yorktown 202 years earlier.

In the years since Dr. Goodwin and Mr. Rockefeller first shared their dream, much has been done to discover what this place was—from the time Dr. John Potts set his stakes here until Jefferson removed the seat of government. More has been done to restore it to that home of slave and gentleman, silversmith and silver-tongued orator, a city of practical crafts, complex economy and cunning preindustrial technology, at once a hamlet and seat of empire. Williamsburg has become both antique resort and historical laboratory. As its work continues, more accurate images of two centuries ago appear, images that often add to the picture of the past and sometimes contradict our previous understanding of colonial life.

It is doubtful whether Williamsburg will ever again exert the extraordinary—nay revolutionary—impact that it exercised on the eve of America's War for Independence. In terms of culture, economics and politics, this city led the land in a way that it never can again. Yet the town that was home to two thousand souls lives again as a museum, theater and time capsule in one to preserve the physical evidence of the past that both instructs and inspires—a restoration that restores its visitors in many ways. Looking back over the centuries, colonial Williamsburg and Colonial Williamsburg have several sorts of histories. Their combined story starts as one of exploration, planning and creation; then becomes one of destruction, deterioration and loss; and finally emerges as one of reconstruction, discovery and recall. This place was founded, planned, built and abandoned, then rediscovered, recovered, restored and examined. Volumes of formal "history" have been written about the historic eighteenth-century town, while its twentieth-century resurrection is the keystone of a new historical force, the restoration movement. This book will try to sketch the city from the waning of the seventeenth century to the dawning of the twenty-first.

In 1632, the Assembly convened and, among its other business, addressed the matter of having Middle Plantation—the future Williamsburg—"staked out and paled in"; 147 years later, in 1779, a legislative act turned history's back on the erstwhile capital, apparently for good. Yet 147 years later, in 1926, a venture began on the basis of a handshake and a dream. It was a partnership between two men certainly, but more important it joined vague visions and hard dollars in an uncommon cause. Who can say what the next 147 years will bring?

The stream of time flows on.

ABOVE: Iconic Williamsburg: The Fifes and Drums, following their major, step out once again on Duke of Gloucester Street, their backs to the reconstructed 18th-century Capitol building of the Virginia colony, their faces staring into the 21st century so that the future may learn from the past.

OPPOSITE: In a misty hour after dawn, two horses graze among trees—as their sires did two centuries earlier beneath oaks long since felled for lumber and ship spars.

THE COLONIAL PERIOD:

Jewel in the Crown of the Empire

1

Soon after his Accession to the Government, he caused the Assembly, and Courts of Judicature, to be remov'd from James-Town, where there were good Accommodations for People, to Middle-Plantation, where there were none. There he flatter'd himself with the fond Imagination, of being the Founder of a new City. . . . There he procur'd a stately Fabrick to be erected, which he placed opposite to the College, and graced it with the magnificent name of the Capitol.

—Robert Beverley, 1705
The History and Present State of Virginia

Williamsburg would become a jewel in the crown of British Empire. Yet its founding resulted from failure, from accident, pestilence and other misfortunes that assailed Jamestown, which was, in a word, a disaster. Virginia's first government had been seated in entirely the wrong sort of place.

From the beginning Jamestown's pestilential swamp beset the settlers with "Fluxes and Agues," despite the imposition of English America's first sanitary code in 1610. Within the compound Governor Sir Thomas Gates prohibited not only the "unmanly, slothfull and loathesome . . . necessities of nature" but laundry and pot washing as well. Yet contagions continued, spread no doubt by bad water from the shallow wells and by the marsh's mosquitoes. Settlements established south of the James and upriver near the falls fared better: "There did not so much as one man miscarry, and but very few or none fall sicker," a chronicle recorded. The writing was on the stockade wall.

Jamestown remained the capital because the colony had more pressing problems to address than relocating: security, relations with home, trade, agriculture (especially in the cash crop tobacco, which was planted in the very streets). Motions to move the capital were heard as early as Gates's day, but the colonists were preoccupied with surviving, making their livings, getting ahead. Then as now, life is what goes on while we're making other plans. If Jamestown was not an ideal city, at least, like Everest, it was there. If it escaped destruction by Indians in 1622, Englishmen running amok half a century later made up for that.

In 1676 a wellborn newcomer from Suffolk, Nathaniel Bacon, challenged his cousin-in-law, Governor Sir William Berkeley, over the latter's benign Indian policy, which successfully confined natives to reserved areas. Bacon inspired the massacre of tractable Indians, raised a rabble—some say a rebel army—and laid siege to Jamestown. When Governor Berkeley fled to the Eastern Shore to marshal his forces, Bacon entered Jamestown and burned it to the ground in a nighttime blaze that struck fear into men's hearts as far as the glow was visible. The firebrand might have reached greater heights, but a month later he died of fever—a case of Jamestown's Revenge?—and Berkeley reclaimed his ashen seat.

Taking vengeance, the governor hanged Bacon's followers, some at his estate and others at the place called Middle Plantation. This central site between two rivers on the high ground above the peninsula's narrowest spot already boasted a hamlet with a church and crossroads. It was the place where royal troops had been quartered and Indians agreed by treaty to live apart under English sovereignty. Then it was here that the Assembly, bereft of a capital in 1677, met at the home of one Captain Otho Thorpe and in its wisdom decided to restore the seat of government to Jamestown.

PREVIOUS PAGES: A man's wheels made manifest his station in life no less in the 18th century than today. Thus the governor's coach was a masterpiece of vehicular design, with a graceful wishbone suspension made of tempered steel and leather, an exterior painted with the care of Chinese enamelware and the motive power of a matched team of blooded horses.

OPPOSITE: A royal governor ruled over all he could survey—actually the narrow scope of Palace green as seen from a palace balcony. Just as the divine right of kings declined through the 18th century, the power of the royal governors in Williamsburg waned with the rising clout of the elected body, Virginia's House of Burgesses, which would eclipse the governor and his Council. Late in the colonial era the Baron de Botetourt held sway by personal popularity and political persuasion—until his enlightened rule was cut short by death and followed by the blundering arrogance of a lesser man.

Given the magnitude of the troubles that befell his administration, it was inevitable that Berkeley would be recalled to England. He was replaced in 1677 by Thomas Culpeper, a baron and friend of King James, for whom he performed one particularly noble service. Mindful that the Assembly had presumed the exclusive prerogative to tax Virginians since 1623, Culpeper nevertheless proposed a royal levy on exported tobacco. Predictably, the Assembly opposed it, but Culpeper had not been sent to govern because he was a fool. First, he promised certain rewards to certain burgesses if they would support his original bill, for example, to the elected Speaker of the House a lifetime seat on the appointed Council. Then Culpeper agreed to an amendment seemingly in a spirit of compromise: Tobacco carried in Virginia ships would be exempt from the new duty, giving the colony's captains a competitive edge. Through these maneuvers he got the bill passed subject to royal review. The king accepted the act, then exercised his acknowledged right to veto amendments, and the colony's advantage was annulled. Culpeper and his successors—uniquely in these colonies—were thus freed from having to bargain with the legislature for the funds to pay their salaries. In the meantime, Jamestown was rebuilt on its ashes. The city grew beyond its original walls until the autumn of 1698, when disaster struck again. The statehouse, fourth building to fill that function since the colony's birth, burned in a fire of mysterious origin. For reasons unrelated to the fire, a new governor arrived a few weeks later and threw his considerable weight behind the logical decision to move the seat of government.

The new executive was actually returning to Virginia, so the tangled tale of his administration (and the founding of Williamsburg) starts earlier. First a soldier, then a professional administrator and prototype colonial civil servant, Francis Nicholson eventually governed colonies as distant as South Carolina and Nova Scotia. Often champion of governmental reforms and a man of many talents, he seemed a paragon in some respects, though he had three besetting sins: a chronic thirst, an apoplectic temper, and an unrequited fondness for rich young women.

Nicholson had come to the New World in the 1680s as an infantry commander and served in New England under Governor Sir Edmund Andros. He swore loyalty to the deposed King James II in 1688 and opposed the succession of Parliament's choice, William of Orange, whose coronation signaled the end of royal rule by divine right. But he answered for that back in London and two years later was restored to royal service—this time in Virginia. Serving with distinction from 1690 to 1692, he opened new trade with Indians, inspected the frontiers, improved the militia, established a postal system, and provided both moral and financial support to the idea of erecting a college. This last notion proved crucial.

A college for Virginia had first been envisioned upriver in 1617 by King James I (he who won lasting fame for commissioning the Holy Bible's most poetic English translation). Possessing missionary zeal and captivated by exotic Pocahontas during her brief stay in London, King James had wished to educate "the children of the Infidels"—before the massacre of 1622 dampened such ardor in English hearts. The college idea then lay dormant through the reign of James's ill-fated son Charles I and the Puritan interregnum. It was revived in 1660 with the restoration of the martyred king's son Charles II, though by now its new goals had become "the advance of learning, education of youth; [to] supply the ministry and promotion of piety." Still it remained only an idea. Charles II's Catholic brother James II came to the throne and went into exile and King William was crowned before the idea arose again. Now it was championed by an ambitious minister trained at Marischal College, later a citadel of the Scottish Enlightenment.

The Reverend James Blair, the bishop of London's new representative in Virginia, won endorsements from the colony's clergy, the Council and notably Governor Nicholson, who was then

ABOVE: No portrait of Francis Nicholson survives, but the governor left his mark—both in this seal used to brand wine bottles and more grandly on his plan for the city of Williamsburg, "jewel in the crown of empire."

OPPOSITE: The Reverend James Blair made his mark in the institution around which the city grew, the College of William and Mary. He founded it, having persuaded his king and queen to charter a school in Virginia, then named it in their honor. To fund the school, he accepted gifts from any source: royal coffers, pirates' swag, the estate of the scientist Robert Boyle. Named president of the college, which is symbolized by the image of the Wren Building, he sat for this portrait, attributed to Charles Bridges, after 1735.

serving his first term. Possessed of persuasive powers that were nearly Rasputinian, Commissary Blair traveled to London, where he won Queen Mary's support and through her King William's. In 1693 he convinced the monarchs to substantially endow the college that would bear their names. (The commissary also raised private funds, including a gift from imprisoned pirates as a quid pro quo for helping to secure their freedom. More respectably perhaps, the executors of the scientist Robert Boyle's estate donated a large portion of income from his Yorkshire home, Brafferton Manor; hence the building that houses the Indian School at the college was named the Brafferton.) Bearing the only royal charter ever granted a college in English America, he returned to Virginia where the Assembly named him president of the college for life and the king appointed him to the Council. The legislature then debated several Tidewater sites and resolved, according to the modern historian Rutherfoord Goodwin, "That *Middle Plantation* be the Place for erecting the said College of *William and Mary* in *Virginia* and that the said College be at that Place erected and built as neare the Church now standing in *Middle Plantation* old Fields as Convenience will permitt."

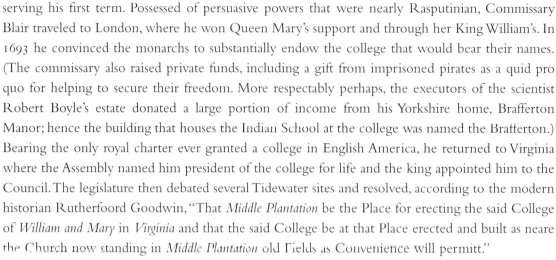

The city that Governor Nicholson planned was very grand for its time—despite the encroaching wilderness. Duke of Gloucester Street stretched straight as a string for a mile from the Capitol to the college, yet a carriage passing its length would vanish from view twice, so deep were the ravines.

Meanwhile, in one of those shuffles that colonial administration was heir to, Nicholson was recalled to England, then named governor of Maryland while his old boss succeeded him as head of the Virginia government. Sir Edmund Andros was ensconced in Jamestown when Commissary Blair returned from England and the two quickly quarreled (as indeed Blair quarreled with—and bested—almost everyone who crossed him). When Blair fell sick and couldn't preach, Andros appointed another minister to fill the Jamestown pulpit; recovering his health, Blair raged so violently about the affront that Andros suspended him from the Council. A witness observed that the first college building's foundation was laid "with the best Solemnity we were capeable" on August 8, 1695. But dignity deteriorated from there, when the king restored Blair to his Council seat and the feud between governor and commissary grew hotter.

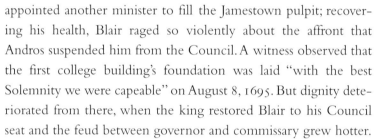

Andros accused Blair of unbridled conduct and Blair replied with volleys of charges: everything from antipathy for the college in general to making off with bricks meant for its construction in particular. He spread tales of gubernatorial error as far as his pen could reach, writing Nicholson in Maryland that Col. Philip Ludwell, the best man to oversee the college's construction, had begged off. "The reason he gives out Publickly is his age. . . . But he sticks not to say among his Friends, that he sees no possibility of carrying it on in this Governors time." Journeying back to Virginia, Nicholson vainly tried to mediate and was arrested by Andros for his pains. Blair went all the way back to England and brought charges against Andros before the archbishop of Canterbury. In Andros's place, Blair and such worthies as John Locke secured the reappointment of Nicholson, who had officially supported the college plan and personally subscribed £150 to it. For the moment, Williamsburg had champions at the head of both church and state.

The returning governor was as ambitious, able and headstrong as Commissary Blair, his patron pro tem—even if he was less adroit in their ultimate contretemps. Nicholson's principal accomplishment in Maryland had been to design the new capital city of Annapolis after he had secured the removal of the capital from St. Mary's City (a stronghold of Catholics whose loyalty was distrusted by the restored House of Stuarts). His plan for Annapolis far up the Chesapeake featured open squares and major buildings set in circles to command the views up radiating streets. The design, a mixed success, departed from English tradition to reflect new urban vogues exemplified by Sir Christopher Wren's ambitious and unfulfilled plans for rebuilding London after the Great Fire of 1666.

Arriving in Jamestown weeks after the statehouse mysteriously burned, Nicholson willingly addressed the challenge presented by its charred remains. Knowing the old site, he disliked it. If a new statehouse were to be built, why not raise it in a pleasant and healthy place worthy of the distinction? There was already "the beginning of a town" seven miles away, as a student at William and Mary declared: "A Church, an ordinary, several stores, two Mills, a smiths shop, a Grammar School, and above all the Colledge." A goal clearly in mind, Nicholson began politicking to get his way, for though the governor's office had won certain new prerogatives after Bacon's Rebellion, his powers as chairman of the Council were limited to that of *primes inter pares* ("first among equals"). Perhaps he commissioned a survey without troubling other authorities about it. Certainly he consorted with Commissary Blair, still his ally, for on May Day, 1699, the college hosted a grand fete for the colony's populace and its establishment—the burgesses and Council with Nicholson at its head. The celebration featured student oratory to prove rhetorical prowess, and one scholar's address offered persuasive arguments for locating the seat of government near the young institution: "The Colledge will help to make the town . . . [by] the very numbers of the Colledge who will be obliged to reside at this place viz. the president and Masters . . . with such servants as will be necessary for the kitchin, Buttery, Gardens, wooding, and all other uses." Further, the student declared, the institution would attract "Tradesmen, Labourers, Shopkeepers, perhaps Printers, Booksellers, Bookbinders, Mathematical instrument makers, nurses for the sick. . . . By this method we have an opportunity not only of making a Town, but such a Town as may equal if not outdo Boston, New York, Philadelphia, Charlestown, and Annapolis; and consequently such a Town as may retrieve the reputation of our Country." The colony "has suffered by nothing so much as by neglecting a seat of trade, wealth and Learning, and by running altogether into dispersed Country, [i. e.] plantations. If ever we would equal these our Rivals, we must contrive to joyn our heads and purses together . . . learn to improve our shipping and navigation, our trade and commerce, our minds and manners, and what no man can do singly, by a friendly cohabitation and society to do jointly with one another."

A fortnight after May Day, one Benjamin Harrison, burgess, presented the student's prescient speech to the Assembly and formally proposed moving the capital to the college precinct. Meanwhile Theodorick Bland had surveyed the area's irregular boundaries and the miles-long rights of way leading to two landings on the nearby creeks. That task must have taken considerable time, yet Bland finished his survey map on June 2, 1699. Five days later the burgesses authorized the building of a city on the site his plat depicted. Nicholson signed the act into law the next day, as well he might, evidently having written a good deal of it.

This "Acte Directing the Building of the Capitoll and the City of Williamsburgh" at once stipulated the creation of both a building and the surrounding town. It is a remarkable document for its double focus and its syntax:

> And forasmuch as the Generall Assembly and Generall Courts of this his Majesties Colony and Dominion cannot possibly be held and kept at the said Capitoll [building] unless a good Towne be built and settled adjacent to the said Capitoll suitable for the Accommodation and Entertainment of a considerable Number of Persons that of Necessity must resort thither[;] and whereas in all Probability

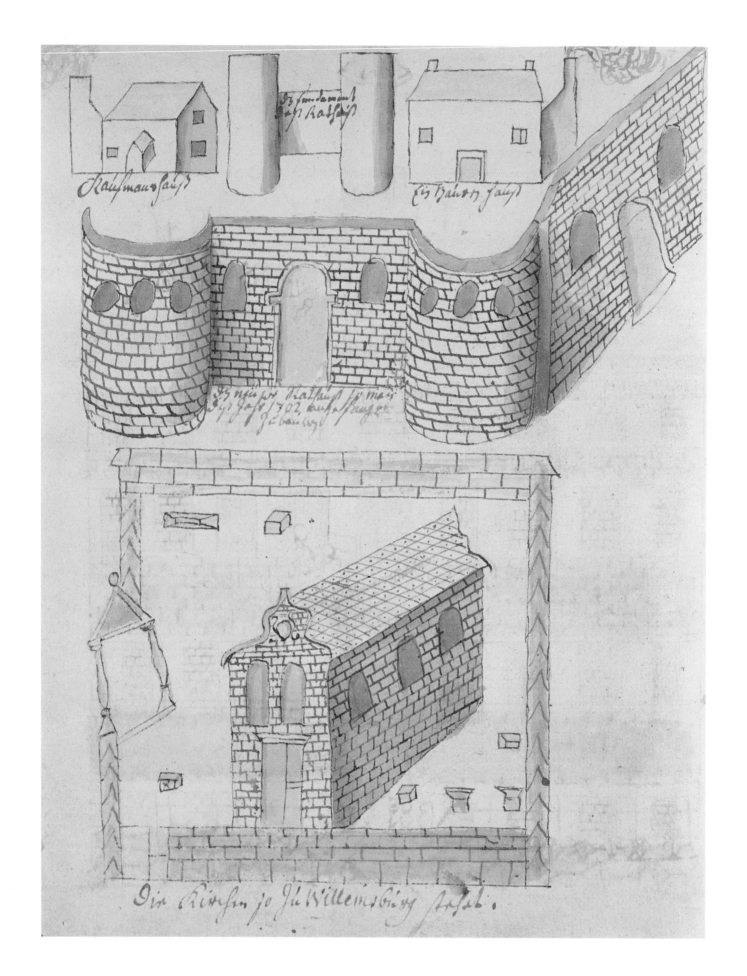

it *will* prove highly advantageous and beneficiall to his Majesties Royall Colledge of William & Mary to have the Conveniences of a Towne near the same[;] *Be it therefore enacted by the Authority aforesaid and it is hereby enacted[:]* that two Hundred eighty three Acres thirty five Poles and a halfe of Land scituate lying and being at the *Middleplantation* in *James Citye* and *York* Counties . . . shall be and is hereby reserved and appropriated for the onely and sole Use of a City to be there built and erected.

The act went on to reserve a specific plot 475 feet square for the structure to be "caled and knowne by the Name of the Capitoll," a term not used in America before.

Nicholson's original bill—for certainly he was the principal author—was marvelous in its particulars as the act went on to read like a zoning code. It specified sixty-foot-square lots for warehouses and such at the public landings on the two creeks, which gave access to the York and James rivers respectively. It directed that the town be divided into half-acre lots; that houses be set back six feet from the main streets; that dwellings measure at least twenty by thirty feet; that they stand at least ten feet high at the edge of the roof.

Building regulations would be written by "Directors appointed for the Settlement and Encouragement of the City of Williamsburgh." With Nicholson again the first among equals, these directors were empowered to "make such Rules and orders and to give such Directions in the Building of the said City and Portes not already provided for by this Act as to them shall seem best and most convenient": Twelve freeholders from the neighboring counties of York, New Kent, and James City were chosen to appraise the value of properties expropriated for the city; ownership passed to six trustees who were then commissioned to sell town sites and use the proceeds to repay the original owners.

Sales were conditional; a purchaser was required to build a substantial dwelling within twenty-four months or the land would revert to city ownership. While house size and material depended on the parcel—one needn't build two minimal houses on a double lot—all properties were to be fenced within six months of occupancy. Similar conditions could be applied to other parts of town at the discretion of the directors.

Having sketched the town in considerable detail and laid ground rules for its development, the act paid homage to royalty at home. It named Queen's Road, which led to a "Port or Landing Place" on Queen's Creek, "in Commemoracon of the late Queen Mary of blesed memory." It stated that Archer's Hope Creek, which ran to the James, "shall for ever hereafter be caled and knowne by the Name of *Princess* Creek . . . in Honour of her Royall Highness the Princess *Ann of Denmark.*" It declared "the said main Street . . . in Honour of his Highness William Duke of *Gloceter* shall for ever hereafter be called and knowne by the Name of *Duke of Gloceter* Street." (This eleven-year-old princeling was heir apparent to the English throne by an act of Parliament that established the line of succession through the deposed James II's fertile second daughter, a Protestant. Princess Anne conceived eighteen times but delivered only five children successfully, and none of them reached adulthood. The little duke died in 1700, and two years later the crown devolved to his mother—as Queen Anne—when King William died.)

Knowing that History does not reward the modest, the governor seized the prerogative to name the next largest streets Francis and Nicholson for himself. The rest took the names of realms in the growing empire, for this royal governor was careful to observe appropriate amenities often very grandly, as would happen when news arrived three months after the fact of King William's death and Queen Anne's coronation. Nicholson designated a holiday for some weeks off in order to have time to plan properly. As a Swiss traveler recorded, he hosted a day of both deep mourning and splendid revelry.

ABOVE: Nicholson's plan vanished but in 1702 Francis Louis Michel, a Swiss traveler seeking a place for a settlement, sketched the town's landmark buildings. The College of William and Mary appears in its original form before the first of several fires led to alterations.

OPPOSITE: Michel drew the Capitol with its unique rounded wing ends (above) and the first brick Bruton Parish Church with its enclosing wall and a scattering of tombs.

The "Frenchman's Map" of
1782 illustrates Nicholson's grid
plan of eight decades earlier.
Roads slanting from the west
end of town past the college
(left on map) may have figured
in a cypher of the royal initials
"W" and "M." No traces remain
of similar cyphers—which early
writers hint at—near the Capitol
and Market Square (near center).
Perhaps Nicholson offset the
central green like a diamond;
thus, the main street would split
to go around it, forming diago-
nals for another pair of cyphers.
Probably drawn by French army
officers with an eye to housing
troops, the map shows topography, dwellings, even outbuildings.
It proved indispensable to restorers because it located structures
and, for instance, apparently confirmed a report that catalpa trees
lined Palace green.

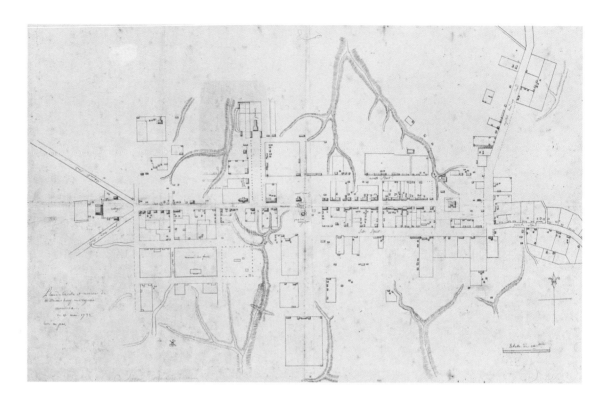

Most of the populace converged on Williamsburg for the occasion; two thousand militia from
six neighboring counties were in attendance, to say nothing of two Indian queens with two score
"of their most distinguished warriors and servants." Grandstands were erected before the college,
and musicians appeared on the college balconies. "On the uppermost were the buglers from the
warships, on the second, oboes and on the lowest violinists, so that when the ones stopped the others began. Sometimes they played together. When the proclamation of the King's death was to be
made they played very movingly and mournfully." Nicholson appeared in mourning astride a white
horse draped with black and Commissary Blair's eulogy moved people to tears. "Considerable
marching and counter-marching" continued until noon when the musicians abandoned dirges in
favor of livelier airs. Riding a new horse, Nicholson reappeared in a blue uniform covered with
braid and the new queen was proclaimed to rousing cheers and salutes from cannon. Nicholson
refreshed his honored guests "right royally" while "the ordinary persons received each a glass of rum
or brandy with sugar." The ceremony was then repeated at the building site of the Capitol and "the
Governor entertained again as at noon" as toasts "were repeatedly answered by guns and buglers."
That night when the master of ceremonies came a cropper at setting off the fireworks, the governor mounted his horse to oversee them himself. Nor did the revelry end there; it was all repeated
the next day at Nicholson's grand behest.

Whether as governor of Virginia per se or executive director of Williamsburg, Nicholson
claimed the role of urban planner even before the town was chartered. Given his worldly sophistication and experience, he was probably the most qualified man in town for the job, if hardly the
most popular. The lay of the land physically limited the town's options, and traditions of English
town design dating back to the period of Roman occupation dictated constraints at least as distinct.

Nicholson took it upon himself to design a city that was classic in some respects and progressive in others. While he had ideals, it was not to be an ideal city; the Tidewater was not Elysium
after all, but a ramble of woodland, pasture and gullies; his chalk was not indelible, nor was the slate
perfectly clean when he began. The main building of the college, already in place, faced almost due

east toward the old brick church. A road, or horse path in some people's view, came north up the peninsula, sensibly avoiding steep ravines by meandering along the top of the ridge. It followed the most level route, then split at the college, one path slanting off to Jamestown and the other toward Henrico and the eventual location of Richmond.

Topography and tradition combined as the locations of college and church virtually dictated a central avenue running due east from William and Mary. Tradition alone dictated a grid pattern of parallel and perpendicular streets. But Nicholson was aware of the new aesthetics that architects and planners like Sir Christopher Wren were championing at home in the dawning of a newly urbane age. A principal tenet on the rise was the importance of the grand view to show off stately edifices and simultaneously bring order to their surroundings. With these principles in mind, Nicholson ordered a boulevard ninety-nine feet wide. It ended at the foot of the first college building which the colony's promoters soon insisted (erroneously) had been designed by the master himself. As one correspondent described, "The Building is beautiful and commodious, being first modelled by Sir *Christopher Wren,* [and] adapted to the Nature of the Country by the Gentlemen there."

The street's other end, just short of a mile away, would be anchored by Nicholson's Capitol. Why didn't he place the latter building exactly a mile from the first? Alas, any rationale (if he had one) was lost scant years later. Even visitors, diarists and historians of his own generation could only surmise many details of his original plan once Nicholson had moved on. Nonetheless, his plan envisioned a main street linking the two premier edifices of the town, nay, of Virginia and even of the English colonies in America. No other American city of the period would boast such impressive buildings nor display them so grandly.

Cross streets would lead to large lots—sites for especially stately homes made all the more impressive by their placement—and Nicholson planned one site as grander than all the rest. Instead of an ordinary north-south passage across the main street alongside Bruton Parish Church, here his plan allowed a grand crossing with a ceremonial avenue twice as wide as Duke of Gloucester Street. This would provide a most spectacular vista when the inevitable governor's house would be built on the estate at the south end, a mansion the designer might have known he would never see.

At the risk of offending local tastes Nicholson embellished his grid design with diagonal streets to border open spaces and form royal initials. As the college mathematician and cleric Hugh Jones reported in his boosterish *The Present State of Virginia,* Nicholson "laid out the city of Williamsburg in the form of a cypher, made of W and M." Gentleman Robert Beverley put the worst face on it in his *History and Present State of Virginia,* which suggested a plurality of cyphers: The governor "flatter'd himself with the fond Imagination, of being the Founder of a new City. He marked out the Streets in many Places, so as that they might represent the Figure W in memory of his late Majesty King William, after whose Name the Town was call'd Williamsburg." If his statement sounds sour, Beverley had been burned by Nicholson's decision to move the government seat from Jamestown, where he held considerable property, and he evidently coveted the return of the capital to its original site.

The Colles maps of 1789 were a convenient and easily carried edition of route maps published for travelers. Each sheet showed a stretch of main road (this one divided into three adjacent portions) linking principal towns in the newly independent states.

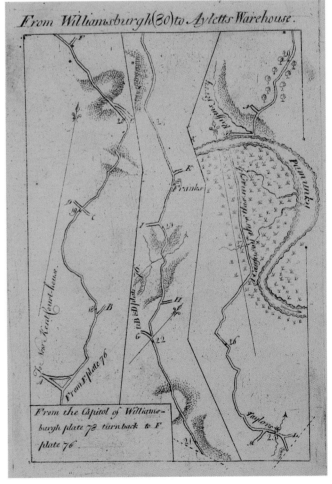

His Royal Highness Prince William, Duke of Gloucester and heir to the throne, displays a regal bearing at the age of nine, about the time Williamsburg's main street was named for him. The lad died two years later and two years before the death of his godfather, King William III, for whom the city was named. Thus, the boy's mother, Queen Anne, assumed the crown in 1702 to become the second of five monarchs to reign while Williamsburg was capital of the royal colony. This portrait is attributed to Edward Lilly.

While much of his design would stand the test of time, Nicholson's royal cyphers disappeared—almost as quickly as he did. The reasons for his departure were trivial and political. The governor offended powerful competitors, among others Commissary Blair and Beverley, who were his equal in nursing powerful grudges and engaging in mighty pettiness. Though he was gifted in several practical disciplines, Nicholson's violent temper and legendary thirst added fuel to his adversaries' fire.

In one recorded opinion, this worthy was "born drunk"; an impression memorably strengthened when a naval officer requested money to service his ship for the voyage home. Then occupying apartments in the college, "The Governour flew out into such a Passion against the Comiss^{rs} of the Navy calling them all the basest Names that the Tongue of Man could express, & with such a Noise, that the People downe in the lower Roomes caime running up Stairs." The witness testified that others ran down as best they could, including one merchant captain wakened from sleep thinking that such a row could only mean the building was afire. He fled before putting on either his pants or his wooden leg. Yet another time, Nicholson suffered a famous "love-fit," forced presents on seventeen-year-old Lucy Burwell, and generally acted the fool. When she refused his suit he threatened her and the man she meant to marry as well as any minister who would perform the ceremony.

The business over Lucy Burwell was the last straw for Commissary Blair, who once again applied to his friends in high London places. (More important, perhaps, power in Parliament had changed hands twice and even the most adroit politician would have been hard-pressed to keep his fences mended beyond an ocean that took one to three months to sail across.) So Nicholson was replaced in 1705 by Edward Nott, and the powers who remained in Williamsburg set about to undo what they could of the former governor's work. They removed his coat of arms from the Capitol and erased the cyphers that adorned his city plan. He wasn't gone a month when the Assembly amended his act, which directed the building of the city and Capitol in the first place.

In short order the Assembly and new governor appointed new directors, empowering them to make changes in the plan. They were authorized to "enlarge the Market Place and to alter any of the Streets or Lands thereof where the same are found inconvenient"—though Duke of Gloucester Street "shall not hereafter be altered either in the Course or Dimensions thereof." That course was straight in Bland's original survey plan, but the Reverend Hugh Jones hinted that it might not have remained so: The "noble street" became "mathematically streight" only after Nicholson departed and "the first design of the town's form is changed to a much better [one]." Whatever change occurred, it also pleased Robert Beverley who wrote in the second edition of his book that the streets were realigned "from the fanciful Ws and Ms to much more Conveniencies."

His considerable political accomplishments aside, this able if unbridled governor left legacies beyond his name on Francis and Nicholson streets. But for him there might not have been a college at Middle Plantation. (However powerful Commissary Blair might become, he was green when he first championed the borrowed dream of a college in his ecclesiastical domain.) In his first term, Governor Nicholson's gifts of money and support helped the idea become a reality; in his second term, his political gifts seated the government near the college. Finally, though his early plan for the town's design was altered, its basic form survived. It was Nicholson who sketched the town, made it Virginia's capital and drew Williamsburg around the seat of government. Whatever arose here grew from his brief vision.

Even as royal power waned, the governor's opulence waxed—as these furnishings reflect in the central room of his private apartment in the Governor's Palace. Based on an inventory of Lord Botetourt's belongings, his accoutrements boast ornate gilded mirrors, a crystal chandelier, a sophisticated secretary and ornamental china.

When Williamsburg became a city in name, it also instantly became capital of a strapping colony then on the verge of feisty maturity with a population of sixty thousand souls, the most populous of the crown's American dominions. The new city was born as the intended hub of a vital and complex community. Like the scion of a noble family who comes into his inheritance before coming of age, Williamsburg was in charge of a domain before it grew up. In a manner of speaking the city had been endowed an estate with a wealth of living traditions as well as all its burdens.

Chosen to play spiritual, intellectual and administrative roles—to fulfill many functions—the city had aspects of its eventual persona before it was born. What it lacked, of course, were the support structures both physical and intangible: first the major public buildings, then the offices, shops and dwellings along with a body politic to animate the idea of a capital.

This was an instant metropolis. Metaphorically speaking it did not have to invent the wheel; its coming residents, both rustic and passing elegant, had all sorts of working contrivances already: habits, ways of doing business, courts to settle disputes, and the like. These people called themselves English and the gentry in particular identified with the mother country, looking more slavishly to London for guidance in matters of taste with each passing year. These emotional bonds were strengthened by the facts of economic dependence on England, a dependence that was reinforced by laws that favored the mother country as a trading partner and gave her certain monopolies. Both blood and banking—through the coin of tobacco, which earned its growers credit with English merchants—bound Virginia to Britain.

Yet things were also different here. While both "the finer things" and necessary hardware like hammers and nails came from across the sea, outlying plantations sustained life. The plantation had become the linchpin for city and colony, for the overarching economy and social structure alike. The royal government at home desired colonial communities to resemble those in England both socially and physically. But conditions often dictated otherwise, and even the most loyal leaders here often decided against English precedents out of simple necessity.

Climate alone made an enormous difference. Temperatures could range a hundred degrees in a year and humidity vary from arid winter to sodden summer; thus, some materials favored in England were virtually useless here. Then there was the shortage of other building stuffs: stone, for starters, which was simply not to be had around the Tidewater. Instead of solid rock, the peninsula was made of clay, which became bricks when shaped as mud in wooden molds, then air-dried and stacked into hollow "kilns" fueled with hardwood and burned for a week. There were also middens of oyster shells that were burned as well to provide lime, a sine qua non for vast quantities of mortar. Yet if the peninsula lacked stone for building, it possessed forests of such height and variety that the first-comers thought they had found an inexhaustible supply of ships' masts, building beams and firewood. Another difference was that England's provincial capitals had grown helter-skelter for

OPPOSITE: As Rome rose in marble and Angor Wat in native limestone, Williamsburg was built of its region's abundant material: wood at first, then bricks "burned" from local clay. Builders enhanced the appearance of walls with a complex pattern of wide red "stretchers" and shiny blue-glazed "headers" known as "Flemish bond." They molded and carved special shapes for pediments, scrolls and dentil work and surrounded doorways with bricks polished to a smooth matte finish, cementing them with the slimmest applications of lime mortar.

more than a millennium, while Virginia's was cogently planned and built in mere decades. The public buildings here would also receive especially prominent placement of a sort unknown in most English cities, where even the grander edifices tended to take their chances willy-nilly among the rest.

If Williamsburg was rare in being designed, it was unique in that it did not have to accommodate the sort of commerce that choked growing New York and made Philadelphia a busy shambles. Their sites were chosen for their natural harbors; transportation was the key to these communities' very survival while growth and trade remained principal reasons for their existence. Here by comparison, the new capital did not need to manhandle and store huge amounts of goods (viz. tobacco) which were handled on plantation wharfs, in warehouses along Chesapeake tributaries, and at the planned public landings on Queen's and Princess creeks. This infant, instant city could concentrate on better things than serving as a plain port and moving goods. Spared the need to be very muscular, instead she would be smart—both intelligent and chic.

Of course the young city would engage in some commerce, if only to cater to inhabitants, seasonal visitors and the curious travelers attracted by her growing reputation. But her forte was beyond business. Her cornerstones were found in the cerebral estates of college, church and Colonial Government. Three cornerstones then? No, four, as it happened in a stroke both symbolic and ironic, because one of those estates would be made manifest in twain: Government would be represented by the legislative and judicial Capitol and by the residence of the royal executive governor.

The College, its construction slowed by Blair's quarrel with Andros and by a shortage of skilled workmen, was originally intended to be a quadrangle around a central court. But only the front range and one wing were built in those years, a chapel wing decades later, and the enclosing fourth side not at all. (Academic instruction had not waited upon the completion of the first college building, however; classes were first conducted nearby about the time the foundations were laid in 1695.) Nonetheless with the handsome front and the northwest wing raised by the second year of the new century, Virginia's first historian Robert Beverley could report "In this part are already finished all conveniences of Cooking, Brewing, Baking, &c. and convenient Rooms for the Reception of the President, and Masters, with many more Scholars than are as yet come to it; in this part are also the Hall and School-Room." In 1702 it could be said that the college population included a president, rector, grammar master, usher, writing master, and twenty-nine students in the grammar school.

The brick building itself was laid up in English bond with alternate courses of stretchers (bricks laid lengthwise) and headers (bricks laid end-to). By one count it consumed 840,000 bricks, most of them "burned" nearby of clay dug on the spot. In appearance the building benefited from the application of a newly celebrated code of rules that harkened back to the Renaissance and even farther to classical times. Sir Christopher Wren had declared that beauty was to be found in nature, and his designing heirs concluded that nature was geometrical—hence the vogue for employing geometric forms.

However formally the building's design conformed to aesthetic equations, the young college's small community didn't need such grand accommodations, which soon acquired other tenants as well. While the Capitol was being built, the Assembly, Council, General Court and governor found apartments here until they started using their own building in 1704 and occupied it fully the next year. Alas, they moved none too soon, for hardly had the lot of them moved than the college was destroyed in a fire of mighty spectacle.

Nicholson himself had warned that the college chimneys were too small: "A fire can't be made in them without running the hazard of its falling on the floor, as it once happened" in the secretary's office. In the Great Hall wooden girders ran "through the middle of the hearth whereby no use can

ABOVE: The ornate tomb of Governor Edward Nott, imported at public expense, bears the epitaph: "By the Sanctity of his Moralls and the Mildness[,] Prudence and justice of his Administration[,] he was Deservedly Esteemed A Public Blessing while he Lived & when He Dyed a Public Callamity." All this for a man who served just over a year. Like many immigrants, he failed to "season" in the New World.

OPPOSITE: The new city soon boasted the grandest buildings in English America. Drawings engraved in copper about 1740 and possibly intended to illustrate a history of Virginia show (top row) the front of the college with its flanking Brafferton Building and President's House (middle row, left to right); the Capitol, rear of the college and Governor's Palace. Discovered two centuries after it was made, the so-called Bodleian Plate would provide priceless information for the restoration of the colonial city.

The college's original facade gained this new cupola and right-angled pediment when it was rebuilt after the disastrous fire of 1705. Over the course of the next two centuries it burned as least twice more and was altered several times before the Restoration returned it to its 18th-century appearance. Traditionally called the Wren Building, it resembles some work of English master builder Sir Christopher Wren though no proof survives that he designed it.

Built in stages the Wren Building was conceived as a quadrangle surrounding a central court, which never received its enclosing fourth side. Seen today from the rear (above), the restored main range shows the odd roof hips depicted in the Bodleian Plate. The south wing contains the chapel (bottom left and right), now restored with graceful restraint. Memorials on the walls commemorate colonial leaders including Commissary James Blair and Governor Botetourt, whose remains once lay in vaults beneath the floor.

be made of it." The room used by the Council had a fireplace with "some plank laid just under it insomuch that at Christmas 1702 . . . the wood under the hearth took fire & was almost all consumed before it was discovered."

It fell to Nicholson's successor, Governor Edward Nott, to inform the government in London: "I am sorry that I must give Your Lord[shi]ps the melancholy news of the burning of William & Mary College. On the 29th of October between 11 and 12 aclock at night, a fire broke out there, wch was got to that height before it was discovered, that it was impossible to save it, the building, Library, and furniture was in a small time totally consumed. . . . I cannot tell what course will be taken to retrieve this misfortune."

Investigators heard hair-raising accounts: "Henry Randolph being one [student] that lodged in the College . . . doth testify that he was then in bed asleep, and one that lay in bed with him cryed out the College is on fire, wch awaked him, and looking up he saw the fire coming over the brick wall into his Room & so starting out of bed he ran down a back pair of stairs." Col. Edward Hill, a member of the Council and early backer of the college, "lay in Mr. Blair's Chamber." Aroused, he fled the building, and "made haste back into the Chamber" to save "what was most valuable." He lugged out his chest, then returned again for a sword, portmanteau, saddle, silver tankard and such truck. Carrying these things away, "If I remember well I had like to be knock'd on the head with something flung out of a window."

Glass for window panes in the reconstructed copy of the original Capitol was made especially for the 20th-century building. Rubbed bricks surround the openings.

Hill's self-serving testimony included the routine admission that he'd gone to sleep with a small fire still alight on his hearth, which some thought started the conflagration. Others suspected foul play, as they had in Jamestown when the old statehouse had burned seven years and nine days earlier. College Master Mungo Ingles bruited the news that Robert Beverley and some others passed the rest of the night "drinking & ranting & carousing." One of them "(but I cannot learn who) was heard to say that if some Thunderbolt of lightning should destroy the Capitol, they might have some hopes of having the Seat of Governmt again at James Town. It's happening at so silent a time of the night, has left us all in the Dark about its cause and nothing but a large field for conjecture to loose it self in."

Nor was that field ever paled, for there were charges of dissembling and cover-up "as Mr. Commissary gives it out, on purpose to divert peoples eyes." An official investigation failed to discover the fire's cause; Duke of Gloucester Street's western vista framed a gutted ruin where the thick walls stood charred and empty for several years.

The eastern vista presented the newly raised Capitol building, with Queen Anne's royal monogram on the drum of the cupola and her coat of arms in the General Court's chamber. Decorations aside, almost every detail of the unique edifice was specified in advance by Nicholson: its H shape, its length of seventy-five feet, the twenty-five-foot interior breadth of each wing and fifteen-foot pitch to the second floor. In conformance with the enabling act, the foundations were four bricks thick to ground level, then in stages the walls became thinner as they rose—half a brick thinner at the water table, the top of the first floor, and the cypress-shingled hip roof. (The waist-high water table was a course of specially shaped bricks that accommodated the change in thickness from broader foundation footings to thinner walls.)

It had sash windows, not casements, which were still more common, and ironwork, glass, paint and stone imported from England. Blithely referred to in the act as singular, the building became plural a few clauses later when it was ordered that "each building" would have flagstone floors. Further, a fifty-foot-long room at "one end of each p[ar]t or side" was specified for the ground floors. Graphically representing the bicameral order of the General Assembly, the building could easily be considered two: "One part or side of which building shall be and is hereby appropriated to the use of the Generall Court & Councill" (whose members sat ex officio for life as judges on the colony's supreme bench). The other wing "shall be and is hereby appropriated to the use of the house of Burgesses," the periodically elected legislative body, "and the offices thereto and to no other use or uses whatsoever." In size and layout each half (or single "building" if you will) departed from the earlier statehouse in Jamestown with its makeshift accommodations. Following the pattern of earlier Virginia courthouses, the Capitol's broad "front" faced Duke of Gloucester Street. But as a twin complex, there was nothing like it in Virginia or anywhere else.

The two parts or buildings were joined by a gallery "raised upon Piazzas." That gallery supported "in the middle thereof a Cupulo to surmount the rest of the building Wch shall have a Clock placed in it and on the top of the sd Cupulo shall be a flag upon occasion." Although the building that emerged was H-shaped, its initial plan appeared otherwise; originally the gallery that formed the bar of the H was to be crossed by an additional gallery. This extra "cross gallery" was abandoned and the main gallery—the bar of the H—was widened. Once intended as a passage between the council room in the west and the committee rooms in the east, it was redesigned as a conference room for joint committees.

Perhaps with the lesson of the Jamestown statehouse fire in mind, the act had not provided for chimneys. At first there were neither fires nor smoking of tobacco inside, a prohibition that lasted only a few years until the secretary complained that dampness was injuring his precious records. Accordingly, chimneys were soon added so the place could be heated in winter. (Almost inevitably, it seems, the Capitol would burn—on January 30, 1747.)

A committee named to oversee the construction had hired Henry Cary to do the work in the spring of 1701. Though he had already built a Yorktown courthouse, he was required to start on a trial basis for a £50 fee before he began collecting a salary of £100 a year. His first order of business was to collect materials: 600,000 bricks at 20 shillings a thousand, oyster shells for mortar at 1

The superior appointments of the General Court reflect the importance of the colony's supreme tribunal. Today it features a glass chandelier, raised bench, gallery and faux marble in the panels painted to resemble stone.

shilling 3 pence per hogshead, and hardware worth over £100 from England. The foundation was laid August 7, 1701, six years to the day after the college. By autumn Cary began felling trees and laying lumber by for "fit scantlings sawd of high land white Oak for the Capitol doore Cases and windowe frames."

He was also ordered to get inch-thick pine planks for scaffolding, inch-and-a-quarter-thick heart pine for flooring and a miscellany of victuals: 20 barrels of pork, 150 bushels of corn and 20 bushels of peas, all this "for diet for the Workmen." Six of them were brought from England and billeted in a kind of exile since a special bill prohibited the taverns from "entertaining any of them or selling them any drink." Other laborers were recruited locally, including four slaves whom Henry Cary bought for £120 from his brother Miles, who was rector of the college, a burgess and clerk for the building committee. When the work was finished, Henry then bought three of the slaves back at cost. When the books were balanced *in medias res,* it was found that £3,822 had been spent and the project was over budget.

The Council first sat in its round-ended chamber on the second floor of the west building on October 20, 1704; the burgesses convened in their chamber on the first floor of the east building on April 21, 1705, and the builder's keys to the Capitol were ceremoniously turned over to the government on the last day of November.

In terms of time, Williamsburg's first cornerstone was Bruton Parish Church, which also became the first to disappear utterly and rise anew. By 1677 the parish boasted two churches in such sad repair that the vestry sought subscriptions for a new one. Councillor John Page gave sufficient land in the area that would become Williamsburg for it, with a churchyard sixty feet deep in every direction.

An "undertaker" (i.e., he who would "undertake" a building contract, not consign a cadaver below) agreed to build the new church for £350. But he found himself in disagreement with two vestrymen and had them arrested. Page himself agreed to erect the Jacobean structure for a down payment of £150 cash and "sixty pounds of good sound, merchantable, sweet scented Tobacco and Caske" from every tithable parishioner for three years running. Mr. Rowland Jones, the "first and most esteemed pastor" according to his epitaph (and eventually Martha Washington's great-grandfather), hired on in 1682 at a salary paid in tobacco (or the currency of tobacco notes) and dedicated the new sanctuary two years later. (At about this time deaths were registered for three pounds of tobacco, while the sexton got ten pounds of tobacco for the necessary digging. One could be buried in the church for one thousand pounds of weed or five pounds sterling.)

The new church was an elaborate brick affair with curvilinear gables, shallow buttresses, a roof slicked with two barrels of tar, and doors specified to be a foot higher and a half-foot wider than the church at Jamestown. As was typical of the period, it was not built very soundly. It required such regular repairs that by 1706 the vestry levied a collection of twenty thousand pounds of tobacco to build anew rather than patch the old. Now the parish fathers sought help from the government as they petitioned: "'Tis very Apparent [that] the Parishioners are very much straightened & often outed of their places & seats by . . . allowing room for the frequent resort of strangers, & more particularly at the meetings of the Generall Assemblies; Courts; Councells & other public occasions." Variously waiting upon each other, the men of Bruton Parish and the burgesses in due time agreed that a grander church was needed than the parish could afford, largely because visitors and transient public officials swelled the congregation mightily. In 1710 the Assembly contributed two hundred pounds sterling from duties on liquor and slaves "Towards the building [of a Church in Williamsburgh And for Making Conveniencys Therein" for royal officials and elected legislators. Moreover, a new governor, who had only just arrived, contributed toward its construction.

ABOVE: Alexander Spotswood: Williamsburg's second master builder. Born in Tangier, the son of a soldier and a career officer himself, he was an active and amiable man. After serving here and acquiring vast estates, he fetched a bride from England and returned to Virginia for the rest of his days. His portrait is attributed to the colonial artist Charles Bridges.

OPPOSITE: The reconstructed Capitol resembles the one that opened in 1705. After it burned in 1747, it was replaced by an edifice that burned too, in 1832. Surviving records, archaeology and a 1730s engraving enabled Colonial Williamsburg's restorers to raise the first Capitol anew as one antipode of the resurrected town.

ABOVE: Out of sight within its brick tower, Bruton Parish Church boasts the original bell presented to Bruton by the merchant James Tarpley. It was cast at Whitechapel Bell Foundry by the men who made Philadelphia's Liberty Bell. It was rung to celebrate the colony's vote for independence in 1776 and to celebrate Washington's victory over Cornwallis in 1781.

OPPOSITE: Appearing much as it did in the late 18th century, Bruton Parish Church is one of America's oldest sanctuaries to follow English Protestant tradition—once Anglican, now Episcopal.

Alexander Spotswood was an affable and able soldier who lacked the connections at court to rise above the rank of colonel. Born in Tangier the son of an army surgeon, he entered the army at seventeen and fought at the Battle of Blenheim where he was hit by a cannonball, which he kept as a souvenir. Like Nicholson in his first term he was actually lieutenant to an absentee governor who had been favored by the crown with a sinecure. (Spotswood served from 1710 to 1722 at a yearly salary of £2,000, of which he paid his superior and patron in London, Lord Orkney, £1,200.) Also like Nicholson, he was a man of diverse talents who would leave his mark on the town. If his predecessor had made the plan, this Scot would perfect it by making Duke of Gloucester Street "mathematically streight" and by adorning the city with several outstanding buildings.

Notably he was invited by the burgesses to "take the trouble of laying it out for Enlarging the said Church and building pews" for all officials. The Council recorded that "the Governor was pleased To answer that he thanked the house for the confidence they had in him, that tho he had never been concerned in business of this nature, he would use his best endeavors." Despite the ubiquity of his efforts, he was more of a seat-of-the-pants army engineer than architect; the felicity of his designs arose from a devotion to mathematical order. As an interested scholar later opined, "It would be wrong to say that in designing Bruton Church Spotswood called Geometry to his aid: he practically handed the job over to her."

Spotswood oversaw the construction of a church in the shape of a cross that lay, by tradition, with its altar to the east. The original plan owed its dimensions to simple geometric ratios; he may have started by having one internal diagonal sixty-six feet—the length of a surveyor's chain. But when it came time to build, the plan was altered. Having agreed to pay for twenty-two feet of the building's length himself, Spotswood then informed the burgesses that since visitors would be "Contented with less Room" he would "Diminish the Wings projected for Publick use." These wings (the features later called transepts) would be open to strangers while the main length of the church (e.g., the nave), was reserved for parishioners, with men seated on the north side in the early years and women across the aisle. Students from the college would use the rear gallery. When the church opened in 1716, the governor's elevated state pew in the east end was "covered with a canopy" on which his name was "written in gilt letters." (When the church proved too small, it gained galleries in the wings and south side of the west end, and then in 1752 an eastern extension that made the chancel as long as the body. It also got its tower with steeple and spire at the west end in 1769.)

Meanwhile, Spotswood had been busy elsewhere: enlarging the Gaol; designing the octagonal Magazine where the colony's arms and ammunition were kept; rebuilding the college; and finishing the governor's residence so grandly that it would henceforth be known—scornfully at first—as the Palace. The Magazine could hardly have been simpler given its elegant octagonal plan: The walls are twenty-four feet high and the roof twenty-four feet more; the diameter of the building, thirty-four feet, is the size of a square whose diagonal is forty-eight feet, or the structure's height.

As the Reverend Hugh Jones wrote, Spotswood also turned his constructive attention to the ruined college: "Since it was burnt down, it has been rebuilt and nicely contrived, altered and adorned by the ingenious Direction of Governor Spotswood." The walls still stood on the original foundations, and they were repaired. To make a more distinguished central entrance, he designed a shallow pavilion below a right-angled pediment. Redesigning the roof, he added a new cupola shorter than the original; now its apex stood sixty-eight feet above the ground, or half the building's length.

Spotswood's crowning architectural work was the Governor's Palace, which had been a gleam in every gubernatorial eye for two decades. A century earlier Sir Thomas Gates had built a residence

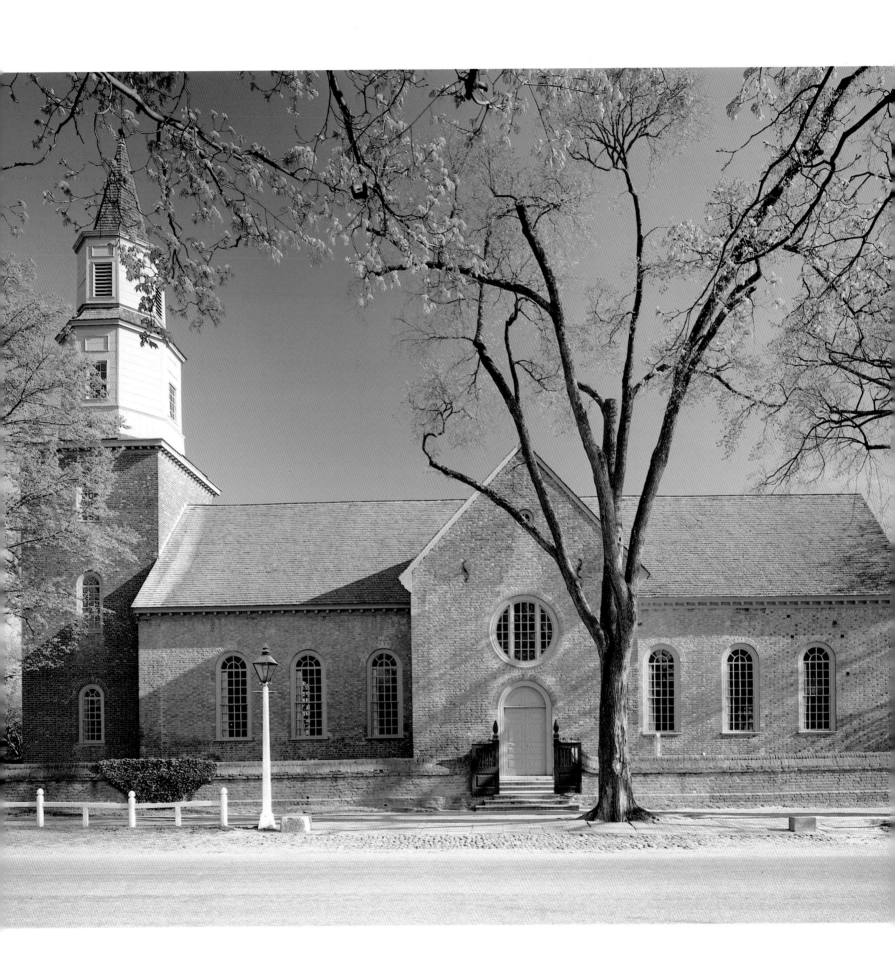

PREVIOUS PAGES: The private apartment in the Governor's Palace reflects the style favored by the last royal governors. The Upper Middle Room's walls are covered in embossed and gilded leather.

THIS PAGE: The Governor's Palace, first begun in 1706, enlarged in 1752 and burned in 1781, arose anew with the reconstruction of Williamsburg. A centerpiece of the new Colonial Williamsburg, it reflects the best research of the 1930s and the best intentions of the restorers. Changes have since been suggested, yet one school of historians would argue that it should no more be altered than a true antique building— in honor of its status as an icon in the discipline known as historic restoration.

of wood, which was later given to Governor Berkeley. Thereafter, resident governors received housing allowances for rented lodgings while London prodded them to build an official house which the burgesses insisted they couldn't afford. Nicholson had made no progress in the matter during his first term in Jamestown, but during his second term in the new capital he persuaded the Council to buy a sixty-three-acre parcel at the head of the broadest cross street. Still, royal and local authorities didn't agree on a way to pay for the residence until Governor Nott had arrived in 1705 and a duty was levied on imported slaves and liquor, like that instituted to pay for the Capitol. The Council invited Nott to design the residence in 1706, but the man was not "seasoning" well in the new country that was hard on immigrants, even aristocratic ones. In June an enabling act was approved by the Assembly; in August Nott's personal constitution gave out and he was buried in Bruton's churchyard.

This act authorized £3,000 for a two-story brick building fifty-four feet long and forty-eight feet wide with "convenient cellars underneath and one vault." Specifying sash windows and a slate roof, the act further called for a kitchen and stable and directed that "in all other respects the said house be built and finished according to the discretion of the overseer," Henry Cary again. He turned out to be somewhat liberal in his interpretation of what constituted an overseer's duties when no royal representative was in the land to oversee him. After spending more than the allotted funds, he charged the colony for his family's victualing, and may have gone so far as to move the family into a building on the grounds.

In any event, when Spotswood arrived on the scene in 1710 he found the residence insufficient and took it upon himself to oversee extraordinary improvements to bring it up to what he considered a reasonable level of elegance. He ended up paying for such amenities as gardens and a "canal" out of his own pocket, though arguments over who should foot the rest of the bill went on and on. Nevertheless, when completed in 1720, the Palace was the grandest residence in the colonies. (Like the church, the Palace would grow even grander over the years. Extensive repair work was completed and the interior most likely remodeled about 1751; a new wing containing a ballroom and supper room was added by 1754.)

The "cittie of Williamsburgh" was coming into its own. As Beverley wrote, "There are two fine Publick Buildings in this Country, which are the most Magnificent of any in America," the Capitol and college. The Reverend Hugh Jones added the Palace to the list: "These buildings are justly reputed the best in all *English America,* and are exceeded by few of their kind in *England.*" (He may be excused the hyperbole; he could not have seen Blenheim Palace, which was begun the year the Williamsburg Palace was first finished.) By the end of Spotswood's term in 1722, the town of 220 acres administered a strapping colony with a population approaching 90,000, and it dominated the local landscape. Where primeval forest lately stood, one could climb any of three cupolas—in Capitol, college or Palace—and see both rivers bounding a peninsula bereft of trees that had been felled for firewood and lumber. By 1716 it boasted that pantheon of artifice, a theater, the first one west of the ocean.

Yet the town still showed remnants of its natural beginnings. If governors decreed a "mathematically streight" street, nature declared it could not yet be level: A carriage negotiating the stately distance between college and Capitol would disappear twice from view, so deep were the ravines.

A weather vane tells the wind and a clock the time on the hexagonal cupola of the reconstructed Capitol.

As the May Day orator had predicted, "friendly cohabitation" of academe and government combined to make "such a Town as may retrieve the reputation of our Country." The college attracted students, masters, servants and merchants who sought their custom. The government seat drew a year-round population of civil servants, along with seasonal tides of legislators and men seeking influence and opportunity along with those bound to them by blood, business or bond. As the Capitol rose, lesser structures multiplied—dwellings that like as not served the dweller's livelihood be he artisan, hosteler, scholar or jack-of-several trades. These buildings were raised by skilled men, who borrowed English design traditions and later found general plans and fine details alike in printed manuals brought from England. To suit the new place they bent these Old World notions into an architecture that simply didn't exist elsewhere.

On many levels this architecture was a marriage—shotgun perhaps, or one of convenience—between substance and style. It joined English forms and traditions with native materials like "heart" pine, superbly straight-grained and everlasting wood cut from the center of trees that had grown slowly for centuries in the Tidewater's dense forests. It suited not only Virginia's climate, with high-ceilinged rooms and one-room-deep plans that fostered ventilation, but also the social lives and mores of its new client-inhabitants. As Hugh Jones wrote twenty-five years after Williamsburg's founding: "Here, as in other parts, they build with brick, but most commonly with timber . . . cased with feather-edged plank, painted with white lead and oil, covered with shingles of cedar, etc. tarred over at first; with a passage generally through the middle of the house for an airdraught in summer. Thus their houses are lasting, dry, and warm in winter, and cool in summer; especially if there be windows enough to draw the air. Thus they dwell comfortably, genteely, pleasantly, and plentifully in this delightful, healthful, and (I hope) thriving city of Williamsburg."

The developing architecture reflected an evolving society in ways both huge and subtle. Builders learned to get more attic space by changing the roof slant: Instead of a plain peaked roof with dormers, for instance, in the late colonial period they adapted the Dutch or gambrel roof, which had two pitches: on the upper part a very shallow slope, on the lower part a nearly vertical slant. As both the economy and social order became dependent on black slavery, the architecture developed ways of keeping the slaves apart. Domestic work came to be performed in detached dependencies, kitchens, dairies and the like—outside the homes of owners who paradoxically felt uneasy at the growing numbers of racially distinct people on whom their economy and comfort depended. Outbuildings, or outhouses as they were called, also evolved in part because they left the house free of cooking odors and heat.

The new architecture did not spring full-born from the brow of some designing Zeus. Instead it was firmly rooted in the tradition of English buildings both humble and grand, though at first it stressed pure utility. The earliest settlers at Jamestown probably built with mud and timber, using rafters cut from saplings to hold their thatched gable roofs aloft. No matter how humble the structure, its

OPPOSITE: On an autumn morning two citizens of Williamsburg open a shop to await the custom of new patrons—as once the newborn city, named capital of the colony, awaited the tides of folks who came from throughout Virginia's growing breadth to attend "Publick Times" twice each year.

single room was called the "great room" or "hall." One of the long walls was broken by an off-center door, while the short wall farthest from it had a hearth and exterior chimney. The floor was packed dirt, the walls daubed clay, though some walls would occasionally boast plaster. A flat ceiling was introduced to serve as the floor above for the simplest of attics reached by a ladder.

The first grand house in Virginia was Governor Berkeley's Green Spring, built on an English model in the 1640s. Called by his wife "the only tollerable place for a Governour," it was among other things the spot where Berkeley hanged some of Bacon's followers and received the royal commissioners sent to investigate the rebellion that blotted his long record of service. (The king's agents would see him recalled to England after Lady Berkeley saw to it that they left the estate in a coach driven by the local hangman.) That house burned in the eighteenth century; an even grander house, built in the 1680s or 1690s, stretched almost a hundred feet along a riverside rise. This one had two rows of dormers and four downstairs rooms (plus a wing probably containing a kitchen). The front door, set dead center, opened into an almost square "hall," the most public room in the house, perhaps in the colony.

In 1665, two decades after the original Green Spring was built, Arthur Allen raised an equally impressive house across the James River. Inherited by his son, a Speaker of the House of Burgesses, it was seized by insurgents in the 1676 rebellion, and though their leader may never have darkened its door, it became known a century later as Bacon's Castle. Shaped like an unbalanced cross, its broad arms contained both the largest room belowstairs, the hall, and a less formal, slightly smaller chamber. The shallow arms, which were the home's front and back, accommodated stairs in the rear and in front a closed entrance "porch" upstairs and down.

Large brick country houses aside, by century's end and Williamsburg's birth the plainest home was still very simple indeed: one oblong room with a loft under the peaked roof reached by a ladder. The outside door was still placed near or on-center of one of the long walls, the fireplace and chimney in the middle of the far short wall. This kind of building could grow, as the house bought by General Court clerk and entrepreneur Benjamin Waller later tripled in size from one-room simplicity to genteel complexity. Waller bought a large tract of land east of the Capitol and sold off the lots piecemeal as a distinct new district of the town. The lot he took for himself had a basic house on it, which then gained additions.

Even as most Williamsburg houses became more sophisticated, the most simple and useful form would abide or often return in such ubiquitous outbuildings as kitchens. Unadorned, the basic building would return in a little bootmaker's shop that would one day stand on Duke of Gloucester Street, a house big enough for two or three men to "stick to their lasts" by the windows.

In one early stage of development, the simple building—whether workshop, store, tavern or most likely, a dwelling with a commercial use as well—acquired an inside partition. Thus the Virginia yeoman entered a narrow "passage" containing a stair to the loft above. The "hall" remained the major downstairs room, still boasting a fireplace on the far short wall. Another practical design, this one never quite vanished either, but was adapted for use as late as the twentieth century.

During Spotswood's term, John Brush paid £4 to buy his freedom from apprenticeship in London. He was admitted as a journeyman into the Gunmaker's Company, a guild, and made his way to Virginia. Perhaps he came at the behest of the governor, who found that "the great part of the Arms in the Magazine and at the Governor's House were much out of repair and unfit for Service." It was Brush who refurbished them as "Publick Armorer," keeper of the new Magazine and a signal member of the community. In 1717 he acquired a choice Williamsburg lot: the one closest to the governor's residence facing onto Palace Green.

ABOVE: Governor Berkeley's great house, Green Spring, intrigued the architect Benjamin Latrobe, who helped design the U. S. Capitol. He sketched it thus in 1796 and wrote: Its "inconvenience and deformity are more powerful advocates for its destruction" though "the antiquity of the old house . . . ought to plead" for its renovation. In this he anticipated the historic preservation movement, which Colonial Williamsburg would both exemplify and champion.

OPPOSITE: The colonial aesthetic embraced practicality to a fare-thee-well, witness the Elizabeth Reynolds House kitchen. Like many in the southern colonies, it was set apart because kitchens often caught fire and incurred more damage if attached to the house they served. Separating the kitchen also served to remove servants and service activities · from the house. To minimize the chore of hauling water, the well was situated near the kitchen door. A paled fence enclosed all to keep out wandering livestock.

The staircase of the Everard House exhibits vigorous details in its carved brackets, which bear leafy decorations very similar to those in the grander plantation house at Carter's Grove. Possibly they were carved by an English immigrant carver and joiner, Richard Baylis.

Looking ahead, Brush built his chimneys at the rear, anticipating the addition of more rooms into the yard toward the separate kitchen, the "necessary" outbuilding (i.e., privy) and other service buildings. The armorer's residence also embraced some new ideas and spaces. As he built it, three rooms probably graced the ground floor: The centered front door opened into the "passage" with its stair; to one side was the all-purpose hall for formal entertaining (now called the parlor), and to the other side was the new "chamber" (today's family room), a more intimate room where the family took their meals and leisure.

At about the same time that Brush was building his house, William Robertson was raising his own on nearby Nicholson Street. Clerk of the Council, gentleman and factotum for a succession of governors, he kept in step with new style—or perhaps barely astride of changing fashion. He built a dwelling that boasted a stair passage and three rooms downstairs, all of them heated by fireplaces serving a single chimney. In addition to the more formal hall (parlor) and informal chamber (small parlor), it had a new amenity called the dining room.

About 1726 the Nicholson Street property was bought by John Randolph, later the only Virginian ever knighted and an eminent man of law whose son Peyton would become president of the First Continental Congress and whose other son John, dubbed "the Tory," would return to England on the eve of the Revolution. Such a distinguished family required a grander domicile than even the Council's clerk, and the two-story house that Robertson built gained an extension in the early 1750s that joined it to a one-and-a-half-story dwelling on the next lot. This work, evidently ordered by the increasingly prosperous and influential Peyton Randolph, nearly doubled the house's size and altered its orientation by 90 degrees; now it presented an impressive and nearly symmetrical façade to busy Market Square. A visitor had to look twice to see that the chimneys did not match.

In 1727, by the time the Randolphs were firmly ensconced, Sir William Gooch came to govern an increasingly prosperous and peaceful dominion. The colony's shipping, once beset by pirates, now sailed freely; Spotswood had seen to that; an expedition he commissioned defeated the notorious

Edward Teach (more commonly known as Blackbeard), whose head was nailed to the bowsprit of the ship that brought his surviving crewmen to Williamsburg for trial and hanging. The Indians were reasonably tractable on both sides of the Alleghenies (until the French would foment them some years later). The tobacco business was hampered by overproduction more than anything else, and locally grown food was plentiful. The old adage that a mother should not get too fond of her baby was almost forgotten as more children began to survive infancy than perished. Periodic famine was no longer a living memory and family life among the gentry was more gracious. The continent's first theater had been built on Palace green by one William Livingston, sometime dancing master and musician, who staged plays by Shakespeare and other entertainments. Virginia was coming of age.

As in England and Europe, most people had more of the amenities once considered luxuries and more leisure than they had earlier. People of middling circumstances were on the rise, and Gooch's twenty-two-year administration seemed a period of prosperity and peace. (This notwithstanding his foray to the Colombian port of Cartagena in 1740. Leading four hundred Virginians against the Spanish stronghold in the War of Jenkins's Ear, Gooch was bruised by a cannonball that passed between his ankles. Adding insult to injury, he caught a fever. The expedition was ill-starred from the start; it was to have been led by former governor Spotswood, who died while embarking at Annapolis.) More thought, however collective or unaware, went into designing the family context, the home. Houses came to be more carefully and artfully planned and, as a result, more distinctly different from other buildings.

Workshops and commercial buildings became distinct too. On Duke of Gloucester Street, Dr. Archibald Blair built a store, which his apprentice, William Prentis, eventually managed in a partnership with some of his master's heirs. This handsome establishment, Prentis & Company, acquired "neat and plain" features. For one, the bricks down to the water table were laid in the handsome and popular Flemish bond—an appealing checkerboard of red rectangles and gray squares as plain red bricks were laid long-ways in a wall, alternating with shiny gray-glazed bricks set short-ways. Between the courses of brick, the shell mortar was incised with straight lines to make the walls appear more uniform. Unglazed bricks chosen for doors and window margins and building corners had their surfaces rubbed perfectly flat. The jack arch above each opening was constructed of specially tapered bricks that together functioned like a traditional keystone arch; as these bricks were wider at the top than the bottom (like a keystone), the arch could not collapse. Further, these rubbed bricks were cemented with pure lime paste mortar, which dried in paper-thin white lines.

Unlike residences, which sat broadside on their lots, Prentis's store and many others presented their narrow, gabled ends to the street. This practice evolved for the sake of commonsense practicality as it accommodated more shops in a given length of street. English experience had proved that commercial buildings virtually filled their lots. Inside a shop the space for shelves to hold a merchant's wares was far too precious to surrender to windows along the long walls. There was room enough for windows on either side of the main door at the front, which offered passersby a look at the goods for sale. In the triangular gable above, another door opened directly into the loft where more goods were stored and an apprentice slept at night, perhaps with an ear cocked for the sound of burglars.

BELOW: The human skeleton of the 18th century was identical to today's but the practice of medicine was not. Witness the hardware in the near case used for amputations (performed without anesthesia) and the set of instruments in the red-lined case, used to break gallstones, a common malady.

OPPOSITE: Herbals, infusions and other popular potions were dispensed in the Pasteur & Galt Apothecary Shop, a building noted for its "rusticated" wood exterior cut to resemble stone.

THIS PAGE: Daily life in the colonies ran a wide gamut, as it does today in reconstructed buildings. Thus a couple and a slave perform household chores in the sparse tenant house (top), and two miscreants wait out their sentences—or wait months for trial—in the even sparser surroundings of the Public Gaol (bottom) where they could count on little more than hominy unless the garden provided better victuals.

OPPOSITE: By comparison, in the lavish home of Peyton Randolph—now newly renovated and reinterpreted—the mistress of the house and her servant lay the table for a sumptuous dinner of savory pies and sweetmeats, all arranged with an eye to symmetry and not at all for caloric restraint. The dietary range between rich and poor was as wide as a continent.

The main room downstairs took most of the space, in keeping with plans provided by the most popular technical manual, Joseph Moxon's *Mechanick Exercises*. In short order this borrowed plan would be amended in the Nicolson Store closer to the Capitol and in the twin stores that the brothers Carter raised. Robert Carter sold general merchandise while James, a physician and apothecary, vended medicines and herbal cures under the sign of the Unicorn's Horn. Their three-story brick building contained two complexes, mirror images of each other. Each front salesroom had a bay window overlooking the street. The back "counting room," boasting the only fireplace, served as office and living room for the family, which slept in chambers above stairs. As was the pervasive practice by now, cooking and other domestic tasks were performed in outbuildings.

In 1738 Henry Wetherburn, operator of the Raleigh Tavern, bought two lots on Duke of Gloucester Street across the street from the Raleigh. Within a few years he built a tavern on the eastern lot, an intentionally commercial structure that resembled a fine house of its day. This rectangular building had four rooms on the ground floor, plus the passage. Patrons entered through a door that centered the welcoming facade with two windows on each side. The four rooms boasted fireplaces set diagonally in the corners; their hearths shared two interior chimneys. The bedchambers upstairs, where guests slept two to a bed, also had the luxury of fireplaces. A front room, too narrow for anything but a servant's cot and chamber pots, was still called the "porch chamber."

The new tavern featured a jerkinhead, or gable roof shortened at each end by a sloping face. This was covered by courses of shingles riven by hand, their exposed ends rounded. The tavern also had sash windows with lead weights and applewood pulleys, and sawn weatherboards, not clapboards (which were split from sections of oak log). Planed smooth for appearance sake, these boards were "beaded"— their lower edges grooved and rounded with a molding plane—primarily for looks. Out back were a dairy and the inevitable kitchen, which featured a room for sleeping, no doubt for the chattel help.

Wetherburn took advantage of all opportunities. When another tavern keeper died, he married the widow—not once but in two instances, thus by law acquiring his competitors' properties, which included the Raleigh Tavern. Enhanced by the practicality of his sworn affections, his business boomed. His clientele included not only travelers and transients attending the Publick Times, but also college scholars and gentry, the new aristocrats of burgesses and Council members. Some of the latter kept impressive part-time residences in the capital for when the General Court was in session and the Assembly convened, but lived in distant manors for the rest of the year. Flush with success and eager for more, in the 1750s Wetherburn expanded his facilities by adding a wing to the west. It was no longer enough to have the Bull's Head Room to serve private dinners and "clubs" of men who met for an evening of food, drink, gaming and conversation. Evidently hiring the man who'd built for him originally, he commissioned the city's largest public reception chamber, the Great Room that spanned twenty-five feet and could accommodate a hundred revelers at subscription balls.

Spanning such a distance required an expensive system of heavy beams and girders and a trussed roof. Like the floorboards of heart pine, the main beams were hand hewn with adze and broadax. Planks and joists from squared logs were cut in a sawpit with a two-man pit saw, one sawyer standing in a trench and his partner above him on a raised trestle. Like as not the heaviest work was done at the carpenter's yard: the beams hewn, the joists sawed and planed, the mortices notched with long straight chisels, the tenons carved to fit into them. Then all the members were pieced together and their ends marked with easily cut Roman numerals as amended by the carpenter's tradition. This way the frame could be built wherever the carpenter liked, then dismantled and carted off for rebuilding on the client's ground; indeed colonial carpenters served customers as far away as the Caribbean by building on the mainland and shipping prefabricated houses to the wood-poor islands.

ABOVE: Like other inns the vaunted Raleigh Tavern served as a social center for residents of Williamsburg and as a way station for all manner of transients.

OPPOSITE: Evidently an itinerant painter occupies the garret in the Raleigh Tavern where the easel holds a portrait in its final stages (top). Other lodging typically held several bedsteads and travelers could not be too fastidious about who shared their sheets.

In the quiet of an autumn dawn, North England Street runs past the homes of some of Williamsburg's leading citizens, leading up to the open expanse of Market Square and, beyond, the Courthouse.

Like many 18th-century buildings, George Wythe's house (even from the back) displays a stately symmetry based on the repetition of certain dimensions. The facade is as wide as the chimneys are tall. The height of the roof equals the diagonal from the centerpoint at ground level to each cornice. The height of the roof edge above the water table is the same as the depth of the house. Below the roof, the facade is twice as wide as high—a double square, one of the tidy forms based on neat ratios that Georgian builders favored. Also popular was the "root-two rectangle" in which a square was lengthened by taking its diagonal as its new dimension.

In 1754 John Palmer, bursar of the college, built a new brick house on the main street lot closest to the Capitol, a lot he and others had occupied before. Nearly twenty years earlier, a jeweler named Alexander Kerr incurred the city's official ire by "setting a Brick-Kiln upon the Capitol Bounds." Thus the Council *"Ordered* That the Directors of the city of Wb take care to remove the Nuisance." Kerr nonetheless built "a well finished Brick House" with "a convenient Store, Coach-House, Stables and other Office-Houses." In the late 1740s Palmer moved in, then one night in 1754 rushed out when another of Williamsburg's plaguing fires wrecked the neighborhood. The fire destroyed the store, where it had begun, and spread to two dwellings, causing damages rising beyond £5,000.

Palmer replaced his house with a new one of brick that resembled the town houses of London and Bristol in its urbane asymmetry. The front door stood atop a short flight of stone steps at the left of twin windows. The door opened into a deep passage, with the stairs rising at the back of the house. This was a "double-pile" home, one or two rooms deep. On the ground floor the hall and parlor each had a diagonal fireplace that shared a single chimney. Outside, the proud facade rose a full two stories from the water table to a steeper, taller roof than the norm. At ground level, the basement windows were guarded with wooden bars. Once the house was raised, workmen failed to fill in the widely spaced gaps in the brickwork where the scaffolding had been anchored, leaving "putlog holes," which birds nested in.

Within a year of the fire, Palmer's peer and Virginia's ranking legal scholar, George Wythe (pronounced "with"), took a wife in Elizabeth Taliaferro (pronounced "Tolliver"). Her father, Richard, was a planter and notably a builder of sufficient reputation to design and construct the new ballroom and supper room wing of the Governor's Palace. It is thought that he raised the splendid double-pile house facing Palace green, which he then gave to the newlyweds with the provision that it pass to their children at their death, or to his other grandchildren if they died without issue. In effect, his wedding present was life tenancy in the house that became one of the most celebrated in Williamsburg for both its elegant architecture and its enlightened occupant.

This was a builder's building, one most likely intended to prove Taliaferro's competence to the world as well as his affection for his daughter. The facade exemplified the new colonial style: balanced, symmetrical and geometric. The imposing double door opened into a central stair passage leading to another double door at the rear that opened onto the gardens. Four commodious rooms—the formal hall, principal bedchamber, dining room, and professor's study—graced the first floor and each was served by an ample hearth. Upstairs were four bedchambers, one of them often occupied by resident students and eminent guests in later years. (The Wythes lived long, though Elizabeth died childless and the widower came to a sorry end. He died in 1806—almost certainly from coffee that had been laced with arsenic by a grandnephew intent on getting his estate. George lingered long enough to disinherit the venal kinsman, who went scot-free because the only witness to his crime was a slave who thus could not testify in court. But these events happened in Richmond a half-century after Williamsburg's architectural flowering and its political demise.)

Williamsburg still had its debunkers of course, like the itinerant clergyman Andrew Burnaby who visited the city in the late 1750s and damned it with faint praise: "Although the houses are of wood, covered with shingles, and but indifferently built, the whole makes a handsome appearance . . . The governor's palace, indeed, is tolerably good, one of the best upon the continent; but the church, the prison, and the other buildings, are all of them extremely indifferent. The streets are not paved, and are consequently very dusty, the soil hereabouts consisting chiefly of sand: however, the situation of Williamsburg has one advantage, which few or no places in these lower parts have; that of being free from mosquitoes. Upon the whole, it is an agreeable residence; there are ten or twelve

George Wythe's desk holds an array of instruments—not just the books of a law professor but accoutrements deemed suitable for any learned man of the Enlightenment: a vacuum chamber for experiments in chemistry and physics, dividers and protractors and implements for designing a multitude of drawings.

gentlemen's families constantly residing in it, besides merchants and tradesmen: and at the times of the assemblies, and general courts, it is crowded with the gentry of the country: on those occasions there are balls and other amusements; but as soon as the business is finished, they return to their plantations; and the town is in a manner deserted."

For most, however, it seemed a capital town. Witness the rise in real estate values: Robert "King" Carter (whose nickname reflected his grand manner and regal three-hundred-thousand-acre domain) left a lot on Palace green to a son whose estate sold it to a London merchant in 1746 for £104. The next year apothecary Kenneth McKenzie bought it for £224, then sold it in 1751 for £537—doubtless with the substantial improvement of a double-pile house that Governor Robert Dinwiddie used while the Palace underwent extensive repairs. Two years later the government sold it for only £450 to Robert Carter Nicholas who turned a neat profit of £200 in 1761. He sold the place to his cousin Robert Carter as a home away from Nomini Hall, the plantation where Philip Vickers Fithian would teach Carter's children and keep a diary that became famous centuries later.

Further downtown in the commercial district near the Capitol end of the main street, a lot went for £350 in 1760. Ten years later it was bought for £600 by James Anderson, the public armorer who owned an adjacent lot and must have seen the writing of revolution on the wall. Early in the war he quickly erected several forges—five connected shops before he was done—to produce nails, gun mounts and other ironwork useful to an army. While he laid stout wooden sills on brick foundations, his walls were most likely covered with rough clapboards. The noises of war were loud in the land, and gracious Williamsburg, a century of evolved architecture notwithstanding, could still employ forms as simple as those found in the colony's rude beginnings.

The colonial capital became a metropolis in form and function if not in size, the epicenter of Virginia if the home of only two thousand souls. Preeminently and inevitably a place of politics, and mecca for everyone having business with the government, the capital was nevertheless a *civil,* social and economic community as well as a collection of buildings. What then of the life of the town? Or rather its many lives? And what role did Williamsburg come to play in the drama of a new nation's birth?

Williamsburg was the precinct of scholars and scoundrels, of gentlewomen and slaves, of indentured servants working off the price of their passage to the New World through years of service to masters who had bought their certificates of indenture. There were gentlemen whose lust for games of chance cost them fortunes; fortune hunters who thrived by investing more daring than capital; Capitol clerks and officials who saw their public duty as a means for private gain; gainsayers, unwilling to let Britain call every shot, who resisted such measures as the ban on farmers raising sheep for local wool; sheepish occupants of the Gaol whose kin brought them delicacies and firewood to wile away their prison terms; wily innkeepers who maximized occupancy by assigning guests to lie two to a bed; lawyers who had trained at London's Inns of Court; courtly thespians who staged such imported dramas as *Richard III* at the colonies' first theater on Palace green and later *The Beggar's Opera* at the Playhouse near the Capitol; a church musician who became the jailer at £40 a year to augment his organist's income of £25; printers who served as postmasters, assuring their publications a wider circulation; a black preacher with the engaging name of Gowan Pamphlet. Severally and separately, they made a town.

The center of their city was central to everything except politics (which had its nexus at the Capitol). Here stood the Magazine beside the field where the militia mustered, and where revelry and bonfires celebrated royal births, coronations and the arrival of the crown's new governors. The Customs House was also here. A James City County courthouse stood nearby across Francis Street until it was replaced by one on Duke of Gloucester Street that served both county and city. Misdemeanors and civil disputes were settled in this edifice; burgesses were elected on its steps as freeholders cast their votes aloud for all to hear before balloting became a secret act. Near its portals miscreants found swift justice at the whipping post, stocks and pillories. (Since a felon could lose an ear, a man who parted with one in a tavern brawl often came to court to seek a writ proving he wasn't maimed by judge's order.)

Market Square itself was self-evidently named. Governor Nicholson planned its use, which the city charter ratified in 1722, designating Wednesdays and Saturdays as market days. Farmers and other vendors gathered to sell food and goods of all sorts—first in rude stalls, later in a one-story frame building of some rough dignity that provided shelter for butchers' stalls. Slaves and land were also auctioned here (and at the Exchange between the Capitol and Raleigh Tavern, which dealt in tobacco and livestock as well). Here too occurred the three-day fairs mandated by the city fathers

OPPOSITE: In the central hall or passage of the Peyton Randolph House, a gentleman portraying Randolph pauses to view goings-on in the rear garden. Peyton Randolph's attention to detail when he expanded his house is shown in his choice of costly walnut for the doors and windows.

to start on April 23 and December 12 each year. Stray animals roamed the streets and fowl ranged free (fences required by law did more to keep animals out than anything in), yet human affairs were actively and strictly regulated by government in the eighteenth century. Witness the all-important taverns, institutions of singular significance in a town whose population would swell during Publick Times. Year-round the taverns were social centers and business places as well as way stations.

After 1638, when the Assembly first set the price for a meal or a gallon of beer at six pounds of tobacco (or eighteen pence in "ready money" i.e., cash), Virginia's inns, taverns and ordinaries—call them what you will—were closely overseen. At first the royal governor granted commissions to innkeepers, then the prerogative to license them passed to local courts. By the time the Capitol was dedicated, regulations governed the sale of bottled drink and established true weights and measures (e.g., four gills made a pint, two quarts a pottle). Limits were set on credit, with none allowed to customers who owned less than two servants or £50 in property. Penalties were established for illicit sales, and punishments fixed for gambling and drunkenness. Sailors, servants and students were barred from taverns lest they incur debt or cause damage that could not be recovered in a lawsuit.

Before a tavern opened, the court reviewed its location and the character of the proprietor, who was required to post a substantial bond. Each March the Hustings Court in Williamsburg set prices that taverns could charge for food, drink, lodging, even for a horse's keep. Those who overcharged were fined, those who reported scalpers were rewarded. By mid-century the annual license fee was thirty-five shillings; the bond was fifty pounds in "current money" (i.e., Virginia currency) and the proprietor who failed to get a license could be fined or sentenced to a whipping.

Bottles in the Palace kitchen hold a multitude of fluids: red wine, Rhenish (presumably a Rhine vintage) and English catsup.

The fare was varied. In the Bull's Head Room Henry Wetherburn served turkey, veal, chicken, fowl, calf's head, chicken and asparagus, lamb, tongue, pork, Scotch collops, fish, venison, beef, mutton, bacon. The celebrated diarist and gentleman William Byrd II, who daily recorded even his diet in code, dined at Jean Marot's ordinary variously on roast goose, roast beef, fricassee of chicken, mutton, fish, roast veal. To drink, Marot offered wines from Madeira, the Canaries, Portugal, and Germany; brandy from France; English and Bristol beer; cider; and aniseed water in addition to the spirits he produced in two stills. Another hosteler served imported red and white wines, Hock, shrub, arrack, cherry brandy, raspberry brandy, and citron water in addition to the inevitable rum made from molasses and a rum made from cherries too. There were ales and porter to be had, along with beers made not only from barley but persimmons and corn husks. The diverse punches—one recipe called for beer, brandy and sugar—were served by the bowl, and they were celebrated in their own right. The price Thomas Jefferson's father paid an in-law for a two-hundred-acre tract of land, Shadwell, was "Henry Weatherburn's biggest bowl of arrack punch." Drinking was the pastime of colonists of every station, while gambling was considered the privilege of the better folk and taverns were one place where they gamed.

Virginia gentlemen played whist, billiards, dice, backgammon, draughts and "the royall and most pleasant game of the goose" (a board game somewhat like our Parcheesi)—often for stakes as high as whole plantations. Many were ruined. When Williamsburg butcher John Custis lost heavily one night and died of a cut throat by morning, a coroner's jury ruled his death *felo-de-se,* a suicide, and his estate was confiscated by the crown. William Byrd III, who would hazard £500 at a time, gambled away his inheritance, ended up bankrupt thanks to his addiction and also died by his own hand. Loaded dice were not unknown, nor was violence. Col. John Chiswell, in-law to the distinguished Randolphs and a burgess, killed a rude Scot in a country tavern. Jailed in Williamsburg and then bailed out, he took an overdose of laudanum to avoid the shame of trial, according to rumor. Whatever personal prices were paid by sporting men, the proprietors of the inns profited from their custom.

BY PERMISSION

Of the Worshipful the MAYOR of WILLIAMSBURG

(For the BENEFIT of Mrs. PARKER)

At the old THEATRE, near the CAPITOL,

By the VIRGINIA COMPANY of COMEDIANS, on FRIDAY the 3d of JUNE, will be presented

The Beggar's Opera.

Captain *Macheath*, by Mr. VERLING.

(Being his first Appearance in that Character)

Mr. PEACHUM,		Mr. CHARLTON.
LOCKIT,		Mr. FARRELL.
MAT of the MINT,		Mr. PARKER.
NIMMING NED,	by	Mr. WALKER.
Crook Fingered JACK,		Mr. BROMADGE.
BEN BUDGE,		Mr. MALLORY.
FILCH,		Mr. GODWIN.

Mrs. PEACHUM, and LUCY LOCKIT, by Mrs. OSBORNE.

JENNY DIVER,		Miss DOWTHAITT.
Mrs. COAXER,	by	Miss YAPP.
Mrs. SLAMMEKIN,		Mrs. DOWTHAITT.
MOLL BRAZEN,		Mr. WALKER.

Mrs. DIANA TRAPES, by Mr. PARKER.

Miss *Polly Peachum*, by Mrs. PARKER.

After the Opera Mr. GODWIN *will perform the* DANCE *called*
The DRUNKEN PEASANT.

PEASANT,	by	Mr. GODWIN.
CLOWN,		Mr. PARKER.

To which will be added a FARCE, called

The ANATOMIST,

OR

Sham Doctor.

Le MEDICIN (the French Doctor) by Mr. GODWIN.

Old GERALD,		Mr. PARKER.
Young GERALD,		Mr. CHARLTON.
CRISPIN,	by	Mr. VERLING.
MARTIN,		Mr. FARRELL.
SIMON BURLEY,		Mr. WALKER.
ANGELICA,		Miss YAPP,
DOCTOR's WIFE,	by	Mrs. DOWTHAITT.
WAITING WOMAN,		Miss DOWTHAITT.

BEATRICE, by Mrs. PARKER.

The MUSICK *of the* OPERA *will be conducted by* Mr. PELHAM, *and others.*

In 1716 America's first playhouse opened on Palace green, where colonial Virginians attended plays by Shakespeare and other classical writers. A second theater, near the Capitol, in 1768 announced the New World debut of the London hit *The Beggar's Opera,* performed by the Virginia Company of Comedians with music conducted by Peter Pelham, renowned organist of Bruton Parish and keeper of the gaol.

It was the tavern keepers who organized subscription horse races at the track just outside town. "Quarter racing" was the early eighteenth-century rage, and Virginia horsemen developed a famous breed of sprinters, the first quarter horses, until longer distances became popular for racing. By mid-century, Williamsburg had a mile-round track, and match races of three four-circuit heats attracted bettors from all over, which just increased the taverns' business. Innkeepers, who sold a variety of imported goods on the side and forwarded mail, also profited from the trade attracted by cockfights. On the whole theirs was a very busy and lucrative trade. The value of one proprietor's bed linen amounted to £20, nearly the annual salary of a skilled tradesman. Several innkeepers owned as many as twenty slaves, or more than enough to work a country plantation.

Every class of traveler patronized these establishments. As acting governor in 1726, Robert "King" Carter stayed in a tavern when business kept him in Williamsburg, though he was the most extravagantly landed gentleman in Virginia. George Washington patronized Mrs. Vobe's establishment on Waller Street and then followed her to the King's Arms; for a time he favored Christiana Campbell's, where tips ran up his bill to more than £4 in 1768. When his wife and stepchildren accompanied him, he stayed at Richard Charlton's across from the Golden Ball. A few years later a German traveler found his lodging expensive but elegant: "Black cooks, butlers, chamber-maids, make their bows with much dignity and modesty; were neatly and modishly attired."

As habits changed so did regulations. By the 1760s the Raleigh Tavern served as a lecture hall (hosting one notable discourse "on heads," i.e., phrenology). With taverns increasingly becoming the meeting places of men's social clubs and intellectual societies, so, too, students came to frequent them legally; thus Phi Beta Kappa was founded by college men in the Raleigh's Apollo Room in 1776. In celebration of one event of public importance, a newspaper reported, "there was a ball and supper at the King's Arms tavern which the Ladies graced with their company; during which the populace concluded their rejoicing, by a repetition of the healths round a large bonfire. The whole day passed with the greatest joy, decency and unanimity." (Few ladies stayed overnight in taverns. By and large these were rowdy places where men caroused late into the night, often passing out before making it upstairs to a shared bed.)

If gentlemen frequented the taverns for recreation, they also entertained at home. In part this tradition arose out of practicality; the three hundred families who ran Virginia's society, economy and politics all knew Williamsburg, but lived on their far-flung estates for most of the year. To visit a friend or cousin like as not meant traveling a substantial distance and spending the night; to celebrate a wedding meant a house party that lasted several days. In this era of rising aspirations, middling folk, like their social superiors, devoted greater energies to finely orchestrated recreations in a manner that was quite new. After reading Greek and Latin on arising, William Byrd II wrote that he "danced" in the morning; it was his exercise. For others it was a social activity—what quality people *did* when they got together.

To entertain themselves and each other they also made music by singing, bowing, strumming, plucking and blowing as the instrument demanded. Robert Carter of Nomini Hall and Palace green, according to his children's tutor, Philip Vickers Fithian, owned and played "Harpsichord, Forte-Piano, Harmonica, Guittar, Violin & German Flutes [i.e., recorders]. At Williamsburg, [Carter] has a good Organ, he himself also is indefatigable in the Practice," observed Fithian. (The "Harmonica" mentioned was an instrument perfected by Benjamin Franklin. It comprised a set of spinning glasses that made musical tones when touched, just as a wine glass vibrates when one runs a wet finger around the lip.) Fithian, a candidate for the Presbyterian ministry from New Jersey, was commissioned to teach Carter's two sons, five daughters and one nephew everything from the

BILLIARDS.

ABOVE: Today near the Courthouse steps 300-odd years later children test the stocks that once held ne'er-do-wells in humiliating public punishment (top). The engraving, printed in London in 1780, satirizes a bewigged hustler and his dupes.

OPPOSITE: Colonial fathers (and children too) engaged in many games that abide with us still—billiards on a twelve-foot table now housed in the Raleigh Tavern, for example (top). Backgammon was played in the Geddy House Parlor.

English alphabet to Greek grammar in addition to reading, writing, "Cyphering" et academic cetera. Itinerant specialists instructed the Carter clan—and many visitors—in the social arts of musical performance and dancing.

Not only did people entertain at home, they adorned their residences with furnishings imported from England (shipped by agents who bought the tobacco that provided the colonists their distant credit). Fine porcelains, tall clocks, mirrors and rich fabrics all came from England; so did the styles of furniture, clothing and manners that the colonists copied almost slavishly. By mid-century, imported brocade and chintz were preferred fabrics; a choice Chelsea serving piece or figurine graced tables and mantels in every modish home. This was an age of balance and delicacy, of Handel, Mozart and the minuet, of Thomas Chippendale's chairs and Josiah Wedgwood's tureens. Virginia's aristocracy had the leisure and wherewithal to indulge in all these and more while middling folk cultivated their own heightening sensibilities.

As the colonists looked to England for guidance in the finer things of life, they also learned to provide them for themselves. A royal governor might bring suites of elegantly decorated hunting arms with him, but Virginia gunsmiths also made beautiful (and very serviceable) rifles, tools that combined base metallurgy with pure artistry in form and decoration. The councillor who sent abroad for a serving table and chairs had to wait six months or more, and then perhaps got only what the cabinetmaker happened to have on hand. To get exactly what he wanted, he'd pay more for local cabinetry because skilled labor was dearer in Virginia than England (while freight charges were absurdly low in empty westbound ships that had come to fetch tobacco). But growing demand supported growing industry. Men like Benjamin Bucktrout and Anthony Hay made up elegant pieces to precise specifications; if so ordered, they could borrow the selfsame devices of pattern and adornment that their peers in London used. Often using native woods and locally developed techniques, they made chairs, tables and sideboards that resembled London's latest as described in Thomas Chippendale's *Gentleman and Cabinet-Maker's Director*—and sometimes surpassed them in quality.

Clearly, accomplished artisans were at work in Williamsburg, despite the absence of guilds, which controlled crafts and professions in the Old World. James Geddy and his sons cast brass and bronze fittings, silver candlesticks, pewter plates and tankards. Unable to legally import raw silver from England—one of the many trade restrictions imposed by the crown—James Craig did a handsome business nonetheless. His patrons brought in salvers and coffeepots of dated design and bade him melt them down to make new ones in the latest style. He also wrought gold and made jewelry too.

If the colony had imported taste, it nonetheless found native talent in Williamsburg to produce desired amenities. There were wigmakers, milliners, tailors, bootmakers, bookbinders and shopkeepers of all sorts selling local notions made after English models. Apothecaries who imported the latest medicines from England also pushed homegrown cures such as rattlesnake root and ginseng, native drugs claimed to be as potently all-curing as any bottled potion for everything from snakebite to social disease. Like innkeepers, the apothecary, surgeon and "practicer of phisic" had their fees regulated by law for about two years around 1736, a year also notable for a new sort of license— the permit to publish.

For a century and a quarter Virginia was barred from producing one sort of commodity—the printed word. Gentlemen owned books; some libraries contained several hundred volumes, most of them classics and all of them imports. Governor Berkeley had railed in the seventeenth century that "learning has brought disobedience, and heresy, and sects into the world, and printing has divulged them." Further, he believed that publishers' stock-in-trade was "libels against the best government." In England the printing press was allowed in only four cities before 1695; in the Old Dominion, a

ABOVE: Today's costumed interpreters join hands in the first figure of a cotillion.

OPPOSITE: Engraved three centuries ago a rapt gentleman and lady trace squiggly trails across the floor to edify subscribers in the mysteries of the minuet. This plate in dancing master Kellom Tomlinson's *The Art of Dancing Explained by Reading and Figures* (1735) diagrams the dance's final steps and the arm positions that the partners must perform. Virginia gentry learned many arts through printed manuals and leaflets imported from England, font of their manners, conventions and fads, but the complicated minuet was best learned from one of the many dancing masters in Virginia.

OVERLEAF: The Wythe House dining room, its table laid as if diners had just adjourned for a dance in the adjacent parlor, displays near-perfect balance (save for the corner cupboard). Even the dishes upon the table are laid out in almost perfect symmetry. The parlor in Peyton Randolph's house displays symbols of his wealth: a gilded mirror, brass fire tools, cross-stitched fire screens and porcelain vessels imported from the exotic East.

Gloucester County man imported one in 1680, was ordered by the Assembly to print the acts it passed that year, and then charged with operating a press without a license. It would be half a century before printing resumed here in Governor Gooch's time. In 1730 William Parks came from Annapolis to take up the duties of public printer for Virginia. First his work was confined to printing official documents, laws enacted by the Assembly and the like; in time he built a paper mill to make his stock and published all manner of material: medical manuals, agricultural tracts, political pamphlets. These proved Berkeley's infamous point: A publisher could criticize governments or governed alike, spread seeds of dissent or contentment, disseminate ideas and even misinformation.

In 1736 Parks established the weekly *Virginia Gazette,* the colony's first newspaper, which survived him and two subsequent owners, each of them employees who bought out the business that enjoyed monopoly status. In 1766 Alexander Purdie ran the *Gazette* and favored the royal governor's view of news and events. Yet there were other sides of the story to be told, and enough interest in goings-on around America and elsewhere to support competing journals. By 1775 Williamsburg boasted three independent papers, all of them named *Virginia Gazette.* Berkeley might have anticipated the results of so many published voices and no doubt he would have dealt with them summarily a century earlier. However, many things had changed in the generations following Berkeley's rule, among them the methods of governors (who had to rule largely by persuasion rather than fiat), economic conditions, intellectual attitudes and political relationships both within Virginia and with the mother country.

The parental metaphor is telling; the colonies were growing up, and like adolescent children becoming impertinent, even rebellious, while England became less permissive and even more demanding of her offspring. Always the most populous of the British colonies, by 1750 Virginia had more than 230,000 inhabitants. She had come a cropper in terms of mineral wealth and natural resources, but tobacco proved an immensely valuable export. (This despite the fact that its market price could vary more rapidly even than its growth could wear out the land.) The evolving plantation system that produced it depended on vast tracts of virgin land or fallow ground and on a perennial supply of cheap labor. As indentured servitude provided less and less manpower, slavery became the keystone of the tobacco economy, and blacks accounted for forty percent of the population. Among worse things, this meant that farming had become a capital-intensive business since slaves were expensive to buy, if cheaper to maintain than free men. All this tended to concentrate economic power in the hands of a relatively small number of families who by now were all related by marriage several times over. As this coterie came to dominate the colony's economy, so these men also controlled politics. A virtually hereditary aristocracy had come to rule Virginia, and struggled to keep that power just as others tried to seize a share through hard work, shrewd investment or marriage.

The "Manor Plantation," seat of influence and source of wealth, was a microcosm in many respects. Fairly self-sufficient, it resembled a feudal fiefdom by the second quarter of the century. As William Byrd II mused at Westover, his plantation home on the James River, "I have a large Family of my own, and my Doors are open to Every Body, yet I have no Bills to pay, and half-a-Crown will rest undisturbed in my Pocket for many Moons together. Like one of the Patriarchs, I have my Flocks and my Herds, my Bond-men and Bond-women, and every Soart of trade among my own Servants, so that I live in a kind of Independence on every one but Providence.... I must take care to keep all my people to their Duty, to set all the Springs in motion and to make every one draw his equal Share to carry the Machine forward."

In such a place, the scions learned about governing early. A young Byrd's supremacy over personal servants was obvious in early childhood, while his liberal education was geared to provide all the sorts

ABOVE: George Booth, a Virginia planter, "shows some leg" (above) as he stands in the approved posture—one knee cocked to display a well-muscled calf. His portrait, by the artist and dancing master William Dering, includes sculptures (possibly fanciful), accessories added to the scene to prove the gentleman's gentility—or his aspirations.

OPPOSITE: A gentleman's pleasures knew no limits. In colonial days Williamsburg famously had a racetrack where one-on-one match races were a favored sport among the gentry.

of knowledge required to oversee agriculture, operate businesses, invest money and govern the folk of this New World Elysium. The boy raised to run a Virginia estate was also expected to do his share beyond its borders—initially by overseeing the temporal affairs of the established Church of England. In this era church and state were closely joined and the two heavily influenced each other. Not only was church attendance required of all freemen by law, but gentlemen with any political ambition at all began their careers on church vestries, where they conducted the business of the parish. Vestry seats were held for life; vacancies caused by death were filled when the surviving vestrymen chose their late colleague's successor. The gentry came to control each parish (as soon as there came to be a gentry), and power in parish affairs became all but hereditary too. The young aristocrat—even one with the most lackadaisical sense of noblesse oblige—would then seek out a post as a justice of the peace from which he would administer the temporal affairs of his community. Most young gentlemen took commissions in the militia and thus acquired military influence as well. As soon as they were able, the ablest of the lot would seek election to the House of Burgesses.

While nobody was looking, it was in this House that the first American revolution occurred. In Sir William Berkeley's day, the governor's appointed twelve-man Council dominated over the lower chamber, which comprised two members elected from each county. But as the number of counties increased to 59 by the 1770s, the number of burgesses swelled to 122—118 from the counties plus 4 from the college, Williamsburg, Norfolk and Jamestown. The Council, composed of gentlemen chosen by royal governors (and thus likely to be sympathetic to royal causes), never grew in size; it soon lacked the manpower to dominate the business of colonial government as it had previously. After 1750, perhaps as few as two laws were initiated in the Council; by weight of numbers and other changes the freeholders' chosen representatives had essentially assumed control.

Modeled on the House of Commons, the House of Burgesses was a deliberative body. As it grew, its more numerous members voiced more varied opinions, which were carried farther and wider both in private letters and in the growing public press. The colonists, firm in their belief that they

RIGHT: Virginia's legislators discuss the defense of the ever-expanding westward settlement.

OPPOSITE: Costumed interpreters in the House of Burgesses review a bill.

The mightiest weapons of all: pen, the paper on which to write resonant words and a shaker of sand to dry the ink. The quill comes from a living goose, and the marbled paper from the shop of Williamsburg's living book-binder behind the Post Office on Duke of Gloucester Street, while the well-used shaker and inkpot might have belonged to a Virginia gentleman who used them to write verbal shots that shook the world. Yet this letter opens with personal thoughts, and it is in such relics as these that historians find priceless information about daily life in 18th-century Virginia. Personal letters, journals, diaries, ledgers and such are treasured by modern scholars as they seek deeper understanding of our antecedents' lives. Colonial Williamsburg sets great store in its collections of such papers and ephemera.

were loyal Englishmen, also believed that tradition and the Common Law conferred upon them rights and privileges that could not be overruled by a distant Parliament or colonial administrators. Ever since civil war had rocked England, deposing the king (to whom Virginia remained loyal), Virginians had demonstrated their willingness to differ with political leaders at home. They called themselves Englishmen and honored whoever wore the crown while they learned to demand rights due them as royal subjects. (All agreed they could not reasonably be represented in the national legislature that sat at Westminster an ocean away.)

There was a mortal ambiguity in all of this. The key to wealth and opportunity still lay in land, and the land lay in boundless tracts to the west. Though London repeatedly tried to prohibit it, westward expansion occurred willy-nilly despite threats from French colonists beyond the Alleghenies. King George II rushed in both to defend his interests and to provide the royal protection that intractable pioneers had come to expect. Thus began the French and Indian War, a New World manifestation of the Seven Years War that involved all Europe. Simultaneously, this period saw new leaders coming to Williamsburg, which, as the capital, was centrally involved with goings-on in the west, and everywhere else for that matter.

In 1755 Gen. Edward Braddock marched grandly on Fort Duquesne (later the site of Pittsburgh, Pennsylvania) only to have his troops surrounded by an Indian force who butchered those who did not flee in panic. Braddock was killed, and Governor Dinwiddie then named the most proven Virginia officer, George Washington, as commander of all the colony's forces. Three years later British and colonial troops retook Fort Duquesne (which was renamed Fort Pitt in honor of the king's minister), as the tide turned against the French and their native allies. In the same year, Frederick County sent Washington to Williamsburg as a burgess.

In 1760 the king died, to be succeeded by his grandson George III. Two years after that William and Mary student Thomas Jefferson started reading law with the multitalented George Wythe, Williamsburg's burgess, a leader in its intellectual establishment, eventually the first law professor in an American college, and first among Virginians to sign the Declaration of Independence. In 1763 the Treaty of Paris certified Britain's victory in the Seven Years' War and her substantial gains in North America; France ceded Canada, and Spain abandoned her claim to Florida. That same year the young lawyer Patrick Henry gained fame as an orator in a celebrated lawsuit known as the Parson's Cause, a tangled affair that saw the Privy Council intervening in the matter of Virginia ministers' salaries. Henry soon became a burgess too.

Meanwhile, the king and Parliament were seeking new sources of revenue. Hard economic times had fallen on Europe; Britain's national debt had doubled as a result of the recently won war, which had been all the more expensive for the defense of the distant colonies. After a series of lesser money bills imposed new duties on goods, word came that Parliament meant to pass a Stamp Act requiring that documents such as deeds, licenses, newspapers and whatnot bear a stamp, for which the colonies would have to pay. Patrick Henry, though burdened by an upstart's reputation, delivered his Caesar-Brutus speech in the House of Burgesses. He railed against the act as a tax imposed by England's legislature, Parliament, despite the Virginia Legislature's presumably exclusive right to levy taxes in the colony. Henry offered seven resolutions of which five were adopted, the most extreme by only one vote. So hotly worded that some thought them treasonous, these resolves were opposed by such resolute men as Wythe and Peyton Randolph, who exclaimed in Thomas Jefferson's hearing, "By God, I would have given 500 guineas for a single vote." Next day Henry was absent, the five resolutions were reconsidered and one, the most extreme, rescinded. The editor of the *Virginia Gazette* had considered them too harsh to print, but all Henry's proposals quickly found their unex-

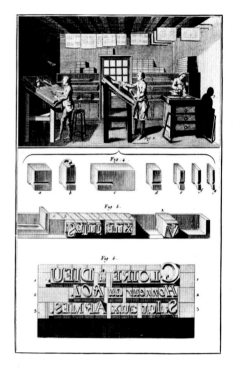

By the 1760s newspapers were a force to reckon with as they spread news, facts, opinions and rumors alike—much as today's media. How to set type and actually run a press was one of the many arts that literate Americans could learn "by the book" so to speak—in this case Denis Diderot's *Encyclopédie*, which was first published in France in 1751.

purgated way into a few other newspapers and spread throughout the colonies. In the meantime Governor Francis Fauquier, one of the most able to serve the crown in Virginia, dissolved the Assembly for challenging the constitutionality of Parliament's legislative supremacy. Legally emasculated by the governor's order, this colony's leadership could not send representatives to the Stamp Act Congress. Nonetheless Fauquier sent word to London that the Stamp Act, which by now had been passed, could not be enforced.

Henry's sentiments, if not his expressed resolves, found support in Virginia and elsewhere throughout the colonies. Opponents said the Stamp Act, written by a distant legislature, imposed a de facto local tax contrary to precedents established in Jamestown. For months the Stamp Act was the main topic of conversation. In Williamsburg it was debated in the Capitol, in the taverns and around the polished tables of the city's leading citizens over their long midday dinners. When a hero of the recent war returned to Williamsburg from England as distributor of the stamps, he had the ill luck to arrive during Publick Times. A crowd followed George Mercer to a coffeehouse hard by the Capitol where he was greeted by Governor Fauquier; the crowd became a mob, and Mercer only escaped injury or worse when the governor escorted him away personally. Next day Mercer resigned his commission and the hated stamps were placed for safekeeping on one of His Majesty's ships at Norfolk.

In some instances opposition to the Stamp Act was more subtle. Virginia justices of the peace and judges declared their hands were tied; since Mercer failed to deliver the necessary stamps, they could not conduct court business. While they continued to try murderers, probate wills and such, they declined to handle civil suits to the despair of colonists' creditors in England.

British wares such as this inflammatory teapot were imported into the Tidewater in the 1760s. The creamware vessel probably came from Cockpit Hill, Derbyshire.

In 1766 Governor Fauquier received word and announced the repeal of the Stamp Act, prompting revelry in the streets, an illumination of the town, and grand celebrations in the taverns. All seemed forgiven for the historical moment; Fauquier clarioned the king's benevolence in resolving the crisis (and invoked good Enlightenment principle to propose the building of a mental hospital, the first in the colonies). The Assembly proposed raising a statue of King George to honor his beneficent wisdom in repealing the improper tax. Still, that year was pivotal in several respects.

A cabal of "hot burgesses" invited printer William Rind to relocate from Maryland, since they could not trust the present *Gazette* publisher to air their opinions fairly. Also, Peyton Randolph was elected House Speaker after a most remarkable revelation. His political patron, John Robinson, long-time Speaker and treasurer of the colony, had very generously abused his official duty of retiring dated currency or tobacco notes (the certificates of ownership of tobacco casks that were used as money). Robinson had provided funds from this pool of supposedly obsolete money to various gentlemen in need. After his death it became clear that more than £100,000 in bad debts were outstanding. Robinson had not taken any of it for himself nor profited—except by winning friends and perhaps their votes. The most direct result of this revelation was the corporate decision to separate the duties of treasurer and Speaker. Thus Speaker Randolph saw Robert Carter Nicholas, long a leader of the conservative faction in the House of Burgesses and an antagonist of perfect probity, take the mantle of treasurer. (Like every colonial officer from county clerk to governor, he was entitled to a small percent commission on all the work he performed; but he never took a penny more than his due.) Thus, power in the liberal House was diffused.

While many problems and misunderstandings exacerbated relations between the several colonies and England in the next few years, Virginia remained closer to London than most. Alas, her good governor Francis Fauquier died in 1768, though he was succeeded by a most congenial and elegant gentleman in Norborne Berkeley, Baron de Botetourt, who arrived in a royal coach drawn by six matched grays. The new governor impressed hoi polloi and won the affectionate admiration of finer folk like Anne Blair, an avid correspondent who spread Botetourt's fame through her letters. A man of dignity and protocol, he presented himself at the Capitol, heard his commission read and took his oath there. When he banqueted at the Raleigh, the town was illuminated for him.

It was a lovefest; as one paper declared, "All ranks of people vied with each other in testifying their gratitude and joy that a Nobleman of such distinguished merit and abilities is appointed to preside over, and live among, them." For his part, Botetourt declared he would defend the traditional rights of colonial legislators: exemption from arrest, protection of their estates, freedom of speech and debate. As he had been a favorite in the royal court, so, too, he became remarkably popular in Virginia. If the colonists learned that he had been involved in a financial scandal and had tried to bribe the Lord Privy Seal to save his fiscal skin, they didn't care. The bachelor governor was almost instantly the most beloved in Virginia's memory. He endowed gold medals at the college "for the honour and encouragement of literary merit." Until he had furnished the Palace to his taste, the leading lights of town took him to dinner. He captivated the populace with his gilded coach displaying Virginia's coat of arms and silver-mounted harness—gifts from the king, who evidently hoped to save his able and hardworking friend from the worst rigors of his recent financial ruin.

But trouble had been brewing elsewhere. Since Parliament's passage of more revenue measures in the form of the Townshend Acts in 1767, colonists and British authorities were clashing with greater frequency and rancor. One of the acts forbade the New York legislature to sit, and in 1768 Massachusetts called for concerted action by all the colonies in a pamphlet that Parliament banned. Despite the prohibition, Virginia's burgesses—which Jefferson joined in 1769—debated the Massachusetts proposals; in response to a new threat they passed resolves much like those that had answered the Stamp Act, albeit in more respectful terms. The king's ministers had unearthed an ancient law: men accused of treason outside the realm could be taken to England for trial. The burgesses reiterated their exclusive right to tax Virginians, their right to petition the crown and to communicate with each other. Pledging their loyalty to King George, they also begged him to abandon the notion of spiriting Americans to London for trial, an act that could bring only "dangers and miseries." Under orders to suspend any Assembly that endorsed the Massachusetts proposals, Botetourt summoned Speaker Randolph to the Council chamber and with memorable dignity declared: "Mr. Speaker and Gentlemen of the House of Burgesses, I have heard of your Resolves and auger ill of their Effect. You have made it my Duty to dissolve you; and you are dissolved accordingly."

Quite simply he had invoked the royal prerogative to dismiss a legislature, a prerogative that was the linchpin of the king's power. That might have been that—had the House stayed dissolved, as it did when Fauquier had dismissed it a few years earlier. But the burgesses adjourned to the Raleigh Tavern down Duke of Gloucester Street and resumed their colloquy in the Apollo Room. Electing Peyton Randolph as their moderator, they declared themselves an association and deliberated a proposal brought down from northern Virginia to ban the import or use of British goods. Once fully drafted and debated, eighty-nine members of the "dissolved" House signed it. On that afternoon, May 17, 1769, elected representatives of an American citizenry defied royal authority with remarkable effect: They reconstituted *themselves* a representative government. They demonstrated that they didn't need the king's permission to act or represent the people.

Nonimportation became a matter of fact; the governor reportedly said privately that he supported the demand for repeal of Parliament's "obnoxious acts," and life went on. When Botetourt marked the king's birthday with a sumptuous Palace ball, "a numerous and very brilliant assembly of Ladies and Gentlemen attended." When the burgesses held a ball at the Capitol in the governor's

Francis Fauquier, one of the abler colonial governors, dealt with the Stamp Act crisis in Virginia. When he announced its repeal by Parliament in distant London, a ball and an illumination celebrated the event on June 13, 1766. His portrait is by Richard Wilson.

honor, their ladies attended in gowns made of homespun. (The boycott seemed a promising economic weapon, but its first casualties were those Britons most sympathetic to Virginians' interests, namely their agents and suppliers. This led to the charge that rebellious acts were being inspired by deadbeats who meant to welsh on their English bills.) When the Assembly convened again the following winter, Botetourt predicted a happy resolution to past problems and swore to faithfully present the colony's cause to London. Virginians believed the honorable and popular man to be true to his word, but he could not be so for long.

Botetourt fell ill of a fever in September 1770. When he died Williamsburg's three bells—in the college, Capitol and Bruton Parish Church—all tolled. Six members of his Council and Speaker Randolph bore his pall; Norborne Berkeley was buried in a vaulted brick crypt beneath the chapel of the College of William and Mary. To celebrate his memory, the Assembly commissioned a splendid marble statue of him to be placed in the piazza of the Capitol.

John Murray, Earl of Dunmore, a Scottish peer descended from the royal Stuarts, was appointed to become the next governor. His selection seemed to prove London's growing insensitivity to the colonists and ineptitude in coping with an already inflammatory situation. As patriot Richard Henry Lee wrote a few years later, "If the administration had searched through the world for a person the best fitted to ruin their cause . . . they could not have found a more complete agent than Lord Dunmore." Having just recently been named governor of New York, he got off to a bad start before he even reached Williamsburg by trying to wriggle out of the assignment. (It didn't help that his letters on the subject were published and Virginians found them insulting.) When he arrived in 1771, he rudely summoned the Council to the Palace—contrary to tradition—and took the oath of office there. As custom dictated, the town was illuminated for him; his only bow to precedent was to call for new Assembly elections.

Dunmore, who liked high living and brought an immense amount of luggage to furnish the Palace, was known as a philanderer by the time his wife and children joined him. As averse to hard work as Botetourt had been dedicated, he declined to meet visitors until he was forced to establish office hours. Oddly, he struck a friendship with George Washington, who found him an able man despite appearances.

When a ring of counterfeiters was discovered in Pittsylvania County, Dunmore had them haled into Williamsburg before they had been examined by a local court. The burgesses approved jailing the men whose bogus notes had nearly paralyzed business. But they protested Dunmore's abandonment of due process (no doubt apropos of Parliament's threat to take accused patriots to England). Strictly construing legal precedent and tradition, the burgesses objected that appropriate steps had been skipped by Dunmore's summary prosecution. They then wrote: "The duty we owe our constituents obliges us, my Lord, to be as attentive to the safety of the innocent as we are desirous of punishing the guilty" lest arbitrary justice threaten "the safety of innocent men." Within days the Assembly resolved to establish a Committee of Correspondence to share news of events in England and other colonies.

The pace of escalating events still reflected the distance in nautical miles between the mother country and the colonies and the months of sailing time it took for news (and official dispatches) to cross the Atlantic. The Boston Tea Party, the first notably violent response to a change in taxes levied in the colonies, occurred December 16, 1773. London replied by ordering Boston's harbor closed. When word of that response reached Williamsburg, the burgesses hastily deliberated. They resolved to dedicate June 1, 1774 "as a day of fasting, humiliation and prayer, devoutly to implore the divine interposition, for averting . . . the evils of civil war." Dunmore reacted by dissolving the

Dedicated, politic and able, Norborne Berkeley, Baron de Botetourt, arrived in 1768 to assume the governorship. Despite the troubled times, he became a most popular royal agent and was honored in death with burial beneath the Wren Chapel.

The Raleigh Tavern taproom was one place where Loyalists and dissidents alike gathered to discuss the issues of the day. Yet when the king's governor disbanded the House of Burgesses, the members reconvened at the Raleigh in a clear act of defiance; that is, they met contrary to the royal will as elected representatives of a people (above).

Behind the Raleigh, African-American slaves gathered informally too—and like as not discussed current events as well, including such matters as where their loyalties should lie: with their masters who were rebelling against established authority in the name of God-given liberty? Or with the British who promised emancipation to slaves who would rebel against their own rebellious masters?

On the grounds of the Capitol, cannoneers of the Virginia Militia fire their artillery.

House, to little practical effect. After assembling in Bruton Parish as planned, the burgesses scheduled a convention in Williamsburg for August and called for a congress of representatives from all the colonies. Convention delegates reviewed Jefferson's lately written *Summary View of the Rights of British America* and agreed to strengthen the nonimportation agreements. They chose Peyton Randolph to lead a delegation to the First Continental Congress in Philadelphia, and he was elected the Congress's president by acclamation.

In the meantime, Dunmore's one success came from capitalizing on trouble in the west. Settlers were ignoring royal orders and crossing the Alleghenies into land reserved by treaty for Indians; the Shawnees retaliated with raids and massacres. Dunmore marched to Fort Pitt (which he renamed for himself) while an army of militia under Andrew Lewis met Chief Cornstalk at Point Pleasant. Outgunned and outnumbered, Cornstalk fought to a standoff but sought peace when Dunmore arrived with reinforcements. Having planned a campaign in which Lewis took all the risks, Dunmore managed to win brief popularity in Virginia and London, while drawing attention away from more serious problems. For instance, in November of 1774 a band of patriots dumped two chests of tea consigned to Prentis Store into the York River.

By Christmas Dunmore was warning his superiors at home that Virginia was armed to the teeth and recommending that the navy blockade every colonial port. In March of 1775 Patrick Henry declaimed "Give me liberty or give me death" at the Second Virginia Convention in Richmond. The governor soon found it prudent to remove a wagonload of gunpowder from the Magazine. This deed was discovered and Williamsburg's mayor, accompanied by militiamen, went to the Palace and demanded it back. When Dunmore refused, Peyton Randolph and Robert Carter Nicholas managed to disband the angry throng. But a militia force was reported marching from Hanover, Orange and Albermarle counties farther north to seize the powder; in response the governor, who had no troops to speak of, announced he would put the torch to Williamsburg if they threatened him. When Patrick Henry mobilized another militia company to demand either the powder or reimbursement, Dunmore finally defused the situation by paying for the purloined powder.

In the meantime he had boobytrapped the Magazine and laid plans to flee the city. After convening the Assembly in June, he made the empty gesture of suggesting that voluntary payments to the king's treasury might replace taxes imposed by Parliament. Then he fled to an English warship in the dead of night, leaving a regal array of possessions in the Palace: paintings and furniture enough to fill 25 rooms, a personal library of 1,300 books, an orchestra of musical instruments including 3 organs and a pianoforte, 42 barrels and 2,000 bottles of wine, 480 gallons of vintage rum, 300 head of cattle and sheep, 19 horses, assorted coaches, carriages and other vehicles, 56 slaves and a dozen indentured servants.

The burgesses sent an envoy to the ship asking Dunmore to turn over arms and powder that he had cached in the Palace. When he declined, colonists broke in and took the ordnance. (Later his personal property was auctioned off to aid the war effort.) After sending his family home to England, Dunmore would further infuriate Virginians by skirmishing below Norfolk and offering emancipation to any slaves belonging to rebels (i.e., "patriots" in our vernacular) who would join the British cause. By now events had long since spread beyond Williamsburg, though men who had frequented the town were in the thick of them.

In 1775, on April 19 the first battles of the Revolution were fought, at Lexington and Concord in Massachusetts. In May, the Second Continental Congress convened in Philadelphia and Peyton Randolph was elected president again. In June, George Washington had been appointed commander in chief of the fragmentary Continental Army, and days later the British won the Battle of Bunker

ABOVE: In this portrait by Joshua Reynolds Governor Dunmore appears as haughty as his critics thought. Still, this English lord earned George Washington's respect as a dangerous adversary.

OPPOSITE: British satirists saw Virginia's gentry as a mob bent on coercing their betters to abet treasonous pacts—or be tarred and feathered. Events in the colonies supplied comic fodder for London wags before hostilities broke out during the gubernatorial term of John Murray, fourth Earl of Dunmore, Virginia's last royal governor.

Cannon smoke billows over Yorktown's heights as French and American ships blockade Cornwallis's army in this original watercolor from the period, one of many treasured documents in Colonial Williamsburg's collections.

Hill. In July, the Third Virginia Convention met, appointed a Committee of Safety and ordered the formation of two regiments of infantry. That month the Congress adopted a "declaration of the Causes and Necessities of Taking Up Arms," and two days later offered reconciliation to King George, who in August declared the colonies to be in a state of rebellion. Back in Virginia, in October, British forces raided areas around Norfolk.

The calendar turns and in 1776, events accelerate. On the first day of the year Washington raises a Continental flag with thirteen stripes at his headquarters outside Boston, while British ships off Norfolk open fire on American troops who have retaken the town. A month later the *Virginia Gazette* publishes excerpts from Thomas Paine's incendiary pamphlet *Common Sense*. In May, the Fifth Virginia Convention lays plans for a new constitution to govern this domain, and its delegates to the Congress receive instructions—the first of their kind—to propose independence from the crown. On June 7 in Philadelphia, the chairman of Virginia's delegation to the Continental Congress, Richard Henry Lee, offers a resolution for independence, and the Congress appoints Thomas Jefferson to chair a committee to draft a declaration. The following day, June 12, the Virginia Convention, still meeting in Williamsburg, adopts the first Declaration of Rights in America, based on George Mason's draft. A fortnight later the Convention adopts a constitution for the new commonwealth and picks Patrick Henry as governor. Three days after that in Philadelphia, Lee's resolution for independence is adopted by the Congress, and two days later, on July 4, Jefferson's draft Declaration of Independence, is adopted by the Second Continental Congress.

Jefferson would succeed Henry as governor and live in the Palace, which he had sketched during Dunmore's time. But because Virginia settlers were swiftly moving westward, in 1779 he supported a plan to remove the capital to Richmond the following year. A second reason for the move was that Williamsburg was accessible to attackers via the James and York Rivers; indeed, the little city on the peninsula would eventually be occupied by Lord Cornwallis (as was the new capital) on a trek that led him to camp at Yorktown where he meant to find a fleet bringing reinforcements. En route the British used the Palace as a hospital and, leaving an epidemic of smallpox in their wake, retreated down the peninsula, putting the torch to forges and foundries before they left.

Washington's troops—Continentals and French volunteers under the Marquis de Lafayette—chased Cornwallis. They stayed in Williamsburg long enough for the commander in chief to plan his next move, while Cornwallis, for his part, awaited promised aid from the Royal Navy or rescue to come by sea. Pausing until his own massive reinforcements arrived in 1781, Washington accepted George Wythe's invitation to lodge in his stately brick house on Palace green, where he passed a fortnight preparing for the battle. From there, he marched south and laid siege to Cornwallis's entrenched army, while a French fleet sailed up the Chesapeake to cut off escape or reinforcement. Thus surrounded, Lord Cornwallis surrendered. In practical terms the Battle of Yorktown won the War for Independence, and British power hereabouts went the way of Williamsburg's: It ended.

Each year companies of volunteers muster and camp in the old colonial capital, recalling scenes that led to America's Independence. In 1781 General Washington marshaled his troops at Williamsburg, where he awaited reinforcements before marching down the peninsula to Yorktown where his superior forces besieged the blockaded British army. Lord Cornwallis surrendered, leading George III to acknowledge his loss of the thirteen colonies in the war of liberation that ignited a revolutionary movement that spread around the globe and continues to this day.

THE PHOENIX YEARS:
Decline and Resurrection

2

The ravages of the rude hand of time meet the eye in every quarter of the town. . . . I never walk the streets without experiencing the most gloomy sensations, but it is a kind of pleasant melancholy, that the mind rather courts than despises. It is a dignified pleasure that is always experienced in the mind when viewing the vestiges of departed greatness.

—A Student in 1804

If there was no good "natural" reason for Williamsburg to be here in the first place—no strategic, commercial, or geographical advantage that dictated her location—therein lay her tragic liability, an almost fatal flaw. Having been created by the stroke of a pen, she could be erased by fiat too. The removal of the capital to Richmond in 1780 was such a stroke. It left Williamsburg bereft. Designed to govern, the city lost its *raison d'être*. The charter had been annulled, and Williamsburg began its long, slow decline into village status. Once a seat of empire, it became a backwater bench. The Capitol building, which had burned in 1747 and been rebuilt along very different lines six years later, stood empty. If a symbolic event were needed, the year after Virginia's new state government departed, another conflagration lit up the sky: The Palace, symbol of the royal presence, burned in a fast hot blaze and collapsed into its ample cellars.

With neither industry nor commerce to speak of, the people who had frequented Williamsburg in political seasons went instead to the new epicenter of the growing Commonwealth. Men involved in the business of government, like George Wythe, abandoned the place for the new capital city. Men of business who depended on the patronage of government per se or the custom of government people, like blacksmith and armorer James Anderson, followed them there. The courthouse remained, as did the city's first cornerstone, the College of William and Mary, which fell on very hard times. But for these two old institutions, and a new one, the city could have wasted away. One needn't look farther than five miles away at Jamestown to see a place that perished when human events took a new course and fickle History turned her back.

The younger institutional neighbor in Williamsburg had its ups and downs in a kind of counterpoint to the city's fortunes. As Shomer Zwelling illustrated in *Quest for a Cure,* his history of the Public Hospital for Persons of Insane and Disordered Minds, it went through many transformations. Happenstantially founded—as *invented* perhaps as the town itself—it was the brainchild of one generation of Virginia's enlightened leaders.

The hospital's first champion—back in 1766—was Governor Francis Fauquier, a member of the Royal Society in London and, once he reached Virginia, a leading light in the colony's intellectual fraternity. As a man of the Enlightenment (which knew no geographic bounds), Fauquier was a student of science and natural philosophy, a devotee of music and good works. No doubt he knew that a new sort of institution was rising elsewhere and thought to place his city in the vanguard of social progress. London had raised Bethlehem Hospital, better known as Bedlam; France had opened madhouses; Pennsylvania Hospital was reserving separate wards for deranged patients.

Fauquier proposed this hospital to the House of Burgesses under curious circumstances—right after word arrived that Parliament had repealed the hated Stamp Act in response to the uproar it raised in the colonies. The governor's address to Virginia's legislature began by espous-

PREVIOUS PAGES: The "canal," once enjoyed by Governor Spotswood, goes nowhere in truth—rather like Williamsburg itself after Virginia's government removed to Richmond. So the erstwhile capital city stagnated for fully a century and a half before its rediscovery and then its rebirth at the hands of one local clergyman and an army of architects and historians from the North, the so-called "second Yankee invasion of Williamsburg." Indeed, this even marked a second Reconstruction as some buildings would be restored and others rebuilt on the traces of their original foundations.

OPPOSITE: This house facing Market Square was the home of St. George Tucker who came to study at the College of William and Mary in 1771 and stayed on. An officer in the militia that became part of George Washington's army, he returned to civilian life and earned fame as a lawyer and civil libertarian, then in turn taught law and lived out his life here. The house passed down through generations until its last resident, Tucker's great-great-granddaughter, died at the close of the second millennium. Now it serves as a hospitality center for faithful supporters of Colonial Williamsburg.

ing lofty sentiments about how beneficently the crown and royal ministers had responded to the Stamp Act crisis. It ended on a very different note, indeed a sort of tangent, as he recommended building America's first public hospital exclusively for mental patients. The governor endorsed "legal confinement" for those who "cannot help themselves" and medical efforts "to restore to them their lost reason"—all this after putting as handsome a face as possible on England's surrender of principle in the recent Stamp Act showdown. Were the disagreements between king and colony akin to common lunacy? Weeks later the burgesses passed a pair of resolutions that suggested the legislators might have linked these issues too. First, they proposed to erect a statue honoring the king who had restored "ease and happiness" to his colony; second, they hoped to improve the lot of "persons who are so unhappy as to be deprived of their reason." By 1770 no less a moralist than Treasurer Robert Carter Nicholas expressed the fear that "Lunaticks and other unhappy objects of insane minds . . . will multiply too fast in this country." All was not right in the mind of the body politic.

After Fauquier's death in 1768, Norborne Berkeley, Baron de Botetourt, arrived to represent the crown, becoming a governor of incomparable noblesse oblige, political politesse and popularity. His gilded coach wowed the populace; his "condescension" (then a social virtue) pleased all, as when he happened upon a gaggle of sweltering gentry one summer evening and joined their songfest. A winning politician, he went out of his way to oblige. When the colony's legislators deemed a madhouse reasonable, he graciously endorsed their bill—since granting this desire could not hurt the king's interests.

OPPOSITE: The city's only "growth industry" for six generations was the Public Hospital. Unlike London's infamous Bethlehem Hospital, "Bedlam," which Hogarth drew decades earlier, it emphasized treatment over incarceration.

BELOW: Abandoned by history, the erstwhile seat of empire seemed as ruined as Lord Botetourt's statue in the crumbling Capitol, where in 1796 the itinerant architect Benjamin Latrobe sketched it "deprived of its head and mutilated in many other respects." Richmond had became capital of the new Commonwealth in 1780, and Williamsburg began its decline.

The hospital's design was drawn by Robert Smith of Philadelphia, who had raised Carpenter's Hall there and Nassau Hall for a young college in Princeton, New Jersey. The building contract called for "hard well burnt Bricks and laid with good Mortar," a cypress-shingled roof and inch-and-a-half-thick flooring. The commission for construction went to Benjamin Powell, the able builder who repaired both Capitol and Gaol and raised Bruton Parish's tower. Though this first-class building took longer to build and cost more than planned, the asylum accepted its first patient in the fall of 1773.

The building was an imposing edifice, proof positive of the colony's enlightened sense of social rectitude. It contained all of twenty-four cells, an apartment for the keeper and a meeting room for the supervisory court of directors who numbered such luminaries as Wythe, Nicholas, brothers Peyton and John Randolph, and John Blair, Jr., grandnephew of the celebrated commissary. Serving gratis, these gentlemen as a group reflected Virginia's tradition of responsible leadership as well as any and better than most. So too the protocols they established made manifest the best thinking of this time and place. As the final arbiters over who would be admitted and who released, the directors accepted only those patients considered dangerous or curable. They would not admit chronically harmless lunatics, alcoholics, paupers and the like; this was neither prison nor extended-care facility.

The first visiting physician was Dr. John de Sequeyra, who in 1770 attended Botetourt's last illness ("a bilious fever and St. Anthony's fire"). By birth an Englishman (of Portuguese Jewish descent), he had earned a medical degree at the University of Leiden and been in Williamsburg since 1745. At the hospital, he examined patients upon their admission and once a week thereafter; since the patient population was rarely more than fifteen, he continued his private practice. By the end of his twenty-year tenure, patients were receiving such state-of-the-art treatment as diagnosis by phrenology and therapeutic jolts from a static electricity generator. The full-time resident keeper (at £100 a year) was James Galt, who qualified for the post by having been keeper at the Gaol. His wife came with him as matron (at £25). Thus began a connection between this family and the Hospital that lasted for generations.

Until the hospital opened, people of unsound mind had been lumped with paupers, beggars, vagrants, poor orphans, and the like—haphazard wards of a parish. Some were placed under the care of people who took in unfortunates for pay; others were imprisoned for lack of an alternative, such as the Virginian "under great insanity of mind . . . [who] was committed to the publick Gaol for preventing mischief he might otherwise have done, and which every body apprehended he would commit." Most people did the best they could at home for mentally deranged loved ones; Patrick Henry cared for his beloved wife Sarah when she suffered extreme "melancholy" after the birth of her sixth child, what we would now term a post-partum psychosis. In a deepening depression, she mutilated herself until placed in restraints, a straightdress. As her condition inevitably worsened absent any effective therapy or intervention, Henry outfitted a basement room in his manor, Scotchtown, with windows to provide light and views, and assigned two slave women to attend her until death relieved the madness in the twentieth year of their marriage.

Now as in London and Philadelphia, Williamsburg had a special place for such woebegones (though Patrick Henry did not avail Sarah of it). Now people with the best of intentions were contriving procedures for persons whose illness was impalpable—although these treatments were naive and often contradictory. The "unhappy object," i.e., a patient, might be made more tractable by a baleful stare since "dread of the eye was early imposed upon every beast of the field" and mad people were considered bestial in some respects. Since the humors were still blamed for almost any human irregularity, "mania" and "melancholia" were seen as the results of one internal imbalance or another. Thus mental patients were variously bled or blistered with salves. They were given drugs; if opiates or sedatives didn't prompt the right results, stimulants were administered. If induced constipation didn't balance the humors, the answer might be found in a laxative. Since one school of thought held that madness was voluntary (albeit a malady that could cause brain lesions), harsh treatment was encouraged to help the mad choose rationality. The "plunge bath" or dunking chair involved the patient's total immersion and might quiet the violent or stimulate the lethargic. When the patient was not undergoing one of these regimens, he or she was allowed brief exercise in the "mad yard" and then left alone—often for long periods. Those who couldn't be trusted were restrained in irons affixed by the blacksmith.

As for the hospital's successes in restoring reason to the mad and the once-mad to the world, there were some. In its first five years, thirty-eight patients were received. Eight were "restored" to sanity and discharged; four were released to friends or family and ten died. Of the rest, fourteen were still confined in 1778. Whether or not these results satisfied the community, the coming war soon took its toll and in 1781 the hospital was closed for want of funds. A traveler at the time wrote that the "Bedlam-house is desolate, but whether because none are insane, or all are equally mad it might, perhaps, be hard to tell."

Dr. John de Sequeyra became the first visiting physician to the Public Hospital. He treated George Washington's stepchildren and introduced the tomato to Virginia. He arrived in Williamsburg about 1745, when William Dering may have painted this portrait.

Exhibits in the reconstructed hospital show how conditions changed over time—a little. An 18th-century cell (above) has little more than a pallet on the floor. A century later, more sympathetic or humane keepers provided patients with beds, even fiddles, in their rooms (below).

In 1800 William Galt succeeded his father James as resident keeper to become second dynast in the family of keepers and physicians at the hospital.

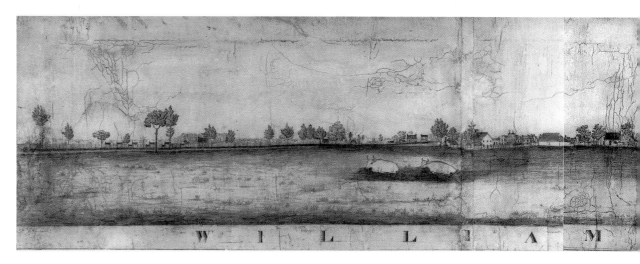

Reopened a few years later, the hospital notably became a state-supported facility. James Galt remained the keeper until his death in 1800, when his son William took the job. Upon Dr. de Sequeyra's death in 1795, the medical work was accepted by Dr. Philip Barraud (who left for Norfolk a few years later) and by James Galt's brother, Dr. John Minson Galt, who had studied in Paris and Edinburgh. He was succeeded in turn by his son, Dr. Alexander Dickie Galt, who was visiting physician until his death in 1841 when his son, Dr. John Minson Galt II, took the new title of superintendent.

During the first quarter of the nineteenth century, nearly forty percent of the hospital's patients were ultimately released as cured; then the rate started falling off even as the size of the inmate population grew. Alexander Galt kept up with the latest medical literature and was aware of new European notions that insanity was an illness that could be cured by "moral management" and kind treatment. But change was slow in coming, especially since the state redefined the hospital's role and enlarged it as a custodial facility. It grew to four major buildings by 1833, a year after Williamsburg lost the last vestige of its former political greatness when the second Capitol burned. During Dr. Galt's tenure, however, and spurred on by concerned legislators, treatment became more humane. The more reliable patients were encouraged to take Sunday excursions, play musical instruments and work in the keeper's vegetable garden, which led to charges that the keeper, cousin Dickie Galt, was taking advantage of them.

Andrew Jackson's Populism spread in many directions as the second quarter of the century gathered steam; one was to improve the lot of prisoners and patients, even those in the newly named Williamsburg Lunatic Asylum. Here John Minson Galt II became the man of the hour. He organized activities from lectures to carpentry and fancy needlework, one of the manifold expressions later called "folk art." He trained his staff to concentrate on a patient's sane features rather than insane aberrations. He treated the inmates with kindness, mesmerism and warm baths. He replaced restraints with opium and claimed to cure almost half his patients (though it is fair, if sad, to say that his knowledge of addiction and pharmacology proved wanting). Accepting slaves as patients, he trained one of his cured blacks as an attendant. The doctor himself became a charter member of an organization that would become the American Psychiatric Association. The Enlightenment was long gone, but this Galt was an enlightened practitioner of a discipline then in its infancy that was intended to ease needless human suffering, psychiatry.

John Minson Galt II was also a loyal and devoted son of the new Confederacy. When Union forces finally captured Williamsburg at the end of the devastating Peninsula campaign in 1862, he

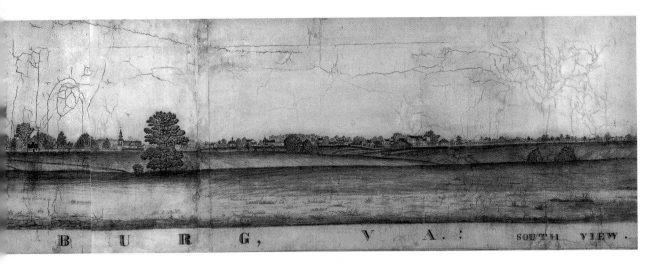

B U R G, V. A.: SOUTH VIEW.

was distraught. To calm his nerves, he took a dose of his own medicine, laudanum, the heady blend of opium and alcohol that seemed so felicitous for his patients. The prescription might have served a de facto addict, but it killed good Dr. Galt.

There were nine buildings now, with nearly three hundred patients, and the hospital was sacked during the Yankee occupation. When it was repaired and reopened in 1866, the most common cause of mental breakdown among new patients was now the ghastly trauma of "the war." Soon the place was racially segregated, and while some therapeutic programs came into being, ten years after Appomattox only five percent of the patients were considered curable. When a new superintendent instituted furlough programs, he was forced out and Williamsburg's once progressive institution became almost exclusively custodial. In early summer of 1885, when its population was approaching five hundred, a fire broke out in the old main building and destroyed it—remarkably, with few human casualties. The original edifice, dedicated to the enlightened treatment of lunatics, was razed at a time when the "warehousing" of mad patients came into vogue. Virginians from around the Commonwealth who went "to Williamsburg" were not expected to return; about the only destination here for outsiders was a place to which most were committed for life.

In a manner of speaking, things were even worse at the college. When war broke out between the states, William and Mary's president, professors and every undergraduate answered the call to the colors. For all but one of them the shade was gray, according to oral history. During the war the Wren Building was variously fortified, fitted out as a Confederate barracks, equipped as a Union hospital, and burned (for the third time since Nicholson's day) by a mutinous cavalry unit from Pennsylvania. The president, Benjamin Stoddard Ewell, spent two decades vainly seeking reparations from Washington. While classes had been suspended for various periods during both the Revolution and the Civil War, in 1881 William and Mary closed for lack of money. But Ewell (whose brother had been a general at Gettysburg) kept the charter alive by ringing the bell at the start of each academic year. Briefly, the insane asylum was about the only game in town. In 1888, the college reopened with a state appropriation to train public school teachers. So it went for Williamsburg: down, up and down again until the next century.

One child who must have heard Ewell's annual tolling of the bell was Catherine Brooke Coleman, whose mother was descended from St. George Tucker, an illustrious alumnus and law professor at the college. Living just down Nicholson Street from her ancestor's old house, the eleven-year-old girl was stricken with appendicitis (probably) and died during one of those

EASTERN LUNATIC ASYLUM   North View

Renamed the Eastern Lunatic Asylum, by the 1850s the hospital looks like a fashionable spa in an engraving with gentlefolk strolling the grounds—no doubt to ease the minds of patients' kin if not the patients themselves (top). By 1884 the main building had gained a third floor (below). The enlarged structure soon burned to the ground but the institution as a whole continued to grow.

Septembers when William and Mary was closed. A year after her daughter's death, Cynthia Beverley Tucker Coleman invited the girl's playmates to form the Catherine Memorial Society in remembrance. In the habit of southern gentlewomen, the young ladies learned to sew for charitable profit; they sold their stitchery and in springtime collected ivy sprigs and daffodils to sell as well. The girls sent the proceeds of these activities to Bruton Parish Church. Indeed, within two years of their first meeting the Catherine Memorial Society had donated $300 to buy a communion table and repair the heating system. By 1887, the girls were striking further afield. Mrs. Coleman appealed through the Christian journal *Southern Churchman* and raised enough money to repair the churchyard's round-crowned brick wall and restore the broken tombstones. The Catherine Memorial Society's name came to be carved in the stone of several markers.

Bruton's churchyard looked better than it had in decades, but the town was still a shambles, a shadow of the dimly remembered capital of an erstwhile colony whose heirs had not yet recovered from losing America's most devastating war. The Palace and Capitol both lay in ruins. The Magazine was now a storage shed. Various lots had been sold off from the public greens. The college boasted all of six professors plus a president, no more than in the seventeenth century. The most viable institution was a madhouse complex of such miserable repute that town residents traveling elsewhere would tell new acquaintances they came "from near Richmond" rather than admit that Williamsburg was home. This was the place where "two thousand lazy lived off one thousand crazy," according to local wags. All this had come to pass because of the loss of capital status, the loss of the war and, perhaps, the loss of Williamsburg's self-respect. Still, all was not lost.

The "new" Public Hospital, reconstructed to its original 18th-century appearance, opened as an exhibition building and gateway to the DeWitt Wallace Decorative Arts Museum in 1985.

Intrigued by the Catherine Memorial Society's success in restoring shards of Williamsburg's once proud heritage, Mrs. Coleman got together with Miss Mary Jeffrey Galt of Norfolk, a kinswoman of the medical dynasty. Through the good offices of Governor Fitzhugh Lee—his wife was keenly interested—they chartered the aptly named Association for the Preservation of Virginia Antiquities. Though its headquarters would soon be removed to Richmond, it gained a statewide membership. And for obvious reasons the APVA became a substantial property owner in Williamsburg—or perhaps insubstantial comes closer to the mark, given that its acquired properties had greater symbolic value than practical worth. A real estate firm, for example, willingly gave the Capitol site to the new association, which capped the foundations with concrete lest scavengers continue to rob the bricks. The group's first purchase was the "Powder Horn" (as the Magazine was then called), which was soon repaired and opened as a simple museum. Within a decade, Mrs. Coleman's group was given twenty-two acres at Jamestown, where it restored the most ancient church tower (dating from about 1639) and began work on a sea wall to save the island from encroaching tides. Virginia's heritage was being secured if not resurrected.

The APVA was founded in 1889. That year one William Archer Rutherfoord Goodwin, a twenty-year-old orator and moralist from the Blue Ridge foothills, set out in the world. He sojourned in Richmond to test his vocation and decided to enter the ministry.

What had once been Virginia's colonial capital would never—could never—have become Colonial Williamsburg but for one man's dream and another man's fortune. The two prime movers were not related like the proverbial chicken and egg. One undeniably came first; the city's resurrection was conceived by a minister who had a remarkable imagination.

As he himself declared in *A Note-Book of Memories,* years before he met his patron, the Reverend William Archer Rutherfoord Goodwin was a man "possessed." First there were the binding legacies "of a southern temperament and a New England conscience" that he likened to a "combination of rheumatism and St. Vitas dance." Afflicted by contrary drives from birth—and pursuing every interest with impressive intensity—he was both mystic zealot and Episcopalian patriarch, antiquary and trendsetter, an unabashed patriot whose view of race relations was in keeping with his times. He was a tireless builder whose joy came in the work itself; rarely would he enter the edifices he had raised. A cleric dedicated to worthy works (and finally to one cause), he was to have been remembered as a mendicant; a son entitled a memoir (which was never finished) *My Father Was a Beggar.* So be it. Goodwin did not beg for himself, but strenuously for good causes: missionaries abroad, William and Mary's endowment fund and finally for the historical rebirth of historic Williamsburg.

In pursuit of these interests, he seized likely benefactors by the emotional throat and throttled them, or mesmerized them, holding them transfixed like the Ancient Mariner. If that did not work, he seized their lapels and held them fast while he talked. "He wouldn't let you go," says one man he often collared. "Begging" for him was like repairing bicycles for the Wright brothers; he elevated an oily business to a new vocation and changed the world somewhat. To his credit and undying memory hereabouts, he invented Colonial Williamsburg as surely as Wilbur and Orville put together the first airplane with horse glue and baling wire. It simply could not have happened without him. To get things started, on the basis of nothing more than a handshake and a dream, this man of the threadbare cloth persuaded John D. Rockefeller, Jr., to parcel out more than $2 million. With this pre-Depression fortune he bought a town lot by lot in his own name in order to raise the colonial capital like a phoenix. In short, Goodwin was a genius. As Hamlet was "to the manner born," this man drew breath to resurrect the colonial capital. It was almost in his genes.

"Inheritance has made me constantly mindful of the rock and the stream from which I sprang," he wrote, tracing his Virginia lineage to a Yankee grandfather who came south in the 1830s to study theology. "A man of austere piety," according to the heir who had a nose for metaphor, grandfather possessed a doctrine "strongly perfumed with the mingled odors of the Mayflower and of brimstone that had come out of hell." Entering missionary work for the diocese of Virginia, Grandfather Goodwin married an army surgeon's daughter, Mary Archer, and settled in the Blue Ridge Mountains to raise four sons. Half of them became ministers in turn; this clan's men took to pulpits like mockingbirds to treetops. A third son went west and became a judge in the Arizona Territory; the fourth, John Francis Goodwin, entered business in Richmond before the Civil War "in partnership with his uncle, Mr. William Archer, after whom I was named." Their business was

OPPOSITE: Clad in a tapestry of bricks laid in the pattern called Flemish bond, the reconstructed Capitol stands on the site of two earlier capitol buildings. Flemish bond features red bricks laid longways as "stretchers" alternating with blue-glazed bricks set shortways as "headers."

iron, which no doubt seemed promising stock at the time. But "in after years, when making love to several Richmond girls," the heir would write in 1924, "I often looked down from Gamble's Hill at night into the seething and molding masses of iron which continued to flow through the furnaces after my father and uncle had retired from the Vulcan Iron Works." Retired? More likely Messrs. Archer and Goodwin had been ruined by the war, if not the peace called "Reconstruction," a word then innocent of architectural meaning.

Like the flower of his generation's gentry, John Francis Goodwin had answered the call to arms. He took a captain's commission in the Confederate Army and was never the same again, "his health having been undermined during the War." As his firstborn son explained it, he followed doctors' orders "to remove to the country" with his wife, née Letitia Rutherfoord. He packed the family back to Norwood, in rural Nelson County below Charlottesville, where one of his sisters had married the local doctor, who promised expert medical care gratis. There they lived in genteel poverty, farming poorly and collecting rents from tenants. Captain Goodwin, CSA ret., served as senior warden in the local parish and his wife ran the Sunday school.

The Reverend William Archer Rutherfoord Goodwin sports a mustache and steady gaze shortly before his first call to Bruton Parish in 1902. After his second call here, he conceived the idea of the resurrected city, which became Colonial Williamsburg.

Born in Richmond June 18, 1869, "Will" Goodwin was a babe in arms when the family moved. His only brother did not survive infancy; one of his sisters "died of sunstroke" at seven. The scion lived through a smallpox epidemic, measles and a seemingly deathly regimen of chores until at sixteen he ventured off to Roanoke College in Salem, Virginia, where one of the ubiquitous priestly uncles offered free room and board. Testing his possible vocation, Will led religious services at the jail, and one Sunday was locked in for his pains. He sold books door-to-door—the Bible and Mark Twain. He toyed with the idea of studying law.

At prosperous Uncle Thomas Rutherfoord's behest he went to live in Richmond for a year. This benefactor had a motive: It was to give his impecunious nephew "a taste of city life. . . . He sent me to the theater, entertained me sumptuously . . . paid all my expenses . . . and gave me the opportunity of studying Greek. . . . I did my best to suppress any . . . clear call to the ministry of the Church. I stopped going to the YMCA. For a time I entirely stopped going to Church. I danced furiously. I tried to be mildly wild (although I was never led at any time to resort to strong drink)." But his calling was clear.

In 1890 he entered the Virginia Theological Seminary in Alexandria. "On the first night at the Seminary I climbed the cupola and looked down upon the forest in which the Seminary is embossed, and out to the lights of Washington gleaming in the distance. I can well recall the thoughts and feelings which came to me in those silent moments lit with the light of spirit-enkindled emotions." Alas, he did not specify what those thoughts and feelings were. As would often be the case, where patriotic matters were concerned, Will Goodwin assumed everybody knew what he meant at the drop of a rubric. He left the particulars unstated, perhaps lest they prompt avoidable discord.

Ordained a deacon, he was assigned to St. John's, a poor parish in the middling city of Petersburg, south of Richmond. The neighborhood boasted five saloons within a block of the church. It was here that one of his most remarkable talents blossomed: He became a fundraiser. Preaching that "most of the poverty in the parish resulted from the drink evil," he persuaded one bar owner to give up the business. He established a "dry" social club and said men flocked to it. Finding the wherewithal to replace the plain wooden church with one of brick, he left the tower a blunt stub for reasons of economy—until a shopkeeper across the street paid for the steeple to save himself from facing an eyesore.

The young minister raised some $8,000 a year for the Bishop Payne Divinity School. This little seminary prepared "colored students" for the ministry, and Goodwin found teaching there an experience of "invaluable benefit." Ahead of his time in many respects, he would testify in favor of a law "prohibiting little children from working all night in the cotton mills" and he would lecture the protestant Masons on religious tolerance when Al Smith ran for president, the first Catholic candidate for so high an office. But in matters of race, he walked in step with most white Virginians of his day. Of his divinity school pupils, he wrote, "Truth had to be made very simple" to them. "The thought and study necessary to present the truths of redemption to these earnest but uncultured people demanded clearness of thought and simplicity of language, or else there was a complete failure to secure results." He called one of his teachers "an ignorant Yankee" for fraternizing with blacks and inviting them home for dinner. "This, however, did not last very long, as one of them stole all of his silver spoons . . . which resulted in his conversion to the southern point of view."

In 1895 Goodwin married a local girl, Evelyn Tannor, with a bishop and six clerics in attendance, two of them Reverends Goodwin. In the next six years two daughters and a son were born, the last of them (notably for this narrative) the remarkable Rutherfoord who was "so impatient to begin his varied human activities that he arrived before the doctor did." A second son died in infancy leaving Evelyn with the kidney ailment that shortened her life.

Meanwhile, far across the James River, trouble was brewing in Bruton Parish. Advertised as "the oldest [Episcopal] church in constant use in America," it had a future less promising than its past. For reasons lost to parochial history, a rift in the little establishment had developed between minister and vestry, becoming an abyss deep enough to engulf the congregation. With actions threatened in civil and ecclesiastical courts, the bishop opted for a change in personnel and called Goodwin to Williamsburg in 1902.

The new rector seized the challenges that lay ahead, especially in the red letter year of 1907, which marked the tercentenary of Jamestown's founding—perhaps the event that addicted the

Shortly before venturing north to a New York parish the Reverend Dr. Goodwin passes a moment in the rectory. Sitting with him are his first wife, Evelyn, and eldest son Rutherfoord, who became a newspaperman, then returned to Williamsburg where he married a member of Virginia's Randolph clan and grandniece of the bishop who first called Dr. Goodwin to Williamsburg.

young minister to historical commemoration. There was much to be done. As he would remember, "The old town became very much agitated over the question of paving the Duke of Gloucester Street, someone having presumed to suggest that this should be done. [Goodwin himself perhaps?] By many the suggestion was repudiated with indignation. They said that WASHINGTON, and JEFFERSON, and MARSHALL, and MONROE, had walked in the mud. . . . [emphasis in the brittle-paged original, now faithfully preserved by a daughter-in-law]. It was presumptuous for the modern upstarts to insist they were too good to do it." When this grumbling died down, there remained the problem of paying for the job, for this was a most parsimonious town. But the impasse gave Goodwin the golden opportunity to prove his ability to move mountains—a mountain of gravel in this instance. Determined to see the street paved, he persuaded the owner of a distant quarry to donate the stone and talked a railroad president into freighting it to Williamsburg free of charge. Then he convinced the governor to assign prison gangs to shovel it.

Having literally paved the way, the good rector saw to it that Williamsburg would play a key role in the coming festivities, which centered around Norfolk. It didn't hurt his cause that there was virtually nothing left in Jamestown to serve as a focal point, nor any facilities there to accommodate the expected throngs. Neither did it hurt that the Bruton Parish vestry had already agreed "to restore the old Church to its Colonial form and appearance." (Partitions had divided the interior into several rooms, the tower had become a coal bin, etc.) Raising donations "from far and near," Goodwin hired architect J. Stewart Barney to perform Bruton's first renovation in time for the tercentennial; the General Convention of the Episcopal Church recessed its Richmond meetings in order to witness the dedication.

The restored church was reconsecrated with all due pomp and ceremony. President Theodore Roosevelt sent a brass lectern in the shape of an angel (labeled PAX) standing on a globe to commemorate "the three hundredth anniversary of the permanent establishment of English Civilization in America." The angel's rampant wings shouldered a Bible given by the King of England to honor the planting of the Anglican faith in the New World, and even here Goodwin's adroit hand had been at work.

When Edward VII instructed the Archbishop of Canterbury to secure a copy of Virginia's state seal for the Bible's cover, the pastor of Williamsburg found himself engaged in "a somewhat embarrassing correspondence. . . . I replied that I hesitated to comply with the request of His Majesty" because the state seal displays "a very arrogant Virginian" standing rampant over a newly decrowned king and the motto *Sic Semper Tyrannis*. "I ventured to suggest, through His Grace to the King that he might be pleased to use the colonial seal of Virginia which Charles the Second had given Virginia permission to adopt."

Goodwin unearthed this seventeenth-century seal and sent it to Canterbury whence it reached the royal bookbinder. In turn the Bishop of London—successor to the divine who sent Commissary James Blair hence—presented the suitably embossed King James Bible to Bruton Parish. To mark the occasion the princes of Episcopalianism filled the church, along with a host of notable laity including the likes of J. P. Morgan, while a few thousand faithful gathered outside. The immediate celebration was marred only by the Bishop of Washington's announcement that the new Bible had been given by "King Henry the Eighth," who for better or worse had been dead for 360 years by then. The larger occasion was marred by what Goodwin might have considered a personal defeat: He failed to persuade Morgan to become a major benefactor. Goodwin had arranged for the millionaire to ride between church and train station in Williamsburg's finest vehicle, a wagon. The robber baron noted the shabby condition of the harness, and hinted at donating new tack; Goodwin told him that the owner was a college professor and Morgan wrote only a thank-you note, not a check.

ABOVE: The town's rebirth began in 1907 with the celebration of the 300th anniversary of English settlement in the New World, and King Edward VII sent a Bible to Bruton Parish as a commemorative gift. He had asked that Virginia's seal be embossed on the cover and one was—a 17th-century seal, at the Reverend Goodwin's behest— not this one, the official symbol of the Virginia Commonwealth which harkens back to the Revolution with its anti-royal motto *Sic Semper Tyrannus*.

OPPOSITE: Ah the glory that was Greece, the grandeur that was Rome and the gravel that was Williamsburg—after the Reverend Goodwin finagled the paving of muddy Duke of Gloucester Street. This was called the place that time forgot, as when the town fathers cut off the salary of the man who wound the tower clock. One might call it a one-horse town, except the horse is an ox in the late 19th century, scant years before a patriotic celebration led to its miraculous renewal.

Approaching forty, the minister went to England the following year as a delegate to an Anglican congress. He preached at St. Mary's, a fourteenth-century church in Bruton, Somerset, the place whence the Williamsburg parish had taken its name. The Duchess of Marlborough invited him to a garden party and his old correspondent the Archbishop of Canterbury presented him to the reigning king. King Edward asked about his gift of the Bible and Goodwin replied that Williamsburgers listened more devoutly when read Scripture from that copy.

Goodwin was traveling in such lofty circles that his days in Williamsburg were numbered. In 1909 he was called to a far more prosperous parish in Rochester, New York, where his fund-raising techniques blossomed. (Preaching his first sermon on the Fourth of July, he recorded for posterity that his choice of a Gospel reading that particular Sunday enabled him to begin his Yankee ministry with "the southern use of the words 'I reckon.'") A silk parish in a burlap town, his new church, St. Paul's, was led by "men of wealth" whom the young rector visited individually. His message to each of them: "I was not willing that the fact that they had money should stand between us or hinder me from the freest possible conference and intercourse with them." The man who would eventually spend another patron's millions politely demanded that his Rochester vestry vote policy on its merits and not its price. He even tangled with his bishop by advocating more active support of foreign missions abroad. For this he ended up in the diocesan doghouse—barred from conferences—until the mitre was passed to a new bishop.

Goodwin's Rochester ministry was just a sojourn; Virginia remained home. When his wife, Evelyn, died in 1915, he returned to Williamsburg and buried her in Bruton's churchyard. When he sought a second bride, he found Ethel Howard in Ashland, Virginia, north of Richmond, and married her in 1918. He took her back to Rochester, where she bore the first of their three sons a month before her husband turned fifty. Then in 1923 the president of William and Mary invited him to organize an endowment fund and teach religion courses. Once back in Williamsburg, he was called to serve as rector of Bruton Parish a second time.

He had come home again and set his boundless imagination on familiar tracks. As he would later speculate:

Perhaps it was on one of those mild, clear, Virginia nights when I roamed the streets of the sleepy town, and felt the stir of ancient thoughts, visions, prophesies, that arrested the men who lived here, who walked these streets and gazed in admiration at the very same stars that shone on me. . . . How shall we keep forever the vision of those men? How can we impress upon the coming generations their deathless ideals? Why not a shrine to their memory, a living shrine that will present a picture, right before our eyes, of the shining days when the great idea was in the crucible of freedom.

On another occasion he would write of Williamsburg and his neighbors:

Memories lingered here of the things which had been said by those of the olden times. The ghosts of the past haunted the houses and walked the streets at night. They were glad and gallant ghosts, companions of the silent hours of reverie. They helped to weave the stories of the past which have found their way into fiction, into current traditions, and into history. While these stories may not have been always entirely true to fact, they were true to life. They grew as they were told on moonlit verandas or on winter nights by those gathered around a blazing fire whose flickering light illumined the faces of ancestral portraits which still graced the Colonial walls. These ancient personages had been too long silent.

Whenever these lofty notions first came to mind, in February of 1924 Dr. Goodwin traveled north to attend a banquet celebrating the newly chartered Phi Beta Kappa Foundation. Wearing his

The Ludwell-Paradise House was the first building that the Reverend Goodwin purchased for the future Restoration— with a secret patron's money.

The city might be a national shrine one day, yet it was many people's hometown for generations. Destined to become "museums," antique dwellings were homes to plain folk. The dining room in the Tayloe House (above), like many others that would be restored, reflects the busy taste of Victorian America early in the 20th-century. The once "neat and plain" residence built by the Magazine's first armorer—and later called the Thomas Everard House (below)—gained a veranda long before Miss Cora Smith stood in a dark dress with her sister behind its gate about 1920.

Behind the scenes—the Printing Office and Bookbindery occupy the backyard and ravine called Ginny's Bottom.

cap and gown as a William and Mary collegian, the Virginian thanked the assembly for its support of the proposal to build Phi Beta Kappa National Memorial Hall at the college. The building would contain an auditorium, guest rooms and a reconstruction of the Raleigh Tavern's Apollo Room, where Phi Beta Kappa had been founded in 1776. One Dr. George E. Vincent spoke on the educational ideals that the revived honor society would pursue anew. It bears mention that he was president of the Rockefeller Foundation; and that Mr. Rockefeller, Jr., who had earned his Phi Beta Kappa key at Brown University, was chairman of the committee to raise funds for the building. Goodwin met him and, ever the Old Dominion's champion, invited him to Williamsburg. The invitation was politely declined.

Four months later, the energetic cleric was back in New York, this time calling at Rockefeller's Broadway offices with the hope of soliciting a gift for William and Mary, perhaps to restore old buildings. Received by a secretary who heard him out, he soon got a note from another aide: "The letter which you addressed to Mr. Rockefeller, Jr. . . . has received his consideration. He appreciates the circumstances you present, and regrets that he could not wisely make an exception to his policy in the matter of personal gifts to educational institutions." He had foundations to do that sort of thing, and do it in a rather grand manner.

Four days after receiving this news, Goodwin directed his energies elsewhere with a remarkable sheaf of letters to Michigan. First he sent a copy of a booklet on William and Mary's "Romance and Renaissance" to Henry Ford in the "hope that it, will be of interest to you." The same day he addressed to Henry's son, Edsel, an epistle that opened: "Seriously, I want your father to buy Williamsburg." He went on to explain that the city had been capital of a colony that "included the land on which the Ford factory is now located" when Virginia stretched to the Great Lakes. After waxing patriotic about town and college, he enthused: "Other men have bought rare books and preserved historic houses. No man has yet had the vision and the courage to buy and to preserve a Colonial village, and Williamsburg is the one remaining Colonial village which any man could buy . . . It would be the most unique and spectacular gift to American history and to the preservation of American traditions that could be made by any American." Assuring Edsel that he had "no financial interest whatsoever in this matter," he then exercised what could be called prelate's license: "Unfortunately you and your father are at present the chief contributors to the destruction of this city. With the new concrete roads . . . garages and gas tanks are fast spoiling the whole appearance of the old streets and the old city, and most of the cars which stop at the garages and gas tanks are Ford cars!"

The proselyte of patriotism received a letter of thanks for the pamphlet, and shortly thereafter a three-sentence response to his accusatory epistle from Henry Ford's amanuensis: "Your letter of June 13th has been received. We regret that Mr. Ford's many activities are absorbing his entire attention. He is, therefore, unable to interest himself in the matter mentioned." (He was already embarking on some building restorations in Massachusetts and a museum in Dearborn, Michigan.) Goodwin next wrote Henry's brother William Ford, this time omitting mention of the family's culpability in Williamsburg's destruction. Instead he suggested that they come visit, promising the titans of the horseless carriage a ride in a horse-drawn one. If he received the courtesy of a reply, it is lost to history.

But the *Detroit Free Press* got hold of the letter and published its particulars, including the notion that the town could be restored for some $5 million. Papers around the country joined in the hilarity; the *Baltimore Sun* wrote an incredulous editorial, but at Goodwin's invitation sent a man to look around and recanted. The year wound down with little more activity on this front and no further progress, so the next February the cheeky cleric again wrote Rockefeller, recalling their meeting a year earlier. "I am writing to renew the invitation and to suggest that you try to plan to come to

The Thomas Everard House was also enhanced by a ship artfully scratched on a windowpane by Miss Cora's brother H. B. Smith in 1873 when he was a boy.

the College, if possible, early in May. . . . You can bring your pocketbook, or leave it behind." He got another refusal but at least it was signed by Rockefeller himself.

Another year passed and Goodwin busied himself with other things like forestalling the destruction of the old Magazine and contemplating the uses to which he could put the brick mansion built for George Wythe. This home shared the block with Bruton Parish Church and Goodwin coveted it as a parish house. Then in March 1926, word came from the head of Hampton Institute thirty miles south that Mr. Rockefeller would visit there in a fortnight with his wife and sons in tow. That was hardly surprising; Rockefeller generously supported this and many other Negro institutions throughout his life. What delighted Goodwin was the second-hand news that the family wished to tour Yorktown, Williamsburg and Jamestown on their way back north. He responded that in Williamsburg, J. A. C. ("Blackjack") Chandler, president of the College of William and Mary, would roll out the red-white-and-blue carpet.

Goodwin's reply to the Hampton man is interesting in another respect. Half its length is devoted to a separate visit in April by another group of "northern friends," i.e., Hampton Institute benefactors, who wanted to see the College of William and Mary. Chandler would assuredly "entertain the party at lunch at the College," Goodwin wrote. "We take it for granted that the party will be composed exclusively of white persons. It would otherwise occasion you grave embarrassment and criticism, which we would not be willing here at the College to bring about or be responsible for." Thrilled at the prospect of the Rockefeller visit, Goodwin was nonetheless compelled by his sense of southern propriety—and by the Gordian protocols of segregation—to make certain that those other Yankees observed the rules.

After a flurry of letters up and down the peninsula, Goodwin stood by the side of the road on the morning of March 29 waiting for Rockefeller's car. The spot he chose for the pickup: outside Bassett Hall, a house that would figure prominently in years to come. The minister guided the party to the site of the erstwhile Capitol, to Bruton Parish Church and then on to the college for lunch. In the course of the tour young David Rockefeller played the clown and enchanted Goodwin, begging some old photographs for his collection. In the course of the day, Mr. Rockefeller expressed interest in the antiquities and asked if any plans were afoot to preserve the older buildings. Just that once, the voluble minister bit his tongue.

In September Goodwin's request for "a brief interview" with Mr. Rockefeller was fielded by his aide-de-camp, Col. Arthur Woods, who agreed to see him at his convenience in New York. The surrogate interview took place the following month and Goodwin outlined his plan to resurrect Williamsburg. According to Goodwin's faithful secretary, Elizabeth Hayes, "Colonel Woods asked many searching and thoughtful questions, listened attentively, looked with interest at the photographs presented, and, while courteously expressing his personal interest, remained entirely non-committal."

But Rockefeller returned to Williamsburg in November for the dedication of Phi Beta Kappa National Memorial Hall. Between the morning ceremony and evening banquet Dr. Goodwin escorted his celebrated guest around town in a chauffeured limousine borrowed from a Norfolk judge. (No more the borrowed wagon for a VIP.) They stopped at the Wythe House, then being renovated to serve as the rectory, and encountered the caretaker who gave the millionaire some hand-wrought nails found in the woodwork to take back to son David. Miss Hayes reported, "They talked of the educational value which would come from the perpetual preservation of the buildings and colonial greens. Driving down to Bassett Hall, they walked into the woods, past the gigantic oak tree which Mr. Rockefeller greatly admired. . . . After this he said he wanted to walk alone over the

The Magazine, scene of a row over gunpowder between the last royal governor and early revolutionaries, became a private dwelling in the 19th century and later still a livery stable distinguished enough to catch a photographer's eye.

ground . . . in order that he could better study the houses and grasp the situation." That night at the head table, Rockefeller whispered he would put up seed money—a mustard seed amount really— to pay for some architectural sketches of a restored town and Wren Building, the largest building of the original college.

His first day back in New York, the benefactor wrote two long and precise letters to Goodwin. The first asked for photographs of the town and an encyclopedia of information about the Williamsburg buildings and their historic importance. He requested a prioritized list and "a memorandum in regard to the several houses which could most speedily and easily be secured, because of a desire to sell on the part of their owners, because of mortgages or other obligations." Further, he wanted "the financial facts" regarding historic buildings that Goodwin already "had tied up or gotten a hold on." Reviewing "other important points in our conference," Rockefeller seemed interested in "the assembling of this interesting historical material around one or two centers," the Capitol neighborhood and the vicinity comprising Bruton Church, the Wythe House and Palace green. In closing he reiterated "the complete and frank understanding that nothing may come of it and that I am committed to nothing, either now or later on, except as such committals are definitely made in writing."

The second letter anticipated a very preliminary study into the feasibility of restoring "the Sir Christopher Wren building," which the college wanted to modernize. Rockefeller stated with unmistakable clarity that he was only interested in the building from a historical standpoint—not in aiding William and Mary per se—but if the college wanted a feasibility study to learn whether the building could be saved, he'd help out to the tune of $10,000. He stipulated two conditions to Goodwin: "(1) That such assistance should be rendered through you; (2) That it should be rendered anonymously."

On the same day, Dr. Goodwin was writing Rockefeller a letter of plaintive thanks and hard data: "Today I feel like one who treads alone/Some banquet hall deserted: But in Williamsburg we always have the ghosts which abide, even when the distinguished men of the present come, stay for a day, and depart. I have always felt sorry for the people who live in Williamsburg who are incapable of holding companionship with the ghosts, and who do not feel their presence hallowing their ancient haunts. It has been a great pleasure to me to have been privileged to help introduce you to

A host, an army, a swarm, nay a school of scholars in academic regalia musters for the dedication of Phi Beta Kappa National Memorial Hall in 1926—about the biggest thing to happen in Williamsburg since 1907, when the tercentennial was the biggest thing since Yankees marched in during the Civil War. Reverend Goodwin first met his great benefactor during the national campaign to reorganize Phi Beta Kappa and build this hall.

the haunts and homes of these departed spirits. . . .

"You were good enough to ask me to send you a memoranda [sic] of the indebtedness incurred by me up to this time . . . incident to the preservation and restoration work which I have ventured to undertake." Goodwin wrote that he owed $22,000 on the restoration of the Wythe House, its purchase of $15,000 having been underwritten by the Colonial Dames of America. There was $6,000 outstanding on the John Blair House, which he and friends had "rescued from being torn down for a garage" and turned over to the college. "To save the Powder Horn from being crushed in by two buildings, I got a gentleman to buy the lot immediately in the rear of it for $500, and I bought the corner lot in back of it for $1000 (giving my note in the bank). I hope for an additional $1000 to get control of the lot immediately to the west. . . . I have said nothing about the study of the Christopher Wren Building, and will say nothing about it until I receive the letter which you said that you would write. . . . with the perfect understanding that it carries with it no further committal whatsoever on your part. In the meantime [watch this switch!] I wish you would buy Bassett Hall for yourself. It would give you a charming vantage point from which to play with the vision and dream which you see, and it might give me the joy of being your 'playmate' in this dreamland playground."

These men—so often described as opposites—forged a partnership by each one being himself: Rockefeller the circumspect executive, financial administrator and practical philanthropist, Goodwin the visionary and persuader. They did become playmates—sometimes opponents at tug-of-war, sometimes co-conspirators at capture-the-flag. When Goodwin waxed too euphoric, vague or ambitious, Rockefeller knotted his purse strings more tightly even as he encouraged his protégé to reach his stride. (Once Goodwin pleaded that his duties as William and Mary's fund-raiser were distracting, and said he could quit that work if Rockefeller would make a major gift. The patron called his bluff by suggesting that the restoration could wait until Goodwin discharged his obligations to the college.) When Goodwin got wind of a historic residence coming on the market, their pact was put to the test.

The handsome brick house on Duke of Gloucester Street had been owned by Philip Paradise, who lived in London. When the Revolution broke out, Virginia's new government had confiscated the house, which led Philip's friend Samuel Johnson to make a memorable quip about "Paradise's Loss." (After the war, and Philip's death, his daughter, the widowed and eccentric Lucy, returned to

The sun rises on a garden beside Benjamin Powell's home—and on a new day for Colonial Williamsburg.

the house and lived there in her dotage. She grew old and some say addled. Inviting visitors to take an outing, she led them to the porch where her carriage stood and when all were seated inside bade her butler to stand in the traces and jostle them up and down. Two nieces, perhaps greedy for her estate, had her committed to the mental hospital across town.)

In early December, Goodwin wrote Rockefeller that distant heirs wanted to sell the house immediately for the "exceedingly low" price of $8,000. His supplication described the house in detail, noting that a poster announcing Lord Botetourt's funeral had been removed from one of its walls to the college library. Though they had not arrived at a firm plan, on December 7, 1926, Rockefeller fired back a telegram authorizing "purchase of antique . . . at eight." To hide his identity from Williamsburg's Western Union man, he coined a code name that identified him with absolute certainty to his correspondent alone. Rockefeller signed his first Williamsburg purchase order "David's Father."

The informality, which seemed to invite intimacy, was particularly telling, since Rockefeller was habitually formal in the extreme. Unfailingly polite, he called only one associate by his first name, and then because they had been friends in college. At the office he suffered the sobriquet "Mr. Junior," just as his sons would be called "Mr. David," "Mr. Nelson," and the like to avoid confusion. Yet in later years around Williamsburg, he would always be called "Mr. Rockefeller." Here he was uniquely his own man rather than his father's son, which might have been one reason the place came to have such special meaning for him.

John Davison Rockefeller, Jr., was born cautious in 1874, the youngest of five children and only son of the self-made Midas of Standard Oil. His father, John, Sr., had been sternly reared by an all-sufferingly Christian mother and a wayward entrepreneur. (Working upstate New York out of the back of a wagon, "Doctor" William Avery Rockefeller sold patent medicine. He often stayed away from the homes he bought with cash for months at a time—in part because the law was looking for him. After dodging a felony indictment by moving his family to Ohio in 1853, the snake-oil salesman taught worldly lessons to young John by lending him money with interest, then pointedly calling the loan when he thought the boy was strapped.) If the father was a philanderer and the mother a devout recluse, their heir was a deeply religious monomane possessed of a gift for making money. A tithing Baptist from the day he went to work as a teenager, John Sr. let discipline govern his life and the rearing of his children, especially the boy.

Never robust, John, Jr., was small, sedate and shy. Following his father's orders and example, he faithfully kept an account of every penny he spent and only began to blossom after going off to college, where he got along well enough socially and excelled scholastically. Even at Brown, his biographers describe an overweening desire to please his adored mother and stern father. It was here that he met Abby Aldrich, daughter of the senior senator from Rhode Island, Nelson W. Aldrich, whose political influence almost rivaled his eventual in-laws' financial clout. Married in 1901, Mr. and Mrs. John D. Rockefeller, Jr., settled down in New York hard by his parents' home on West Fifty-fourth Street.

There seems to have been little question about his life's work: to manage his father's empire and achieve the public rehabilitation of the man who had come to personify (somewhat unfairly) the evils of great wealth. The scion devoted most of his considerable and highly disciplined energies to the systematic support of worthy causes, always in his father's name. By the time he was fifty, and agreed to help build Phi Beta Kappa National Memorial Hall, he had earned the reputation of a singular philanthropist who was as realistic as he was generous. (When one worthy organization asked for one-tenth of the $1 million it needed, he instructed an aide to restudy the

Mr. and Mrs. John D. Rockefeller, Jr., pose primly in 1901 shortly after their marriage. A generation after the patron's death, one crusty Williamsburger told the author, "I never heard one mean thing said about him, except that he didn't drink."

One man dreamed of restoring this "Cradle of Liberty" to its former state and grace. But dreams require money to become real—and the bigger the dream the larger the bankroll required. The Bruton Parish rector's vision intrigued one of America's most celebrated millionaires, and an informal partnership was struck. Together Dr. Goodwin (left in both photographs) and Mr. Rockefeller embarked on a venture that was nothing short of remarkable.

matter: "Mr. Chorley it's not a question of money, it's a question of what's right.") He had also developed efficient office protocols and clear policies, in part to see that his father's money was dispensed efficiently, and in part to discourage gold diggers. A case in point: Goodwin's first solicitation of a gift for the college had prompted a secretary's formal refusal.

If Goodwin had a dream, Rockefeller had the money and something more, a method of spending to achieve almost any painstakingly defined goal, from restoring the roof at Versailles to making insulin available for American diabetics. This approach was a nebulous asset of almost inestimable value. From the beginning the cautious patron took just one step at a time while keeping the parson on a very tight rein as their common interest progressed. Not that he adopted a special method of dealing with this visionary dynamo; systematic caution was his wont. As an associate would say years later, in dealing with Mr. Rockefeller "one never ventured beyond the scope of the subject of the day." Yet here he found himself working with a zealot who "could leap on his horse and ride every direction at once" as a Williamsburg executive later put it. By habit, Rockefeller would weigh his options, then decide the direction of the next step, take it and pause again. Had they looked far ahead at the outset, it seems unlikely that Williamsburg would ever have been restored. In later years a consensus emerged among the two men's associates, in the words of Kenneth Chorley, the man who ran the Williamsburg show for twenty-eight years: Mr. Rockefeller "had no conception of what he was getting into. Neither did Dr. Goodwin as far as that goes. . . . Nobody really knew what was going to happen" as the pretty dream evolved into a reality of labyrinthine complexity and institutional proportions.

If Rockefeller was a paragon, he nonetheless was a mortal man of his time. By the mid-1920s, America had been seduced by two fickle mistresses, brazen prosperity and the liberating automobile. Never before had people been so mobile or so affluent. Flush from victory in "the war to end all wars," the nation had turned its back on international affairs and taken its own heritage to its bosom in orgies of jingoistic enthusiasm. Further, interest in the arts was on the rise. New York's Metropolitan Museum of Art, a Sunday afternoon stroll up Fifth Avenue from the Rockefeller residence, opened its celebrated American Wing in 1924. Across the land interest was growing in restoring historic buildings and raising new ones in old architectural styles. Mrs. Rockefeller was in the vanguard of cognoscenti; a founder of the Museum of Modern Art, she was also a collector of art, both "modern" masterpieces and the seemingly accidental masterworks of unschooled "folk artists." Meanwhile, as Kenneth Chorley would remember with uncharacteristic whimsy, "Mr. Rockefeller had a great many people sitting around more or less with wet towels on their heads trying to figure out how he could give his money away intelligently."

It was in this atmosphere that the philanthropist haltingly embarked on the miraculous enterprise of Colonial Williamsburg.

Early in 1926 two hunting partners left Boston "in a new Marmon car" for a North Carolina bird shoot. Though no one knew it—least of all the gunners—they were the first gentle wave in "the second Yankee invasion of Williamsburg." William G. Perry, an architect interested in period buildings, persuaded his friend to pause on their return trip and visit the colonial capital. They found "a country town" straddling a concrete highway with a median strip punctuated by utility poles, and they put up at a guesthouse kept by one of Governor Spotswood's descendants.

It was a town where "life was very pleasant," said one native son. "You could almost count the population every morning at the Williamsburg Drug Company." Dr. H. M. Stryker, the dentist, and young Vernon Geddy, a lawyer descended from the clan of smiths and farmers, shared a floor of the local skyscraper, a three-story walk-up. When business was slow they played checkers. The Reverend John Bentley, then curate at Bruton Parish, thought the town "dilapidated in many places. For the most part Williamsburg was a community of people who were just able to make ends meet and live with some sense of dignity and pride. People lived quietly and modestly" while lavishing their energy on flower gardens. Elder spinsters still told sad stories of heroics in the War Between the States. Younger women remembered the glory days of 1907 when the tercentenary prompted people "to cut the grass, paint the shutters and mend their paling fences."

Its central square become a midden of shacks and shanties, Williamsburg "retained somehow a charming quality with many of its houses and buildings quietly reminding one of a notable past," Perry believed. "The principal building on the College of William and Mary, much remodeled, stood as it had since the late 1690s. The Capitol building was represented only by its foundations. A school stood upon those of the Governor's Palace. But the general appearance of the town recalled quite simply the lines and areas of its original plan. It was an example of beneficent [or passive] architectural preservation, unaffected by progress and change. Its remaining buildings had patiently been designed in the vigorous and comely manner of the early 18th century."

Perry was especially intrigued by a stately brick wreck facing Palace green. George Wythe's house "had been abandoned; its doors, front and rear, stood open and ajar; a window sash was missing. . . . Unfurnished and forlorn," it was coveted by the brother of a lady passing by who stopped to chat. "He'd like to remodel it into something useful, like a parish house," the lady said. Learning the stranger was an architect, she suggested he meet her brother, though Perry had to decline. Pressed for time, the Bostonians continued northward by train, leaving the Marmon in front of their boardinghouse.

Months later when they returned for the car (less its dashboard clock and brass lamps), Perry's friend was stricken with appendicitis. While he recovered from surgery, Perry fell in with Dr. Goodwin who by now had acquired the Wythe House with the help of the Colonial Dames of America. Showing the Yankee around, the proud parson said, "I have a decorator from Richmond, and he's come down and helped us on the restoration," a word that gave Perry pause.

OPPOSITE: George Wythe's brick house, residence of the storied colonial law professor and leading citizen, survived two wars and more than a century of renovations before its restoration by Colonial Williamsburg.

Like many homes, George Wythe's was altered often by its various owners. Its plain front of 1899 (this page, top) received a porch (opposite top) in the 20th century, then a fancy pediment (opposite bottom) when Dr. Goodwin made it look more "colonial"—to his eye at least. Finally the Restoration returned it to its original look (this page, bottom) with white trim, the central window returned to its regular size and shutters gone.

"There are many definitions of restoration," he reminisced many years later, and Dr. Goodwin's was one of the loosest, though by no means the least popular, in those days. He was bent on repairing the old building to suit new uses and embody "what he thought ought to have been." The definition Perry preferred was a return to "its original form through studied preservation and reconstruction." But Dr. Goodwin had been hard at work with his usual zeal. He had installed paneling that had never been there before, no matter how closely it mimicked other period houses. This, in Perry's view, "was not 'restoration.'" The decorator had copied the front door motif from the Byrd family seat, Westover, though Wythe's house clearly never had "such an embellishment." As Goodwin led his graciously uncritical guest through the house, he said, "We don't know how to terminate the cornice at this point." Though quite sure the front hall never had a cornice, Perry sketched a new one in a gesture typical of his charm and willingness to help.

Turning down his host's request for a donation in dollars, Perry offered something better. The original doors had lost their antique locks, so he measured the keyholes and marks that remained and promised to send down some old locks he had collected. Delighted by the gift and astonished that the locks fit the doors, Goodwin had them installed. But a sorry admission dampened his effusive letter: "They were just in time for the dedication of the building. Let me thank you very much indeed, but let me also say, and I'm very sorry to have to report, that nine out of the ten keys were stolen that day." So far as Perry was concerned in the spring of 1926 "that was the end of that."

Partner in a firm that specialized in period architecture, he was unaware that Goodwin had already found the priceless key to building his dream when Rockefeller had passed through Williamsburg in March. After the philanthropist returned in November and authorized Goodwin to commission a few architectural drawings, the minister contacted an eminent Chicago architect who declined the job. Not missing a beat, Goodwin remembered Perry and wrote him directly if not succinctly:

"I find myself wondering whether you would be interested to join with me in trying to visualize, and then work out a plan which might be used to interest others in the work of preserving and restoring one or more" colonial shrines. As for the hope that anything would come of it, Goodwin was disarmingly vague. "If by any possibility, having visualized the effects desired, we could succeed in interesting others in the matter, it would be the most spectacular and interesting, and from the teaching point of view, the most valuable restoration ever attempted in America, and I should like above all things to have you associated with me in the preliminary study. We could have a jolly good time doing it together." Perry accepted without even settling on a fee.

Rockefeller had insisted on anonymity; Goodwin didn't even tell Perry he had a patron, let alone one who had already bought an "antique . . . at eight." Nor was the preacher above some timely dissembling. As his faithful secretary Elizabeth Hayes would report, "Dr. Goodwin often said . . . the keeping of this secret would place a terrific strain upon his conscience as a clergyman, but that he was determined to keep the secret and that he hoped to save his conscience."

In fact Goodwin was not above misleading his neighbors or dissembling, as for instance when he stated publicly that he was acquiring properties for the college or that his mysterious "associates" had limited resources. Ingenuous as he might sometimes appear, he was an adept, even cunning solicitor of support for his many causes, a man who kept a looseleaf book of financiers' net worths and personal tastes—for timely reference. His virtuosity comes clear in his letters: solicitous to people whose help he sought; businesslike to those whose services he was hiring; appreciative and even fawning to patrons, yet withal sincere. For all his prolixity, he could tell Rockefeller precisely what he was up to, and then share the intrigue. One 1927 postscript recounted the work of mapping the town with Perry in the dark of night:

I wish you could be here and have some of the real fun that I am getting out of what we are doing. Last night the full moon joined in to help us. We found three College boys who wanted some exercise and with a long steel tape we measured the Duke of Gloucester Street . . . and plotted the houses. . . . Some of the colored folk whom we met must have taken us for maniacs or demon possessed men, and it was fun to see them jump off the sidewalk when they heard the long steel line rattle on the pavement and saw it move. When asked 'What are you doing?' the answer is that we are preparing a map to show people interested in history how to find the historic centers and the historic buildings.

These letters could be packed with information that proved he was moving ahead on several fronts. He dispatched Miss Hayes to the Library of Congress to peruse the *Virginia Gazette* for information about the colonial town. At the college he located the "Frenchman's Map" drawn by a French billeting officer during the Revolution, which he realized "will be invaluable to our study" for its house-by-house plan of Williamsburg. He found descriptions of the Capitol and pictures of the Raleigh Tavern. He persuaded the commander of a nearby air corps post to send a photographer aloft to shoot pictures of the town. Never one to miss a chance to drop a name, he took his own snapshots with "the fine camera" given him by "my friend Mr. R. T. H. Halsey (who is largely responsible for the American Wing at The Metropolitan Museum of Art)." For his own part, Rockefeller encouraged Goodwin with friendly notes and precise instructions.

In May 1927 Rockefeller returned to Williamsburg on the excuse (should public explanation be required) of showing his wife Memorial Hall. Receiving the couple in the newly furnished Wythe House study, Goodwin unveiled Perry's first architectural sketches, then walked them around town. Up to this point, Miss Hayes reported that Rockefeller "spoke always with an 'if.'" As was his habit, the millionaire asked scores of questions "about the future care of the property, about endowment, and what final dispositions could be made of the property. Again and again he cautioned him [Goodwin] not to let anyone know he was showing any interest."

The tale persists that upon returning to the study Dr. Goodwin reminded Rockefeller that they were sitting in the very room where Jefferson read law with George Wythe and then virtually summoned the patriots' spirits to join the colloquy. Whatever impressed him most, Miss Hayes recorded that at last "Mr. Rockefeller said, 'I am not interested in separate centers.'" He was taken by "the proposition as a whole, and a complete thing." Suggesting he'd have little time himself to give the project, "he called Dr. Goodwin 'the mother of the restoration— if a father can be a mother.' He asked if Goodwin would be willing to nurse the scheme along." Would a sinner like sainthood? The parson replied that "he would love it above all things."

They decided that Perry should plat the entire town and Goodwin buy old houses one by one as they became available. Rockefeller was still not committed to anything more than providing the wherewithal; if the plan didn't pan out he might just put the properties back on the market. A few days later

Rockefeller outlined the new phase of their arrangement in a letter that "authorizes my representatives to finance, on the general terms and conditions set forth, any or all of the projects enumerated therein." Another step was taken.

As he proceeded to buy houses, Goodwin was mindful that many were occupied by lifelong inhabitants. "It would be difficult, if not impossible, and I am inclined to think inadvisable" to force anyone out, he told Rockefeller. "If the thought and plan commends itself to you," he suggested a buy-now-take-later approach, allowing residents "to continue to occupy their homes for the few remaining years of their lives, without rent, taxes or insurance." Such terms and $25,000 might induce septuagenarian Peyton Randolph Nelson and his wife to sell Tazewell Hall, once the lavish home of Peyton Randolph's brother John "the Tory" (so-called because he had returned to England when the Revolution broke out). All of $15,000 and life tenancy might wrest two properties from another "interesting character." Possessing one asset—an invitation to the banquet for the Marquis de Lafayette 103 years earlier—Miss Emma Louise Barlow feared burglars. Goodwin reported that the maiden lady "sleeps with six paper bags which she blows up and ties before going to sleep so that she can pop them in case she hears noises in the night which threaten disaster. She has not offered to sell the paper bags, nor is she much disposed to sell her house." But she might consider it if she could stay on.

Rockefeller seized upon the notion of a dollar-a-year rent and "life tenure," the device that enabled Goodwin to buy dozens of houses at reasonable prices. Some people criticized the Bruton Parish rector for pursuing an interest that so clearly conflicted with his pastoral responsibilities. While he was not accused of personally profiting from the transactions, his critics maintained (as a few still do) that he unfairly influenced many naive parishioners. No doubt the pastor enjoyed a unique advantage as a purchaser, and though he never made a clean sweep of old Williamsburg, antagonisms arose that clouded his ministry. Every Sunday one lady rose from her pew and walked out when he mounted the pulpit to preach; she did it regularly, you might even say religiously. Another woman would accost him on the street and ask, "Are you going to preach the Gospel on Sunday? Or are you going to preach about wallpaper? I'm not coming to church if you're going to preach about wallpaper."

It was impossible to keep the campaign secret for long and soon the region was buzzing about the spendthrift parson. If prices didn't rise through the roof, two factors were responsible. For one thing, Williamsburgers knew all about the wages of speculation. Almost a decade earlier a Du Pont munitions plant at Penniman a few miles away had raised a boomtown of fifteen thousand people and house lots were hawked on Williamsburg's streetcorners. But when peace came and plans for plant expansion were canceled, Penniman became a ghost town of 3,778 souls. Judge Robert T. Armistead, who until his death in 1999 inhabited one of the two Duke of Gloucester Street houses that Goodwin never got, remembered his father losing $30,000 the day the bubble burst. Notwithstanding people's reluctance to get burned by another boom, Goodwin used the press to spread his warning that inflated asking prices could smother the historical project he was so rosily if vaguely forecasting.

No doubt, the intrigue was hard on his nerves as people tried to pry from him the secret of his backer's identity. Henry Ford was mentioned as were Harvey Firestone, George Eastman, J. P. Morgan (despite his death in 1913) and just about every other known millionaire. Vernon Geddy, who handled Goodwin's legal work, entered the rectory unannounced one day and heard a reference to "Mr. D." (Goodwin and Miss Hayes had taken to calling their benefactor "Mr. David," a code name adapted from his code name of "David's Father.") To no avail Geddy goaded Goodwin with a bit of

ABOVE: When the controversial president Franklin Roosevelt came to town in 1934, Miss Emma Louise Barlow planned to observe "the 110th anniversary of Lafayette's visit to the city." Living in what became the Historic Area, Miss Barlow remained as one of the town's "life tenants" citizens who sold their homes to the Restoration with the proviso that they and their immediate kin could stay on for their lifetimes.

OPPOSITE: As for the town's other denizens, some seemed content to sit in the shade on Duke of Gloucester Street and watch the telephone poles grow.

doggerel naming every rich man he could think of whose name began with D including "John D." When Goodwin took a short trip to escape the pressure, he wrote a codicil to his will that left the lawyer even deeper in the dark. Each time Rockefeller approved a purchase, his office sent an untraceable cashier's check that Goodwin deposited in his local bank before buying the property in his own name with his own check. The codicil stipulated that in the event of his death, houses that had been bought in this way were to be conveyed to "Colonel Arthur Woods" in New York. Colonel who? Geddy couldn't know Woods was executive officer to a captain of finance.

Goodwin's mysterious business was as much a boon to the young lawyer as it was to the town. "No one had any money in Williamsburg and no one needed any," Geddy would remember. "There was about fifteen dollars that would start out on Monday morning and everybody in town would get their hands on it" before the week was out. (That would change later, when for example a family of shopkeepers pocketed $265,000 for their package of nine lots.)

As the preliminary buying continued, some owners started playing hard-to-get despite Goodwin's open letters to businessmen urging them to cooperate. One night a Chinese laundry burned to the ground; next morning three pillars of the Greek community announced they were ready to sell a movie theater, pool hall, "kandy kitchen" and several stores near the college. One of the sellers admitted the fire scared him: "Suppose my place had burned. I sell quick."

Meanwhile there was speculation in the local press, including a long account about the "Real Estate Boom" in the *Richmond News Leader.* Publisher John Stewart Bryan then wrote Rockefeller and tried to smoke him out: "I do not know whether you have had any role or part in this undertaking . . . as Dr. Goodwin has maintained an impenetrable silence." Bryan's suspicions were possibly not put to rest by Rockefeller's cagey reply. Expressing utter innocence, he wrote, "Let us hope, however, that [Dr. Goodwin's] hand will not be further forced until he is ready to show it, and that so long as he feels it best to withhold the names of his backers, his judgement in the matter will be respected."

By then Bryan's paper had carried an editorial applauding Goodwin and cautiously endorsing the restoration proposal. However, with vain prescience it cautioned against carrying the project too far: "No age can ever quite recapture the spirit of another. . . . For its part the *News Leader* is confident that the restoration will not be carried too far, that its purpose will be to retain rather than to rebuild. Where attempts are made to reconstruct the more famous public buildings of the town, the unescapable limitations will be recognized and historical charlatanry will be avoided."

The acquisitive minister had told Geddy that the first time he earned money plowing as a boy, he saved up until he had enough to buy a book, *Buried Cities Recovered.* Now he was preparing to live it. One day in November of 1927, Goodwin phoned Geddy from Washington and told him to meet his train at the station behind the school on the old Palace grounds. Thinking he wanted a briefing on the latest land titles he had searched, Geddy was amazed when his client declared, "Boy you haven't started. . . . We're going to buy the town!"

Goodwin was returning from a carefully choreographed sojourn in New York's Vanderbilt Hotel. Though still in the dark, Perry had come down from Boston with his latest sketches for a restored town—one of them a nine-foot map—which they set up for display in a guest room. The country minister then asked the urbane architect to wait in his room all the next day in case he was needed. This was too much for even the obliging Perry, who would only agree to sit by the phone every hour on the hour.

Rockefeller arrived alone and marveled at both the map and letters from architectural authorities whose endorsements Goodwin had solicited. He then offered Goodwin a salary to take on the coming work of pursuing the restoration, but the minister declined the offer, saying he could only

The St. George Tucker House remains among the most charming of Williamsburg's original dwellings, the result of having been begun as a single story dwelling, then moved to face Market Square, then enlarged with two additions. Its principal owner was born in Bermuda in 1752 and came to Virginia to study law with George Wythe whom he succeeded as law professor. Called "America's Blackstone," he served as a judge on the state's General Court, its Supreme Court of Appeals and then the U.S. District Court until his death in 1827.

continue to buy houses if he could honestly report he had nothing to gain. Goodwin told his secretary that after his lieutenants arrived, "Mr. Rockefeller took complete charge of the situation." He explained "every detail of the plan in a most masterful way, as though he had lived in Williamsburg for years. . . . He went through the town following the map, explaining the location of every prominent building, giving its history, and significance as it related to the plan, and the reasons why the Restoration appealed to his imagination and interest. . . . Mr. Rockefeller intimated that he would be responsible for the development of the plans as they had been presented."

During the meeting they marked on Perry's map the status of properties purchased, optioned, etc. Meeting with Perry again, Goodwin showed him the map with its color-coded squares. "He was so astonished that he sat down *hard* on the bed. He had no idea that we had accomplished anything like that." And he still had no idea who he was working for.

Now the pace quickened. Rockefeller was no longer to be troubled with details, which would be handled by Colonel Woods, a gracious and able man militantly managerial enough to have been New York's police commissioner. Other Rockefeller aides would continue to review real estate and legal matters case by case. The restoration had become an enterprise of the Rockefeller empire however secret it remained. Soon after the new year, two corporations would be formed, the Williamsburg Holding Corporation to handle the physical work, and Colonial Williamsburg, Inc., to consider future programs.

In December 1927, Goodwin wrote Perry, "At last I am able to . . . report that those associated with me in the Williamsburg Restoration development were most favorably impressed with the plans. . . . I am authorized to retain you and your firm for the further architectural work incident to the further development of the plans and projects under consideration." Goodwin insisted that the matter remain *"confidential.* . . . With this understanding you are hereby authorized to prepare the following full and complete plans," which he enumerated with price estimates: Wren Building, $409,000; Capitol, $188,000; Golden Horseshoe Inn (which was never built), $100,000; Palace, $200,000; plus unspecified amounts for town plans as needed. Perry replied with remarkable poise to the million-dollar letter: "We congratulate you upon your success. We are all agreed that the happy outcome is due to your extraordinary efforts. . . . We all thank you for your loyalty to us and thank you most sincerely."

In March 1928 the *New York Times Magazine* reported that "Historic Williamsburg, once the

Capital of Virginia, will be rebuilt as nearly as possible in the pre-Revolutionary form, and stand as a living memorial of America's Colonial Days." It prompted a flood of mail that nearly swamped Goodwin. Heading home for lunch two blocks away, "I was stopped by three people, did not get home until a half hour after lunch was over, and found two men on the porch waiting for me when I reached my door." He then encountered a lady who wanted to start a tearoom, then a lawyer, and finally "a gentleman and his wife . . . wanting advice as to how to restore Carter's Grove," a plantation upriver that would eventually become part of Colonial Williamsburg. A letter from R. T. H. Halsey offered help locating furnishings, portraits and records in London.

Goodwin received permission to discuss the restoration with town officials—still without naming names—and start restoring the Wren Building (which always seemed to have a life of its own). He'd also been authorized to contact the A.P.V.A., which owned the Capitol site and the Magazine. He admired the organization: "Those devoted ladies of Virginia bent like priestesses over the dying embers of ancient flames and breathed upon them and made them glow again. The fires, rekindled by them, lit the path which led to the fuller realization of the truth expressed by Ruskin when he wrote 'It is our duty to preserve what the past has had to say for itself.'"

But this band of far-flung gentlewomen hedged its bets. The executive committee expressed "its great interest in . . . the rebuilding of the House of Burgesses [*sic*] upon the original site." (The House of Burgesses was a corporate body of legislators; there was never a physical house.) But the ladies wanted the work done within five years or the agreement would expire. They asked for perpetual use of a meeting room in the Capitol, a tablet to commemorate their role and continuing oversight of the building's uses. All that agreed to, they had to poll their entire membership, which turned into a logistical nightmare.

The tangled conditions of this transaction were only a preview of the mammoth complexities to come, for while the Capitol site was owned by a private organization, the restoration plan involved public property as well. Thus a town meeting was called for June when the people of Williamsburg would vote on whether to transfer town acreage to unknown interests—but only after the "second Yankee invasion" became obvious. Strangers with sketch pads, surveyor's rods, slide rules and whatnot arrived on every train; one spinster said, "Well I lived through one Reconstruction, I reckon I can live through another."

As the meeting date drew near, Dr. Goodwin requested an independent audit of Bruton's books, his personal accounts and city land records. The examination uncovered no fiddle-faddle, but it revealed the amount of Rockefeller money he had spent thus far on properties: $2,225,189.87.

Work had already begun on Bracken Tenement, the first colonial building to be restored, when Williamsburg voters met in the auditorium of the high school on the old Palace site to consider two matters of signal importance to the restoration. Posters announced the mass meeting for 8 P.M, June 12, to discuss "a proposal to convey" the town's greens and jail to Goodwin and his nameless associates "in exchange for a new Court House and Jail." Goodwin and Geddy soon breathed easier because June 12 was also Election Day, and Mayor Henderson, who opposed the recent goings-on, was not reelected. The winner, Dr. John Garland Pollard, a politician on his way to becoming governor, was friendly to the restoration idea. He was elected to chair the mass meeting which attracted 450 people—only one-third of them voters. The proposed contract between the town and vaguely named corporations was read and explained. When a citizen asked what was wrong with the present jail, Judge Frank Armistead said it operated on the honor system; a prisoner serving a twenty-year hitch had recently absented himself, leaving a note that he'd be back later. As for the 150-year-old courthouse, it lacked a jury room. Whenever a jury sat (which wasn't often) a clerk

In 1928 the Bracken House became the first dwelling to undergo restoration–even before the scope of the Restoration and the identity of its principal backer were revealed to an avidly curious citizenry.

had to vacate her office "and she always fusses the next day about the cigars the jury smoke."

Goodwin rose to make his pitch. Pointing out that the town's attorney had endorsed the contract, he stressed, "You may be sure that your legal rights will not be overlooked." Indeed, city land would be better protected than in the past when the town fathers had sold off lots around the Courthouse and Magazine. If his syndicate got these lands, "they shall never be sold off" but restored to states "which our ancestors planned. It is the purpose of our associates to make this favored city a national shrine," he declared. "Benefit will come in spiritual as well as material ways. Every business man will be benefitted. It should be a source of pride to you to feel that you will have here the most beautiful shrine dedicated to the lives of the nation builders. We will be the custodians of memorials to which the eyes of the world will be turned. We should return thanks that this place has been chosen as a shrine of history and of beauty. There will be windows built here through which men may look down the vistas of the past. . . . Williamsburg restored will transmit to the future an everlasting memorial of the events which were potent in the founding of the Federal republic and which inspired other nations of the world seeking to lay for themselves the foundations of popular government in liberty and justice."

The room was packed because people wanted to know not only what might transpire, but who was paying for what had already occurred. After further ado, which simply whetted his neighbors' razor-sharp curiosity, Goodwin declaimed, "It is now my very great privilege and pleasure to announce that the donors of the money to restore Williamsburg are . . . [Here he paused, according to his secretary's record]. . . Mr. and Mrs. John D. Rockefeller, Jr., of New York." It brought the house down.

Still a few locals demurred. Major S. D. Freeman accepted "the unpleasant duty to voice the minority side. . . . If you give up your land it will no longer be your city. Will you feel the same pride in it that you now feel as you walk across the Greens or down the broad streets? Have you all been hypnotized by five million dollars dangled before your eyes? . . . What will happen when the matter passes out of the hands of Dr. Goodwin and Mr. Rockefeller, in both of whom we have perfect confidence? . . . We will reap dollars but will we own our own town? Will you not be in the position of a butterfly pinned in a glass cabinet, or like a mummy unearthed in the tomb of Tutankhamen?" Miss Hayes recalled that "his talk was given in a clear, firm voice, with oratorical gestures. When he sat down there was perfect silence."

After short debate, state roads commissioner George Coleman, who lived in the St. George Tucker House, asked for a standing vote. Some 150 citizens rose in the affirmative. According to one record, five voted no, one on the grounds that the ballot should be secret, four on the merits: Major Freeman, lame-duck Mayor Henderson and the sisters Dora and Cara Armistead, cousins of the judge who voted for the restoration but would thereafter be its frequent opponent.

Thus Palace green and Market Square, along with some other plots, were transferred to Rockefeller's companies with the proviso that the public have perpetual access. In return, the town had the promise of a new jail and courthouse along with the prospect of improved streets, sidewalks, sewers, water mains, underground utilities, plantings and a state-of-the-art firehouse.

The story was reported in newspapers coast to coast. A Norfolk reporter was impressed that the Restoration (as it was now commonly called) might spend $15,000,000 to return "Williamsburg to her Colonial simplicity [sic]." Papers everywhere extolled Rockefeller and Goodwin for their vision. For the first time in America's history, a city had the promise of intentional resurrection for patriotic purposes. For the second time in living memory—the first since the town forgot about Election Day (until Geddy's father, the court clerk, belatedly remembered)—Williamsburg got national attention. Rockefeller's money and Goodwin's dream had put the vanished capital back on the map.

Like any county seat in Dixie, Williamsburg boasted a courthouse (above)—indeed one built in 1770—and a hotel with verandas, this one the Colonial Inn that had seen better days. The store (below) once owned by William Prentis had been chased by time's winged chariot so often that it abandoned its horsedrawn carriage trade and now served less gracious vehicles.

As they rode around town in the borrowed limousine after the Phi Beta Kappa dedication, Dr. Goodwin and Mr. Rockefeller mused about "perpetual preservation." Then they walked the woods behind Bassett Hall where there stood a huge tree that took root during the reign of George II. The philanthropist asked, "If I come back some day, can we bring our lunch down and eat it under the oak tree?" It seems such a naive request, almost a child's question by a fifty-three-year-old magnate who had nursed an interest in horticulture since his lonely boyhood on a sylvan estate. That evening the wistful patron made a tentative commitment to the minister's vague dream of restoring the town, and weeks later Dr. Goodwin winningly sent him a Christmas box of holly, mistletoe and running cedar from the Williamsburg wilds. In his thank-you note Mr. Rockefeller wrote, "I have thought many times of that marvelous oak tree which you took me to see and of the fall woods into which we looked. What a wonderful picture it was."

The question remained: Could they give their picture of resurrected Williamsburg a life of its own? That in turn could only be answered by the people they found to help them in the new work of creating a place that had been before. The raising of brick and mortar first depended on flesh and blood: employees, consultants, volunteers and friends; even some antagonists made a difference.

Bound simply by a gentlemen's agreement, Goodwin and Rockefeller had no idea what they were doing—namely, inventing an interdisciplinary tradition. The genius of their plan lay in the fact that there was no plan and not much of a personnel roster to begin with. "Actually there were no people really prepared to administer an undertaking like the one at Williamsburg," Charles B. Hosmer, Jr., would write a half-century later in *Preservation Comes of Age,* his definitive history of the preservation movement. No one had tried this kind of thing before. "New professions, new organizational procedures, and a whole new philosophy of restoration would have to be created. . . . If a physical restoration was to follow, Goodwin had to find contractors, historians, archaeologists, furniture experts, draftsmen, landscape architects and engineers. These professions were available in 1928, but none of them had any experience in the re-creation of a colonial city."

Both Goodwin and Rockefeller had considerable experience in collective enterprise. The rector was a master at marshaling support for Christian good works, the philanthropist a devout believer in backing temporal ventures with the soundest talent his impressive resources could hire. Thus, though they were blazing a trail through an interdisciplinary wilderness, by habit and experience they found able help.

The Restoration required a host of disciplined talents and quickly set out to hire them. By the time the two-corporation enterprise went public, it had acquired an executive officer in Arthur Woods, had hired the firm Perry, Shaw and Hepburn as its architects and retained the contracting company that became Todd and Brown as its builders and engineers. Goodwin had long since instructed Perry to consult two respected architects, A. Lawrence Kocher and Fiske Kimball, who believed that the young discipline of historical architecture should rely on the purest "authenticity."

OPPOSITE: Behind a filigree of wrought iron and autumn leaf at the top of the promenade guarded by the "Twelve Apostles" of yaupon holly, the reconstructed Governor's Palace rises as a monument to Georgian grace, symmetry and grandeur. When originally completed in 1722 (the rear wing with ballroom and supper room coming in 1752), it was the most elegant house in the colonies. The Palace burned in 1781 and collapsed into its own cellars, smothering many objects for eventual excavation, such as clumps of brickwork that revealed their exact bonding pattern to the Williamsburg restorers.

Further, before offering Perry's first plans to Rockefeller, Goodwin showed them to five solons of the American Institute of Architects who endorsed them in glowing terms, which impressed Rockefeller all the more. Strange as it seems, this kind of peer review had not occurred before, yet the Restoration would turn it into a virtual prerequisite for action. Within six months of the town meeting, the Advisory Committee of Architects was formed and began the work it would pursue for twenty years.

Appointment of the advisory committee gave Williamsburg a decidedly architectural emphasis, which seems in retrospect as inevitable as it was initially fortuitous. The complex reasons were happenstantial. For one thing, as Hosmer wrote, "The profession of architecture was already history-minded in the 1920s." Designers had been measuring old buildings throughout the country and borrowing details for office buildings and schools. But kindred professions "were not ready to assume roles of any consequence in a restoration program. Historians merely paid lip service to the idea that buildings could be classed as documents. . . . Landscape architects had restricted their activities mainly to developing city parks and planning gardens for the wealthy. Archaeologists had no experience in interpreting the foundations of buildings from the colonial period because their main interests lay in Grecian, Roman, Egyptian, Mayan and North American Indian antiquities. . . . No large contracting firms had done restoration up to 1928 because no projects had been started that would have needed them. In spite of these obstacles Goodwin and Woods began to assemble a remarkable organization that would help to transform the rector's dream into bricks and mortar."

In 1930 the Restoration's officers stand for a group portrait. Among them are (front row, second from left to right) the Reverend W. A. R. Goodwin, roads commissioner George P. Coleman and President Arthur Woods; (second row, left) attorney Vernon Geddy; (third row, left, center and right) architect William G. Perry, landscape architect Arthur A. Shurcliff and executive nabob Kenneth Chorley.

Among the first to arrive was A. Edwin Kendrew, a junior man from Perry's Boston office. He left his bride, Melinda, at home in Massachusetts because his was to be a brief assignment after all—as he recalled six decades after ultimately fetching her to Virginia. He would spend his life at Williamsburg, rising to the top of its architectural operations and winning many distinctions including an A.I.A. Gold Medal. Coming close on his heels in 1928 was Singleton P. Moorehead, who rented a room in Judge Armistead's home. Finding life professionally challenging and socially inspiring, he also soon found a wife in Cynthia Beverley Tucker Coleman, daughter of the state roads commissioner.

"There wasn't a nice collection of architectural books as you would find for, say Connecticut or Massachusetts," said the Harvard-trained architect Moorehead. The lack of published material "meant we had to go out in the field and measure and photograph." They made full-sized drawings of details, "filling notebooks with sketched plans and elevations." They toured the countryside on weekends and wrote the book on Virginia's vernacular architecture. They examined old buildings, measured them in detail and made precise drawings. They were particularly interested in details: moldings, cornices, chair rails, paneling, staircases, outbuildings, building techniques evident in the "original fabric" of old structures.

"We discovered a very fortunate thing. I doubt if we could have done this job if it hadn't been so": Virginia colonial architecture had rather strict conventions. "There are only a few cornice types, interior or exterior. There were only a few window designs, sash and frames; the use of beaded weatherboard was almost universal. If it was not beaded weatherboards, then it was flush boarding, beaded or not. Shingling methods were all about the same. In chimney and fireplace construction there were seven or eight kinds. . . . Ceiling heights were very consistent. . . . So once you learned the words and phrases, once you learned your bag of tricks, you were in good shape to reconstruct and restore."

The photographs they took and precise drawings they made became a source of details for reconstructions and restorations. They also sent the word out that they were interested in materials from eighteenth-century houses; the Restoration became a steady buyer of dismantled buildings.

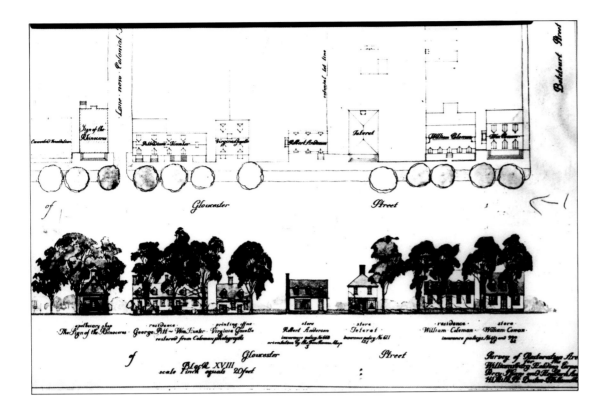

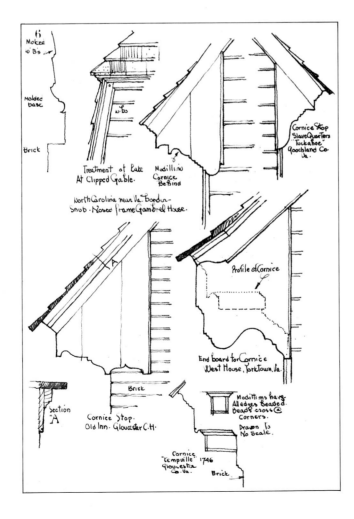

A host of talented people helped resurrect this town. Singleton Moorehead, a junior architect with the firm of Perry, Shaw and Hepburn, recorded architectural details (below) from many Tidewater sources, thus providing a wealth of information about authentic elements to be used in the Historic Area. A plan and elevation of Duke of Gloucester Street's north side (above) exemplifies the precision that this architectural firm brought to bear as it drafted the entire town. The view runs from an "apothecary shop" now called the Prentis Store, to a "store" occupied by one William Cowan, now the Davidson Shop.

FOLLOWING PAGES:
The Governor's Palace and its dependencies would be reconstructed, opened in the 1930s, then reinterpreted anew as new scholarship altered and improved modern understanding of the 18th century. The butler's pantry (left) gained a prime location—at the front of the building off the grand foyer—thanks to new research. The kitchen now displays a bright array of antique equipage.

Many old buildings were bought and stored piecemeal, then used as architectural spare parts after experience proved that moving a house didn't always work; it caused "too much breakage." As they discovered these design elements, they often found that seemingly aesthetic details had practical implications: Shingles finished with rounded ends did not curl and split like those with square ends. Bricks rubbed flat for use around openings offered true surfaces when doors and windows were installed; thus they didn't leak.

As for living conditions, Williamsburg was a mixed bag. The local restaurants were "absolutely foul"; the old Pocahontas Tea Room was visited by rats as well as by people. In self-defense Restoration House was opened, a place where the invaders suffered a steady diet of cold country ham and boiled potatoes until they learned they would get fried chicken if they tipped the waitress. Drink was another matter: The best moonshine was $5 a gallon, and connoisseurs kept six months' supply on hand so it could "age."

Moorehead found his southern hosts famously hospitable, sociable and cultured. The Restoration crowd attended oyster roasts and shad bakes in the country and marveled at visits by touring theatrical troupes that performed Shakespeare alfresco. (*A Midsummer Night's Dream* was memorably canceled when an actor blew a few blasts on a conch horn, which brought every mongrel cur and coon dog howling to the stage thinking a hunt was in the offing.) Alas, the Yankees' idea of a party shocked some locals. The 1930 New Year's Eve blast at the high school featured parody skits on stage, bizarre costumes among the audience and even more bizarre behavior that left some revelers stacked "like cordwood" in the basement. After the celebrants realized they'd almost burned the building down, parties became more private.

(Nonetheless, this must have been a caring community. When a young architect died after a sudden illness in 1931, his colleagues raised a small memorial to him beside the Bruton Parish Church walk. Now the bronze sundial shows the signs of reverent wear; its gnomon has been broken and welded on again; its corners are bright from the touch of passing fingers. "In remembrance of John A. Barrows 1906–1931 Architect Writer Antiquarian." It is graced by an inscription reading around its border: "The shadow fell for a moment upon the hour that marked his death then passed leaving his name and memory illuminated by the eternal sunshine.")

Iconography appealed to the first restorers. Witness the telling business of selecting a seal for Williamsburg. It shows how the Restoration went about its work: In one word, energetically; in another, deliberately; in a third, redundantly. If anything got lost in the shuffle it might only be efficiency, but better that than an unsatisfactory decision made in haste.

By Thanksgiving 1931, it was decided to adopt an emblem: Colonial Williamsburg's own bit of heraldry complete with motto. Perry (in Boston) sent Kenneth Chorley who became president of Williamsburg in 1935 (in New York), a list of sentiments, each one loftier than the last, such as: "For the perpetual remembrance of the thing"; "Honor and protection"; "To remember these things hereafter will be a pleasure"; and more. Perry opined, "To us the motto *Quae Amissa Salva* seems the best of the lot," and kindly translated: "What was lost is safe."

The minutes of a December meeting recorded that "Mr. Perry has presented the proposed seal for Colonial Williamsburg and it was accepted and approved, with the exception of the motto. Dr. Goodwin suggested that we use Ruskin's line 'It is our duty to preserve what the past has had to say for itself,' which was accepted and approved. Mr. Perry is to have this translated into Latin." While Goodwin dug up the rest of Ruskin's prolix homily for Woods to forward to Rockefeller, Perry waited upon his Boston scholars and Chorley demanded action. The next month a letter of accustomed formality went from the principal at 26 Broadway to his principal assistant at 61

Hardly anything took more study and debate among the founders—nor served their purposes better —than the official seal of Colonial Williamsburg with its valiant, ribboned motto.

Even old family photos became useful sources of architectural information. These young people (above) posed in front of what had been colonial silversmith James Craig's house before its demolition in 1907. The enlarged detail (below) reveals not only a child's gaze but details of door placement, window arrangement and shingling. The building today, known as the Golden Ball and reconstructed to its original appearance, once again houses silversmiths who make and sell handmade objects.

The painstaking process of restoring the William Finnie House required the removal of rotten wood and made the place look a mess before its restored beauty emerged.

Declaration for Assurance. No. 486.

Documents as mundane as insurance policies could provide a wealth of information. This one includes a list of dependencies and sketches of a house James Semple owned in 1801. Now called the William Finnie House for an 18th-century occupant, it may have been designed by Thomas Jefferson and anticipates the Federal style of the early 19th century.

Broadway: "Dear Colonel Woods: On the enclosed slip I have presented the various suggestions for a motto for Williamsburg which were discussed the other day. Either of the last two, preferably the last, seems to me the best, namely, 'That the future may learn from the past.' These I pass on to you simply for such further action as you think best. Very truly, John D. Rockefeller, Jr."

The next day Woods instructed Chorley to send his employer's first two choices on to the architects for their opinion. But the day after that Perry sent Chorley translations of the original choice which one classicist rendered as *Vox Am Praeteriti Conservanda* and another as *Nos Oportet Praeterita Tradere*. A week later, Chorley asked Perry, "Are you agreeable in deciding upon Mr. Rockefeller's first suggestion . . . and, if so, would you recommend that it be put on the seal in English or Latin? Perhaps it is too long in Latin." Dr. Goodwin would yet offer something even longer, compliments of a Williamsburg scholar: *Ut Praeteritorum Gloria Posteritatis Memoriae Tradatur* ("In Order that the Glory of the Past May Be Handed Down to the Memory of Those Who Follow"). Perry realized that Rockefeller's favorite was too long in any language for the wavy ribbon he had sketched in anticipation of a conventionally brief sentiment, so he set about redesigning the ribbon to accommodate the extra words, which would be inscribed in English.

Thus the motto evolved: The man at the top gave an order (or made a request); an ad hoc committee of strong-minded men compiled, discussed and presented an array of options to the boss, who shook his head politely and sent them back to try again; that accomplished, in due course he made a sensible selection. As Rockefeller once told an aide: "All my life I have employed experts. I listen to what they say and then I exercise my own good judgement."

To plan the gardens, a project of considerable personal priority for Mr. Rockefeller, Perry's firm recommended a man of twenty-four-karat credentials and eccentric habits. Arthur A. Shurcliff (né Shurtleff), a student of southern horticulture, had helped found Harvard's landscape architecture school with the son of Frederick Law Olmsted, designer of New York's Central Park and Washington's Rock Creek Park. As odd as he was able, Shurcliff habitually wore a black greatcoat and white socks. Whenever he stayed in a hotel he brought a rope and tied one end to a radiator in case of fire. When invited to dinner, he brought his own victuals in a brown bag. When World War II broke out he furnished his living room in Massachusetts with a carriage, stocking it with food and camping supplies in case an enemy invasion forced his family to evacuate.

However eccentric, he was an ambitious aesthete. Time would prove that he was more aggressive in pursuing his own ideas of beauty than in bringing colonial southern gardens into full flower. But if it would turn out that some of his designs were historically fanciful, it bears mention that scholars then knew precious little about colonial gardens. As happened in so many instances and specialties, Colonial Williamsburg itself would be responsible for making the great leaps backward in time. Further, the gardens he designed were soon numbered among the most beautiful in America. Indeed they earned premier status in what the Restoration later called the "Six Appeals of Williamsburg." (The others were architecture, furniture and furnishings, crafts, history and heritage, and preservation research.) Shurcliff designed the splendid formal gardens behind the Palace with its holly maze and ha-ha, which concealed railroad tracks. He planned the anachronistic but lovely Elkanah Deane House garden, fabulous topiaries and several planting beds with elaborate designs.

Shurcliff ignored practical considerations, like budgets, with such aplomb that even Rockefeller laughed in the end. When explaining one plan for the Palace gardens, he pretended not to hear the patron's repeated requests for a cost estimate until the normally diffident Rockefeller shouted for the first time in anyone's experience, "What is the cost?!" Too aloof to have come up with the kind of solid figure the enterprise favored, the gardener said "between two and five hundred thousand,"

OPPOSITE: The study in George Wythe's house again displays furniture and accessories that he might have used and enjoyed: the vacuum pump for scientific experiments on the broadcloth-covered table, the globe in the corner.

which left his usually sedate associates in stitches. Rockefeller answered, "Oh well, let's just appropriate a million and go to lunch."

Shurcliff notwithstanding, the early restorers developed a dedication to historical accuracy. Dr. Goodwin had set an early if naive example with his investigations into what the town had been. When architects alone couldn't come up with the detailed information that soon appeared necessary, more conventional scholarship was called into play and made a substantial mark. Goodwin not only assigned his secretary to examine records, he lured his son Rutherfoord away from a Rochester newspaper job to handle many tasks, one of them historical research. Then the rector commissioned a cousin to search colonial records.

Following the trail back to England in 1929, Mary F. Goodwin haunted the British Museum, hoping (in vain) to prove that Sir Christopher Wren had indeed designed the college building that bore his name. Instead she came upon a catalogue of manuscripts elsewhere that led her to Oxford University's Bodleian Library in search of a copperplate engraving of "a village in Virginia." A few days before Christmas she fired off a message describing what came to be called the Bodleian Plate, a montage of the Capitol, Palace and college executed about 1740. Steel to restore the Wren Building had already been ordered, but a crudely transmitted facsimile of the plate revealed different roof features than Perry and company had surmised. The rear roof of the main range wasn't straight; it featured an odd and totally unpredictable series of sawtooth gables. The Restoration was pleased to make it right.

A paper mulberry shades the oval Orlando Jones House garden. This home was named for the son of Bruton's first rector and grandfather of Martha Dandridge Custis, the merry widow who married the planter from northern Virginia, George Washington.

Painstaking scholars proved their worth many times over. The State Art Commission had special oversight powers regarding the Wren Building, since it belonged to a state college. The commissioners rejected the restorers' plans because of the proposed location of staircases, saying that such a large building wouldn't have had a central stair. Kenneth Chorley mentioned the matter to Governor Harry F. Byrd, a descendant of the colonial patriarchs and as impulsive a politician as he was a faithful friend of the institution that brought national attention to his state. The governor offered to fire any commission members who stood in Williamsburg's way, but Chorley dissuaded him, thinking it would only make matters worse. In any event, the new Research Department found a letter that School Master Mungo Ingles wrote to Governor Nicholson in Annapolis after the 1705 fire. It referred to the stairs "(standing as your Exc[ellenc]y: well knowes) in the Middle of the Pile." This proved the theory advanced by Restoration designers; most important, the building was accurate.

(Confrontations with state agencies changed Mr. Rockefeller's mind about the ultimate disposition of the Restoration. Initially, he'd thought to turn his project over to William and Mary when it was complete. He decided against that course because it appeared that political pressures could be brought to bear on any state institution and he disliked the notion that his legacy might be buffeted by the winds of faddish popularity and the whims of politicians. Beyond that, of course, it became evident that the Restoration might never be finally finished.)

As research efforts broadened, elementary archaeology was given its due. Though James Knight was trained as an architect, he was given the title of archaeologist and assigned the job of combing the entire 170-odd-acre Historic Area in search of building remains. Directing a gang of laborers, he dug trenches one shovel blade wide and a shovel handle apart. When he came to an old foundation, he uncovered it; when he found nothing he simply backfilled. Using the most heavy-handed techniques of the time, he thus traversed the town and found virtually every old foundation—though he ignored soil strata and artifacts, to the consternation of trained archaeologists later.

One who made as significant and far more graceful a contribution was Rutherfoord Goodwin. A man of keen intellect and winning personality, the youngest surviving child of the minister's first wife quickly took charge of education, training, public relations and publications. It was Rutherfoord who hit upon the idea of recruiting hostesses from among the region's gentlewomen and training them in matters of history and Restoration philosophy. He also had them dress in colonial clothes so that they could be identified by (and distinguished from) the visitors who started arriving in ever greater numbers once the Raleigh Tavern opened in 1932. His band of three ladies grew into something that was not considered at the outset, a corps of "interpreters," eventually numbering in the hundreds, to make visitors' experiences "educational."

A skillful scholar and writer, Rutherfoord had both intelligence and imagination. Since Williamsburg started attracting visitors from the outset, he provided a Baedeker in the sort of book once called a "conceit." The choice volume contained his entertaining and accurate narrative written in the style of the eighteenth century along with appendices of historical documents. Printed and bound in engaging mimicry of colonial books, *A Brief & True Report Concerning Williamsburg in Virginia* first appeared in 1935 and sold steadily for more than forty years. Intended as the Restoration's first guidebook, albeit unlike any other, it opens with the telling salutation:

> GOOD FRIEND, what Matter how or whence you come To walk these Streets which are the Nation's Home; Rest for a Time and—resting—read herein, Seek from the Past and—seeking—Wisdom win: For if the Things you see give you no Gain, The LIVES of many MEN were lived in vain.

Sad to tell, Rutherfoord's career at Williamsburg was not an unalloyed success. This despite such random duties as standing in for his father in a movie about the Restoration (opposite Rockefeller who played himself). Without credit, he also wrote a conventional guidebook that sold over three million copies until finally retired in 1985 after thirty-four years in print. Rutherfoord was a "creative" and sensitive person, one among many bound to fall out with the aggressive Kenneth Chorley. It seems to have been a matter of clashing personalities, dissonant purposes, differing opinions and—on Chorley's part—perhaps too much devotion to duty. Hosmer wrote "The restoration needed a 'conscience' and Rutherfoord ably filled that role," but Chorley didn't welcome many players on Mr. Rockefeller's stage.

From the beginning of the Restoration, Chorley was the man from New York who visited Williamsburg most often and most forcefully. His ability, energy and loyalty to his superior were as imposing as his 6'5" frame. "KC" seems to have suffered no inferiors very gladly. Born in England, the son of an Episcopal clergyman, he was raised in a chic New York suburb and turned down an appointment to West Point; instead he sought his fortune in the southwest as a railroad man. He boasted of once working 397 straight days at 12 hours a day before becoming the youngest railyard superintendent in the land. After working briefly for the spectral Henry Ford, he returned east and met Arthur Woods through one of his aristocratic father's friends. Soon he became Woods's right-hand man. Earning Mr. Rockefeller's confidence and affection, he succeeded Woods as president of Williamsburg in 1935 and held the post until 1958; he then acted as a consultant until 1963, when he was elected trustee emeritus, a capacity in which he served until his death in 1974.

Two decades after his retirement and one after his death, Chorley was still remembered variously with admiration, awe, affection and fear. His faithful secretary says that "no executive ever knew how to get so much" from his subordinates. Others say he demanded too much. A Williamsburg physician found himself overworked before Chorley's scheduled visits, which prompted epidemics of gastrointestinal distress among Restoration supervisors. Called "a brute, a boor and a bully" by one bitter survivor, he was a taskmaster. On at least one occasion, he summoned one administrator to his office simply to witness him dress down another. And he required executives to keep letters of res-

The 1788 account book of a builder mentions repairs to the Palace's garden walls that include "putting on Balls." One such stone orb survived in the town and was given by its inheritor to the Restoration, whose own builders had it copied. The original now rests on a restored wall.

Tulips bloom in the garden of the Benjamin Powell House, home of the builder who repaired the Public Gaol, raised the Bruton Parish Church tower and constructed the Public Hospital.

To discover the shapes of things past, Restoration researchers studied whatever material they could find—and learned, among other things for instance, that the Wren Building had a protean facade and metamorphosing cupola. Witness the detail from the Bodleian Plate (top), circa 1740; a background detail (above) from Charles Bridges's life portrait of James Blair (see page 39); an engraving (above right) taken from a pre-Civil War Thomas Millington watercolor; and a photograph (below right) taken in 1882.

The Wren Building's gabled roof undergoing restoration.

ignation typed and ready for signature. Many who knew him would remember him as an ambitious man who coveted power and access to powerful people; a member of the Rockefeller family who saw him operate would remember him as an able and loyal family retainer, indeed "a lackey." (One of the things that irritated several Rockefellers was Chorley's cheek; he loved playing host to visiting dignitaries and when there wasn't a Rockefeller in town he got to monopolize the show. Sometimes he even forgot himself when the family was present. On one ceremonial occasion Mrs. Rockefeller urged her firstborn son, then chairman of Williamsburg's board, "Now John, don't let Mr. Chorley push you out of the carriage.")

Some of Chorley's minions thought him so dedicated to fault-finding that they made certain he'd see something wrong lest he keep them up all night looking for a gaffe. At least once they hung Queen Anne's flag upside down so he could order it righted. Yet he could also be famously generous. He was perfectly capable of rewarding a job well done with a week's stay at a resort with all expenses paid. After Vernon Geddy's unexpected death, Chorley summoned young Vernon, Jr., and said: "I want you to do something for me," namely to serve as Mr. Rockefeller's personal attorney for Virginia matters. It was a bit of business that helped the fledgling lawyer launch a distinguished career. And while whatever quiet credit went to Mr. Rockefeller, it was Chorley who established secret trust funds for several genteel paupers living in the Historic Area.

Chorley was also a very able administrator. As Hosmer wrote, "When one takes Boston architects, New York contractors, and northern money into a Virginia town, it requires great organizational skill and tact to achieve success." Chorley applied the skill within the organization; the tact he reserved for townspeople when it suited him, playing poker, for example, with influential local cronies whom he cultivated and genuinely liked.

Hindsight suggests it was Chorley who made Williamsburg work, albeit at some cost to the people who worked for him, including the talented, if eccentric, Rutherford Goodwin. Mr.

Rockefeller's eldest grandchild, longtime trustee Abby O'Neill, summed him up as adroitly as anyone, calling him "a very powerful and energetic man stubborn enough to get things done." Kendrew, and several others, credit him with another, more nebulous achievement. It was Chorley who kept Rockefeller interested in what was going on in Williamsburg and, when his interest lagged, apparently got the ball rolling again, sometimes by starting a new project that would intrigue his employer. One of the ironies is that this fearsome man adored his gentle-mannered boss.

The Restoration could not have thrived without the aid of devoted outsiders like Horace M. Albright, who had been superintendent of Yellowstone National Park when Rockefeller toured the West in 1924. Later, as director of the National Park Service, Albright found he shared a new interest with the philanthropist, namely the creation of a colonial national monument. Subsequently named the Colonial National Historical Park, this project would physically link three sites that were bound by history in Dr. Goodwin's estimation since "Williamsburg is the continuation of Jamestown and Yorktown is the vindication of Williamsburg."

The idea for a park emerged after Michigan Congressman Louis C. Cramton visited the Wythe House. Connecting the site of the first successful colony, the colonial capital and the battlefield where independence was won, it would feature one of the nation's first scenic highways, but its creation involved a political tangle. In 1929 Albright escorted Cramton's appropriations committee to Williamsburg and found his mettle sorely tested. For example, he was asked to organize a party at Chorley's house after a formal banquet hosted by the governor. Since Prohibition was still the much-flouted law of the land, it would not do to invite a "dry" like Cramton to a "wet" social event. Not knowing which congressmen drank and which didn't, and believing a mistake could be fatal to the cause, Albright showed up at Chorley's party alone. The next day the group was invited to Carter's Grove by Mr. and Mrs. Archibald M. McCrea, who were renovating the 1755 plantation house built by Robert "King" Carter's grandson Carter Burwell. For refreshments, the McCreas "didn't offer" anything but had a bar set up. "The Congressmen pretty nearly broke the antique furniture rushing over."

Back in Washington, Albright began plotting to get the highway approved. Here the problem lay in the proposed route—through an ammunition depot along a stretch of the York River, which Navy brass enjoyed to the limit. In addition to officers' homes overlooking the river, the installation had boat docks, bathing beaches, duck blinds and other amenities of military life. "It was just a little paradise in there, and they were not going to let anybody invade." Even the Park Service director wasn't allowed on the property without special permission. If the parkway-through-paradise proposal went through normal channels, the Navy would block it by one ruse or another. Instead Albright drafted a presidential proclamation, which Secretary of the Interior Ray Lyman Wilbur persuaded President Hoover to sign before the Secretary of the Navy even saw it.

Politicians proved eager to support the plan for a colonial park comprising much of struggling Yorktown, all of Jamestown (moribund save for its ruins) and a right-of-way through Williamsburg. The colonial capital had been considered as a potential part of the park, but a group of townspeople led by Judge Frank Armistead opposed that. As his son would remember it, he opposed placing any part of Williamsburg under the aegis of a federal agency that might override local authority. Armistead had spoken in support of Goodwin's proposition at the town meeting that launched the Restoration, but after that he came to be regarded as anti-outsider in general, anti-Restoration in particular and anti-Rockefeller in person.

His Classical Revival brick house hard by Bruton Parish Church on Duke of Gloucester Street was one of a handful of properties never acquired by Goodwin or Colonial Williamsburg. The judge

Mr. and Mrs. Archibald M. McCrea pose for the photographer at Carter's Grove. They began renovating the ancient manor as their home shortly before Colonial Williamsburg found its stride. Though their work violated many of the evolving tenets of historical restoration, the house still evokes the early plantation and has become an important annex to the Historic Area.

This handsome entrance graces the Greek Revival home on Duke of Gloucester Street, a 19th-century anachronism that survived. Owned by an early opponent of the Rockefeller endeavor, Judge Frank Armistead, it devolved to his son, Judge Robert Armistead, who lived there until his death in 1999. A Greek Revival church did not escape razing during the early days of the Restoration, though it would be saved today as a fine example of a period building— even if of the wrong period.

Wetherburn's Tavern, once again known by its historic name, was one of the last properties on Duke of Gloucester Street to be ceded to Colonial Williamsburg, which researched and restored it with extravagant care. For some generations, the rambling house was called the Bull's Head.

offered to sell this handsome home much later, but at the astronomical figure of $80,000 or twice the going price at the time. Even so, Chorley said turning him down was his worst mistake. Another building that eluded Colonial Williamsburg for years was a Victorian home at the very end of Duke of Gloucester Street by the Capitol, which Armistead's maiden cousins kept as a guesthouse. When Miss Dora Armistead died in 1984, the house was leased to the APVA More than a decade later, a new agreement was struck between the inheritors and Colonial Williamsburg: The Victorian home was moved to a lot outside the Historic Area and the ground below it was excavated by archaeologists in the last decade of the twentieth century. This was a particularly rich dig in terms of artifacts and building foundations; now the coffeehouse that had been there in the eighteenth century awaits reconstruction in the twenty-first.

The last unattainable lots were a scattering of properties acquired by a lady who made the best of the hand she was dealt while, some said, besting the Restoration and all of Mr. Rockefeller's hired experts. Virginia Braithwaite Haughwout, a descendant of the Bucktrout clan of cabinetmakers and builders, lived on Duke of Gloucester Street in a substantial weatherboard building with three brick chimneys called the "Bull's Head" that dated back to colonial times. Popular lore has it that she came to despise Kenneth Chorley and all the Rockefellers, but that was no reason to turn her back on opportunities that their coming presented. By the late 1940s she owned several properties within or adjoining the Historic Area, lots that had been owned in generations past by relatives or ancestors. These included one that she bought at a tax sale on the courthouse steps, local lore related, when she out-bid Vernon Geddy, Sr., whom the Restoration had sent to buy the fourteen-acre tract that fronted on Francis Street next to the new Williamsburg Inn. Geddy had instructions to go as high as $25,000, but every time he bid, "Miss Ginny" raised the ante a few hundred dollars and when he reached his limit, she won the prize.

Mrs. Haughwout decided to build on another site, a gully called Ginny's Bottom that ran from Duke of Gloucester Street to Nicholson Street. Already possessing a home in town, she wanted a rental property, an in-town motel, but her plan fell victim to zoning regulations. She appealed, Colonial Williamsburg opposed her and the matter became a court contest between attorneys whose names would echo around town and beyond. The lady's lawyer was Robert Armistead, the judge's son (and later a judge himself who would confront Colonial Williamsburg over an abandoned family cemetery at Greenhill, the land behind the Robert Carter House). The Restoration was represented by Lewis F. Powell, Jr., later associate justice of the Supreme Court and for a short period chairman of Colonial Williamsburg's board of trustees. After Mrs. Haughwout lost the suit, she rented the gully to Colonial Williamsburg on a ninety-nine-year lease. Ginny's Bottom became the site of the Printing Office, Post Office and Bindery—that lovely colonial industrial park. But Miss Ginny would never see it; she died soon after signing the lease.

She left the use of her several properties to her children during their lifetimes and thereafter to the Bucktrout-Braithwaite Memorial Foundation, which she established. One heir leased the Redwood Ordinary to Colonial Williamsburg for a century. Another lived on the lot bought at the tax sale. This had been improved by the addition of an eighteenth-century building, Providence Hall, which was rescued from the path of a new highway in Providence Forge and moved. The land's value had been further enhanced by the success of the adjacent Inn, which kept growing and needing new amenities like a belle needs balls.

Colonial Williamsburg restored the relocated building, which became a stopping place for heads of state, then built the Inn's Providence Hall wings on the land and added other embellishments like tennis courts. Given the property's rising value and its commensurate rental price, Mrs. Haughwout's original investment would be repaid in rent alone several times over each year.

The heir living in the Bull's Head eventually found the rambling digs too much to handle and agreed to lease them to Colonial Williamsburg with a condition. This had been her home, woman and girl, and she wanted Williamsburg's promise to restore it "sympathetically," a reasonable request. In short order an agreement was reached and the building was treated with more sympathy than the lady could have hoped for. It became the site of a major dig by Williamsburg's historical archaeologist Ivor Noël Hume, who examined it with extravagant care. Then it was restored and reopened under its historical name, Wetherburn's Tavern.

Two years after Mr. Rockefeller was so taken by the "wonderful picture" of the Bassett Hall woods (and by Dr. Goodwin's vision) the new Restoration got its first real picture, Charles Willson Peale's portrait of George Washington. Yet however systematically Mr. Rockefeller worked, he had no clear image of what his new endeavor would create. Among other things, a superb collection of art and furnishings would evolve, because the restored village's buildings would otherwise remain empty shells. An educational institution would arise, too, though the patron opposed an "education" program per se until it was dubbed "interpretation." However grand Dr. Goodwin's vision, neither did he imagine the magnitude of his and Mr. Rockefeller's common cause. In restoring the colonial capital for posterity, the founders' heirs would rebuild a town of some five hundred structures comprising approximately eighty-eight renewed originals or "restorations" and five times that number of "reconstructions," a number that promises to rise in the twenty-first century.

The Restoration's people moved modern intrusions such as a railroad station and the line that served it. They would bury utility lines and reunite the divided Duke of Gloucester Street. They would remove modern stores from its length and relocate them in the new business district called Merchants Square, one of the first planned shopping areas in the land. They would raze almost all the postcolonial buildings, from hovels and shanties around Courthouse green to the splendid Greek Revival church beside the Magazine. They would embark on a program to relocate displaced down-towners, most of them black tenants who found new homes in specially funded low-rent neighborhoods. They would renovate and equip the homes of "life tenants," a process that required the residents to move out for a year or more while the house was taken apart down to the scantlings and put back together better than new.

Predictably the town fathers had something to say about all this. According to city council minutes, Goodwin explained "in a general way" what he had in mind to do around town in 1927. In response, "Whereas the Council has contemplated [drafting a new building code] . . . for some time," it would not do to act hastily. The council decided to address such matters on a case-by-case basis until they got around to writing new codes—at long last in 1947!

The early Restoration's approach was reflected in—and ratified by—the eventual zoning ordinance. It authorized the "restoration or reconstruction and use" of pre-1800 buildings in the Historic Area. "In the event the original foundations have been obliterated," reconstructions were allowed "where there is documentary evidence of the existence of such buildings prior to the year 1800." However, they must be "designed so as to present substantially their original appearance and dimensions" and be put to "a use that existed in this area in the 18th century."

Ably served by the advisory architects and a growing staff, the Restoration settled on a goal that can be stated simply enough: to restore the town to its eighteenth-century appearance. Wisely they decided against choosing a specific year—1770, say—because it was obvious that their blueprint must be a composite based on data from different dates: spottily preserved legislative and land

OPPOSITE: Entirely rebuilt structures restored the *mise en scène* of Williamsburg. Witness the separate kitchen and scullery serving the Governor's Palace. The kitchen in turn was served by terraced gardens on the slope that ended in Governor Spotswood's decorative "canal."

ABOVE: Dr. Goodwin stands in Bruton Parish Church with foreman William Holland near what would soon become his burial crypt beneath the aisle. Though he lived to see the city largely restored to an image of its former self, the rector died before the second (and more complete) restoration of this sanctuary.

OPPOSITE: Removing modern "intrusions" proved a major part of restoring the antique scene, and one ubiquitous eyesore proved surprisingly easy to hide. Utility lines were buried and the poles removed from the offending median strip along Duke of Gloucester Street. It took longer to eliminate another sign of modern times; cars were not banned from this street in daytime until 1974.

records, old letters and diaries, the occasional published picture or amateur's watercolor, and on foundations that could be absolutely dated by architectural or historical means. Further, picking a precise year would mean removing original buildings erected even a year later. It would also have dictated reconstruction of the second Capitol (built after the first burned in 1747), for which no detailed descriptions have ever been found.

The chosen goal—tempered by the determination to avoid speculative answers to historical puzzles whenever possible—predicated two basic rules: Buildings present in the colonial era would be restored or rebuilt; later buildings (with some exceptions) would be torn down or moved away. These tenets were enumerated in the "Decalogue," a set of commandments as sacrosanct around Williamsburg as Mosaic Law in Palestine, and observed about as imperfectly. In some respects a model set of standards for historical restorers everywhere, it provided that:

★ All Williamsburg's buildings of the colonial period should be saved.

★ "Great discretion should be exercised" before destroying any buildings of the postcolonial classical period.

★ All later buildings should be razed or removed from the Restored Area.

★ Other old buildings in Williamsburg should be preserved on their sites, not moved to what became the "Historic Area."

★ "If any reasonable additional trouble and expense" would enable it, an old building should be restored, not razed.

★ Architects must distinguish between the "scrupulous retention" and repair of old structures and "the recovery of the old form by new work."

★ While such work goes more slowly than ordinary construction, "a superior result should be preferred to more rapid progress."

★ Use of old materials and period details "is commendable."

★ Demolition is not an acceptable way to secure old materials, if an old building might be saved on its original site.

★ Necessary new materials should resemble old ones in character without attempts to "antique" them by phony means.

Of course there were slip-ups. The eighteenth-century Jackson House, located outside the original Restoration boundaries on Francis Street, was pulled down prematurely and had to be reconstructed from photos when the Historic Area was enlarged. The Restoration also worked too fast on occasion. As many as three houses at a time might be moved simultaneously, thus blocking three streets. The dust was so thick that once a bulldozer went to the wrong address and knocked down half an original house before the error was discovered. The Greek Revival church on Duke of Gloucester Street was demolished, an event that the next generation of historical architects would call shameful. The original Tazewell Hall, John "the Tory" Randolph's fine home, was moved to make way for the Inn and Lodge.

Within the Restored Area the desired end would be historical fidelity as determined with the help of scholarship, architectural research and archaeology. As luck would have it, the Restoration benefited from the Tidewater's geology. Its clay preserved the details of vanished buildings with telling clarity. Here were signs of two-century-old post holes and foundations that would have long since vanished in other kinds of soil.

As for restorations, one of the first was also the most difficult, in part because it was the largest. Huge, fragile and dogged by various fires, the Wren Building had meandering lines. The engineers developed a delicate method of reinforcing the building so that the old walls supported only their

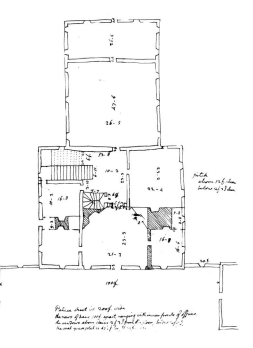

Thomas Jefferson sketched a measured floor plan of the Governor's Palace (above), doubtless with an eye toward improving the edifice. After the capital moved to Richmond and the Palace burned to the ground, his drawing survived as one of the few sources of precise and specific information about the building. Excavation of the Palace site (right) uncovered these predicted foundations.

own weight; floor and roof loads were supported by a new and hidden steel framework. Thus the antique footings, which were not disturbed, now carried only the weight of the original exterior. When it came to replacing the cornice beneath the roof, it had to be made with undulations to fit the curves of the warped structure. "The Wren Building was almost a course in restoration," Singleton Moorehead would remember, while the Capitol was a course in reconstruction and the Palace one in the surprises of archaeology.

Reconstructing the Governor's Palace and Capitol offered a variety of textbook problems, the first being to learn what they looked like. Buried foundations provided considerable evidence, but written material offered even more. The original act that chartered the city and ordered the building of the Capitol survived to serve the Restoration's designers and draftsmen. A sketch of the Palace drawn by Thomas Jefferson—who contemplated improving it—was found among his papers. This provided an accurate, measured floor plan by a premier designer of the era.

But these major structures couldn't be built until the problem of the bricks had been solved; modern suppliers could not provide brick that looked authentic, so the Restoration set out to make its own. Experimenting with obsolete methods and importing brickmakers from the Carolinas, they mixed native clay with water, then packed it into wooden molds for about a day. Removed from the molds, the wet bricks were set out to dry, then stacked—thousands at a time—into a "kiln," a hollow pile as big as many outbuildings. After the structure was sealed with mud, the bricks were "burned" by filling the kiln with firewood and tending the blaze for a week. All these manual techniques were refined by trial and error, though the special glazing found on many original buildings remained elusive. These bricks lacked the characteristic blue-gray glaze on sides and ends exposed to the flames until pine fuel was replaced with hardwood. This produced the right color glazing for the decorative patterns favored in the early eighteenth century. Thus the Restoration replicated the colors of the early colonial period.

As for the distinctive bond of the Palace walls, the restorers found examples in the original building's ruins. When the building had burned in 1781 it had collapsed into its cellars, which meant that excavators in the 1930s found countless "documents" in the buried artifacts: utensils, crockery, tiles, a hart carved in marble to adorn a fireplace (as it would again!)—and sections of wall still bound with lime mortar. Of course, many modern techniques were employed: The Capitol's roof was supported by steel framing and fireproof panels, since they would be hidden from view. When the few sources of handblown crown glass were exhausted, the 1930s restorers found that the cheapest varieties of new window glass had similar bubbles and imperfections. (Decades later, commercial manufacturing techniques made even cheap windowpanes flawless, and Colonial Williamsburg would have to rely on salvage companies for antique glass.)

Exploratory digging behind the Palace ruins uncovered an alarming surprise: a graveyard containing more skeletons than the diggers bothered to count. This prompted action with notable dispatch. Construction crews were pulled off other jobs and ordered to erect a six-foot solid fence at once. (Fiscal niceties, which often took weeks to iron out, went by the boards; they would decide which account to charge it to later.) The governor was notified and the Smithsonian Institution dispatched the preeminent physical anthropologist Ales Hrdlicka to appraise the boneyard. It was known that the Palace site had been used as a hospital, first by Washington's troops, then by both sides during the Civil War. The question remained: Who had buried their dead in the back garden? Examining almost half the 137 skeletons, Hrdlicka decided they came from a homogeneous group of white males (and two females) between the ages of twenty-five and thirty-five. Since few showed signs of trauma, most must have died of disease rather than battle wounds. The few buttons and nails found could not be identified, but seemed to have been made in the eighteenth century. In the end the bodies were reinterred and the place dedicated as a cemetery of Revolutionary War dead. But despite the fence it was discovered that one skeleton now lacked its skull, which apparently had been stolen. This caused waves of anxiety among Restoration executives until they learned that Hrdlicka had taken it for his collection at the National Museum of Natural History.

In the 1930s Colonial Williamsburg was quite simply the most famous destination in Virginia if not in the entire Old South. It received the requisite coverage in *National Geographic,* while *Architectural Record* and *Antiques* magazine devoted entire issues to the newly fabled place. President Roosevelt came down from Washington in 1934 for the opening, or reopening, of Duke of Gloucester Street, which he declared was "the most historic avenue in America." When the Capitol opened, the Virginia General Assembly repaired from Richmond to the earlier capital for the first of its commemorative sessions in the reconstructed edifice. When the Raleigh Tavern opened as the first exhibition building, the preacher who offered the benediction was sufficiently carried away to ask a blessing "in the name of the Father, and of the Son and of the Williamsburg Holding Company."

If the restoration movement had been about to happen in America anyway, the Williamsburg Restoration was its model and its most celebrated exponent, by consensus the single most influential inspiration in the realm of domestic architecture and decor. "Williamsburg style" houses began appearing wherever houses were being built; reproduction furniture and tableware became the rage among people who were buying amenities at all during the Depression. The announcement of Rockefeller's participation in the project had shared newspaper space with the news that Herbert Hoover appeared likely to win the 1928 Republican nomination for president. When the Capitol opened, Hoover was out and bread lines were in. The Depression was on. People hungered for something to cheer about, and they found it here.

When the Governor's Palace burned to the ground in three hours in 1781, it collapsed into its cellars, which became a time capsule of charred debris. In the wreckage Restoration excavators found a shattered marble panel (top), the carving of a hart, which was then repaired and returned to the front parlor mantel (above).

Also uncovered in the excavation of the Palace site was a cemetery dating from the building's use as a hospital during the Revolution. It was rededicated by the Restoration to those unnamed and unrecorded dead.

The opening of the Capitol, Palace and Raleigh Tavern marked a conclusion and a commencement. All the work called for in the initial design and building contracts was finished. The firm of Todd and Brown was dismissed; locals could handle any building work under Restoration supervisors as the need arose. Perry, Shaw and Hepburn was offered a retainer to continue advising the Restoration on architectural matters; the firm's protégé Ed Kendrew, assisted by Sing Moorehead, would handle further design chores as Restoration employees. In later years, the work completed thus far—by 1934—would be called Phase One, though Phase Two had no real beginning. Kendrew would remember that Chorley issued instructions to plan activities one year at a time, with no clear long-term agenda. The decision to make the Restoration a perpetual organization just sort of happened naturally, as inevitably as Mr. and Mrs. Rockefeller returned each spring and fall to their new retreat at Bassett Hall.

To the beholder, the young Restoration looked romantic and conservative in the original sense; it brightened the eye of architectural expert and historical innocent alike, and it stirred every patriotic heart during the most disheartening of times. There were many problems to be solved and unexpected issues to address as the institution grew, and even the New Deal would become involved. The old road from Williamsburg to Yorktown had been paved to serve local military bases during World War I. But once it reached Williamsburg it became Duke of Gloucester Street, the main artery, nay the aorta, through town. Now that an antique *mise-en-scène* had been created, the question arose how to divert the modern automobile traffic so markedly increased by this new attraction. Several alternative routes were proposed, such as cutting through the woods behind Bassett Hall, but none seemed satisfactory.

Dr. Goodwin came to the rescue again, or so he thought when he proposed a tunnel under the Restored Area! This would carry the Colonial Parkway, the road Herbert Hoover's administration had cagily approved, but Goodwin was "practically thrown out of the Rockefeller office" in New York, said Horace Albright who received him next. Having left government for private industry and a seat on the Restoration's board of directors, the former Park Service director thought the tunnel idea "just seemed like a desecration that couldn't be tolerated." That didn't deter Goodwin, who made his pitch to every trustee and official he could reach. After FDR's flamboyant Secretary of the Interior Harold Ickes heard of it, and feasibility studies were made, the seemingly absurd notion of burrowing beneath the Historic Area proved to be the easiest and cheapest solution. Thus the tunnel, by now endorsed by the Williamsburg establishment, was undertaken as one of the New Deal's recovery projects. A curving route was found that skirted the Peyton Randolph House and the tunnel was built by the old "cut and cover" technique of digging a trench and laying the roadway within it, then restoring the surface. The Ludwell Tenement, which had been destroyed during the Civil War, was reconstructed with the help of an elderly resident's recollection, atop the tunnel.

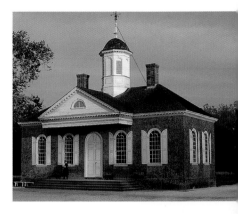

Tazewell Hall, John "the Tory" Randolph's mansion, did not have such a happy fate. It was sold off and towed away in a move as controversial as it was drawn out. As early as 1928 when a Randolph descendant made inquiries, Dr. Goodwin's secretary wrote that the recently acquired home was "one of the handsomest of the colonial homes in Williamsburg and its historical connections make it even more interesting." It was then scheduled to be restored after its occupants' life tenancy expired, though Peyton Randolph Nelson, a crusty old man, wasn't going to budge before he had to. When he got a form letter warning occupants to guard against frozen water pipes, he replied in this vein: "Yours recd &c. I enclose it and mail it back to you for you to stuff it in the waste basket &c. You dont seem to know your and my status—as related to each other. . . . I am the land-lord of these premesis . . . and no tenant of yours &c. & you needn't trouble yourself about what I do here as all my Rights I ever had were reserved to the letter in the Bargain with W.A.R. Goodwin until I die & you do nothing here but what I choose for you to do and you have thus far failed very materially." Relations between the life tenant and the well-meaning Restoration agents declined from there, as did the property.

By 1936, Nelson was sending his water bills to Goodwin, claiming he hadn't used any water anyway because the pipes had broken or some such. Goodwin forwarded a bill to Vernon Geddy with the acknowledgment that "Mr. Nelson seems to hold me responsible for all of his troubles." By now everybody was fed up with Nelson, who was evidently infirm in years, and insisting that the house be allowed to go to rack and ruin. When the old man finally moved to a nursing home, Chorley decided to give up on the building while others argued for its restoration.

The handsome and important mansion at the end of South England Street had been built before 1732 as a showcase, the centerpiece of a "vista." In 1836 it had been massively renovated by Littleton Tazewell, who removed one wing and added a second floor. In 1909 it had been moved aside to allow the straight extension of the street (which passed between the eventual sites of the Inn and Lodge). Bill Perry believed "the picture of Williamsburg will never be complete until the South England Street vista is closed." As late as 1944 he proposed that the home's restoration to its first location be given first priority—even at the expense of all other projects in the Restored Area and even though it was outside the boundary. By war's end the house was vacant, filled with trash and frequented by kids who crawled in through broken windows. In 1948 Chorley wrote Ed Kendrew, "When Mr. Rockefeller and I were in Williamsburg last . . . he asked me why we were holding off taking down that building." The opinions of Kendrew, the Advisory Committee of Architects and

Built in 1770, the Courthouse was probably intended to have columns of English stone, and so four were installed when the town fathers ordered repairs to the building after a fire in 1911. But in fact embargoes and the Revolution had blocked imports from England, so the pediment had stood unsupported for generations, as surviving photos and paintings showed. Thus Colonial Williamsburg removed the columns and restored the facade to the somewhat unfinished look it presented for about 140 years.

The first generation of restorers often included features they thought *ought* to have been here, whether proved or not. In later years CW phased out the less likely speculations—some formal gardens and huge topiary animals —and concentrated on features more certain to have occurred. Thus once elaborate flower beds are planted with more common flowers, though the fancy brickwork remains.

Perry, Shaw and Hepburn notwithstanding, "I think we might as well face the facts: It is not within the realm of possibility that it would ever be moved back or restored on its present site . . . saved from further deterioration. If the above premises are correct, does it not mean that eventually the building will have to come down? If that is so, why not now?"

Kendrew argued manfully that he wanted to study the building's fabric, adding that a "very disastrous blow might be dealt to our good public relationship with the people of Virginia if the greatest tact is not employed in reaching a decision." There were many Randolph descendants to think of, in addition to the apparent violation of the Decalogue. But the writing was on the wall. A member of the House of Delegates bought the house and carted it away for reconstruction on a James River site in Newport News, paying half the price it would have cost to tear it down.

Despite Mr. Rockefeller's misgivings, the Restoration addressed the inevitability of actively welcoming visitors. First the Travis House was restored as a restaurant with a few guest rooms at the foot of Palace green on Duke of Gloucester Street. Originally the home of the Public Hospital's superintendent, and once the scene of a fatal fire, the house would be moved three times before it was finally returned to its original site and dedicated to office space. (This despite the inexplicable sound of footsteps in the night and the faint smell of woodsmoke. A director of research, a scholar who habitually came to work hours before dawn, reported often hearing the sound of someone overhead. No one can offer a rational explanation; but then many original buildings are said to be haunted.)

Some thirty-one thousand people visited the three exhibition buildings in 1934 and the number tripled in two years. It was becoming clear that the old and misnamed Colonial Inn (a Victorian wreck) would have to come down to make way for the reconstruction of Chowning's Tavern. The idea of a new hotel called the Golden Horseshoe had been proposed for the Historic Area, but cooler heads prevailed after much debate. A large building was needed and it was finally decided to build the antebellum-style Williamsburg Inn *outside* the area so as not to impose an anachronism within it. Opened in 1937, it had a restaurant seating 250 diners and 61 rooms for well-heeled guests who could afford the deluxe price of $9.50 a night. It did a busy trade, but people of ordinary means were left out in the cold and the staff proposed to build cheaper accommodations, though Mr. Rockefeller thought the idea nonsense.

The trustees endorsed the proposal to build a lodge at a summer meeting that took place while Mr. Rockefeller was vacationing in Maine. His son, John 3rd (as he preferred to write it), then chairman of the board, agreed to take the news to Bar Harbor with his brother Laurance. The next week board member Horace Albright received a summary invitation to lunch in New York with the paterfamilias, who was not his usually cordial self. He wanted an explanation; another hotel would just be a fiscal millstone around his heirs' necks and the Restoration should not be in the hotel

ABOVE: The Restoration quickly became a sort of time machine as it set out to accomplish nothing less than the reincarnation of Williamsburg. The goal was complex: to discover what the city had been; then to re-create it as it appeared in the third quarter of the 18th century; meanwhile to enable modern folk to visit, enjoy and learn. Not always pure scholarship and finesse, the Restoration often used brute strength. When through-traffic proved a problem, a tunnel was carved through the Historic Area to dispatch intrusive cars underground. The Travis House proved improperly sited, so it was hauled back to its original location.

OPPOSITE: Sometimes the re-creation of Williamsburg necessitated removing "improvements" like chimneys and false fronts from a building like W. T. Kinnamon's garage, which became a gable-ended millinery store.

The Public Gaol stands as a curious survivor, a building begun in 1701, enlarged three times during the colonial period and used by the city for its original purpose as late as 1911. Part of its colonial masonry survives in the restored building now, three centuries after brick was laid upon brick.

business anyway. Albright explained under duress what his own sons hadn't been able to sell him.

After studying the matter, Rockefeller called a board meeting for the next day and had each member of the board explain in detail why he felt a modestly priced hotel was necessary. There were not enough economical accommodations, they said, even in boarding houses like the one the Armistead sisters maintained next to the Capitol; the Restoration would soon be attracting more people than anyone imagined; Williamsburg should accommodate the common man as well as the wealthy, etc. As the meeting progressed, it was clear that Mr. Rockefeller had already changed his mind. John 3rd whispered to Albright, "I don't think we could stop him from building the Lodge" now. Notwithstanding his new opinion, it was a decision that Mr. Rockefeller might regret. Kendrew remembered later that when annual attendance approached the five hundred thousand mark, the patron suggested closing the doors lest wear and tear destroy painstakingly restored buildings.

Colonial Williamsburg came of age in many ways during the 1930s, a decade that saw many changes. Its fabled collections of formal art and the decorative arts, of furniture and furnishings, were begun. Some fifty "major" buildings were restored or reconstructed, among them the Capitol, the Palace, the Raleigh Tavern, the Magazine, the Public Records Office and Market Square Tavern. Many houses bearing eighteenth-century names were renewed and opened as exhibition buildings (the Wythe House, for example, no longer a parish house) while others were occupied as homes. The central town was inhabited again, now by modern families inhabiting a museum. Since the goal had been to restore and reconstruct a living city, what purpose would hundreds of uninhabited buildings serve? Encouraging life tenants to stay on (the unlamented Mr. Nelson notwithstanding) and leasing other houses to Restoration employees would give the town a new life. That had been part of Dr. Goodwin's original dream, to make the hallowed precinct vital again.

Thus a new generation of Williamsburgers grew up in the antique place, among them Goodwin's own "second family." His three youngest boys were rambunctious enough; one is remembered for having baked a cat. (They matured nonetheless. The eldest, William, Jr., a fighter pilot in World War II, would not return from a sortie over Salerno. The able and energetic Howard would join Bethlehem Steel, picking up after a fashion where his grandfather left off in Richmond, and become sales manager for New York. Jack, the youngest, would stay in Williamsburg, a slender pillar of his father's church.) Ed Kendrew raised a brace of girls here. Vernon Geddy, Jr., who would become Rockefeller's attorney in Virginia and later a board member of Colonial Williamsburg, remembers his boyish delight at watching trucks pull down whole buildings and the eerie spectacle of the Palace cemetery digs. Then, as for decades after, children of this town would discover artifacts in the stream running past the Armistead sisters' guesthouse, learn to play fife and harpsichord in the Music Teacher's Room wearing clothes of another era, even to fish in the pond in Bassett Hall woods, which "officially" has no fish.

Dr. Goodwin himself did not see the end of the decade. While his influence slowly declined as the Restoration became ever more professional, his health waned as well, though he was active to the end. He urged the creation of a crafts program to display eighteenth-century trades. He advocated the realistic representation of the entire spectrum of colonial society: slave, artisan, indentured servant, journeyman, gentry. From his sickbed he still managed to raise six-figure donations for the College of William and Mary.

Goodwin is remembered for that remarkable gift; as Chorley told him, "You can raise more money from an oxygen tent than most men can at a desk." He was also remembered for his tenacious persuasion. One elderly lady recalled fifty years later that he once sat beside her on the train to Richmond and seemed intent on hypnotizing her into selling her home to the Restoration. His former curate, Bishop John Bentley, remembers his conviction and thoughtfulness. His own remembrances make his will an interesting, touching document. After his principal heir, his wife, he made bequests to every child and a number of colleagues: To Bishop Bentley the choice of theology books from his library, to his faithful secretary Elizabeth Hayes $2,000, to his sexton $5, to Bruton Church $25. To Mr. Rockefeller he left "the old silver spoon which I dug up between Jamestown and Williamsburg as a token of my heart's deepest gratitude for his friendship, his example and for his generous and gracious consummation of the dream of the restoration of Colonial Williamsburg."

Goodwin saw the second restoration of Bruton Parish Church nearly completed; his funeral was the first service held there and he was buried in a crypt beneath the nave, his head toward the altar in the hallowed position accorded ministers. The stone reads simply: "Here rests the Rev. Dr. William Archer Rutherfoord Goodwin, a native of Virginia, late rector of this parish. Born June 18, 1869. Died September 7, 1939."

A more eloquent inscription graces a wall not far away:

To the GLORY of God
and in MEMORY of
William Archer Rutherfoord Goodwin
Minister, Teacher, Man of Vision
in whose Heart and Mind
was conceived the Thought of restoring the Beauty
of this ANCIENT CITY and who was himself
the Inspiration of its Fulfillment
THIS TABLET
is erected by his Friend and Fellow Worker
JOHN DAVISON ROCKEFELLER JR.
ANNO DOMINI 1941

Speaking at the public reopening of Colonial Williamsburg in 1934, President Franklin D. Roosevelt dedicates Duke of Gloucester Street, calling it "the most historic avenue in America."

THE MODERN ERA:

A Once and Future Williamsburg

3

A FAMILY PLACE IN STASIS,
AN AMERICAN ENTERPRISE EVOLVING

The Leaders: Mr. Rockefeller, Arthur Woods, Kenneth Chorley, Carlisle Humelsine, Charles Longsworth, Robert Wilburn, Colin Campbell

When Dr. Goodwin welcomed J. P. Morgan to Williamsburg, he drove the first millionaire ever to visit there through the village in a wagon. Seventy-six years later when Colonial Williamsburg hosted a Summit Conference, the president of the United States and seven foreign heads of state arrived in helicopters that shook the old foundations and broke some two-hundred-year-old windowpanes. Between those two events a late train once stranded a hapless traveler in Richmond. Times were bad, the weather foul, the night cold. Finding a phone booth on the empty platform, the man was relieved to have one nickel in his pocket, the price of reaching the operator, who became impatient when he couldn't come up with the change to call Williamsburg. "May I reverse the charges please?" he asked, his spirits falling. Before Ma Bell's minion would place the call, she demanded: "Your name?" "Never mind, you wouldn't believe it anyway," said John D. Rockefeller, Jr.

Truth be told, the making of Colonial Williamsburg was not a cakewalk. The route from backwater to world wonder was circuitous at best; the one-horse town was not transformed as easily as the pumpkin into Cinderella's coach. Herein lies one secret of the place. For all the pretty "perfection" some critics have caviled at in its well-groomed Historic Area, it remains an institution built by mortals possessed of all the genius and foibles that flesh is heir to. For all the rock-solid constancy that some perennial visitors seek year after year, it is in a constant state of change. As a corporate organism, and as an intellectual institution, it is always evolving, even undergoing metamorphosis now and then. The questions remain: Why did the founder choose Williamsburg as his remote beneficiary in the first place, then as his perennial retreat and his patriotic locus? Then later, how did it achieve its own independence? To learn the whys and hows, follow the leaders, for it is a story of several men.

~

The answer to the complex first question no longer lies in Williamsburg but in family lore, that body of shared experience and insight that members of any clan know and take for granted. The fact that Colonial Williamsburg was founded by a certain paterfamilias has everything to do with the ways in which it grew. Its evolved character is the product of the human folk who made it, starting with the founding father. Then his successors continued to reinvent it again and into an ever-new image, inspired by their imaginations and the atmosphere of their times, for as one waggish scholar put it, not entirely in jest, "Every generation rewrites history to suit itself"—and to explain itself.

Half a century after the founding, Laurance Rockefeller, John D., Jr.'s, oldest surviving son, saw no mystery in Williamsburg's attraction for both his parents. Unlike in their other haunts, here "they could be just like everybody else." In New York City "Father" was compelled to be on guard against beggars, thieves and fortune hunters alike. By the same token, the Rockefellers lived "behind a wall" at the 2,200-acre Hudson River estate at Pocantico Hills, while their traditional summer home in Maine was another gentrified community possessed equally by every generation of Rockefellers.

PREVIOUS SPREAD: Paths paved with shells and edged with bricks crisscross the Custis Tenement garden in an intricate geometric pattern. In the beds are yellow and orange marigolds, a Middle Eastern plant that found its way to North America via England. The large red lilylike blooms are flowering tobacco (a variety not used for smoking).

OPPOSITE: Costumed interpreters converse as Betty Randolph and her sister-in-law, Ariana, in Mrs. Randolph's "closet," the room that was the office from which she ran her complex household.

A gentleman mounts the passage stairs in the Peyton Randolph House, which now, after a complete renovation and historically correct reinterpretation, more closely resembles its 18th-century original. The custom-made paper replicates a pattern sold to modish patrons in 18th-century London and to those gentry in the colonies who aped their fashions.

Williamsburg was different; John and Abby Rockefeller could claim it uniquely as their own. Their parents had not known it, and once this couple found their haven, it would not become a playground for the gathering clan. "They went there for the self-renewal and serenity, not to bring the family and make a rodeo of it," said Laurance. He remembered with a hint of gratitude that Williamsburg's townfolk embraced his parents and "they mingled with everybody." If many were awed at having a millionaire in their midst, they soon overcame it in light of this middle-aged couple's modest way of living. Edward Spencer, a native who spent a long career at Colonial Williamsburg, remembered Mr. Rockefeller's accepting his older sister's girlish invitation to take tea at ramshackle Palace Farm behind the ruin of the long-gone governors' residence. Others continued to speak—a quarter-century after the founder's death—of Mr. and Mrs. Rockefeller as old-shoe neighbors two months out of every year.

Typically each spring and fall they set up housekeeping in a comfortable house that they bought and decorated to their liking, Bassett Hall. Once ensconced, they settled into the life of the town like cousins. Mr. Rockefeller walked the woods, identifying plants, planning paths with rustic benches on which to rest, hanging a camper's tin cup on a tree beside a stream so that he could drink its pure water whenever he happened by. His wife had the neighbors in for tea and together they hosted supper parties. Abstemious themselves, they never served liquor but once tried to show their liberality by having the butler offer cigarettes after dessert. (Matching their hosts' consideration, not one of the guests lit up, though most were habitual smokers.) The typical evening's entertainment was the seven-o'clock movie in the theater Rockefeller built at Merchants Square. Then by day, he relished his presumed anonymity, quartering the town and checking up on every project armed with a tape measure he carried in his pocket. He studied the dimensions of old buildings and reconstructions alike. Laurance remembers that Restoration executives encouraged this and "went out of their way to make him feel at home."

Mrs. Rockefeller took special interest in community projects. Segregation was the rule in Old Virginia, and when the Restoration prompted a Negro school to be relocated, she made a substantial contribution, and helped equip the sparsely furnished Bruton Heights School so well that some white locals complained about its being the best in the Tidewater. It was the pride of the Negro community and became a vital social center. The Rockefellers supported their own Baptist church, but because the Restoration placed special demands on restored Bruton Parish Church, they endowed a special fund dedicated largely to its music program. When the nation went to war, the flood of tourists ebbed to a trickle except for servicemen from nearby bases, whose admission fees were paid by the Rockefellers, who also established the town's USO center. These relatively small efforts were accepted as the community benefactions of two newcomers to town who happened to have a little more to give than their neighbors.

Of course, because rank hath its privileges, they were able to do certain things that were beyond the grasp of others. On arising, Mr. Rockefeller liked to see the Queen Anne's *Great Union* Flag flying above the Capitol from his bedroom window. The first morning of one autumn visit, he could not see it because a tree had grown too tall; it was pruned back before nightfall. Later he notified Kenneth Chorley, his lantern-jawed aide-de-camp, that Mrs. Rockefeller was awakened at night by the screams of patients in what was by then named Eastern State Hospital. Correcting that took longer to arrange than a tree-trimming, because it required a decision by the Commonwealth of Virginia to replace and relocate the hospital complex that had become woefully obsolete. But in due course, and after negotiations involving the Rockefellers, the College of William and Mary and the government in Richmond, the hospital moved across town and Colonial Williamsburg acquired the original site.

This bedchamber is simply furnished because the inventory compiled after Peyton Randolph's death revealed that this room was the most sparsely furnished in the main house; thus it is interpreted as having often been occupied by the Randolph's nieces and nephews.

Bassett Hall's renovation did not conform to the strict standards applied elsewhere in town. The acknowledged reason was not that the eighteenth-century house belonged to Rockefeller, but that it stood outside the Historic Area—which he had paled, with the town's endorsement. The boundary of the restored area originally ran down Francis Street, but to prevent commercial eyesores from encroaching on the antique *mise-en-scène*, the line had been nudged two hundred feet beyond the curb. Since Bassett Hall happened to be four hundred feet from the street, it remained outside the sacrosanct zone. Thus the Rockefellers had license; they changed Bassett Hall by enlarging the rear wing and added outbuildings as they saw fit, and not only upon ancient foundations. In this the donor was playing by the same rules as everyone else; only he had a hand in defining the boundaries of the playing field. And if he ever found himself losing, he could even change the players.

When Colonel Woods retired as chairman of the board in 1939, the oldest of Mr. Rockefeller's five sons succeeded him. John 3rd served ably through the war years and into the troubled times of the early Cold War and McCarthy Era. But by the early 1950s, it is remembered, he started setting new goals for the Restoration (as it was still called thereabouts). His widow, Blanchette, said decades later, "John had very strong feelings about it as an educational institution as well as a museum." So deep was his interest that the couple spent one week a month there, more time even than President Chorley, who tended to run things from New York. At John 3rd's behest Williamsburg began hosting frankly educational programs. Foreign visitors and groups of promising young people were invited to debate great political issues. Emissaries were dispatched to distant places to learn about life abroad, even in Socialist countries. Conventional wisdom around town holds that in promoting these intellectual adventures John 3rd clashed with Chorley who found such projects suspect. Thus, the story continues, Williamsburg became too small for both of them, and Mr. Rockefeller reluctantly decided that his son was more expendable than Chorley. As senior staffers tell the tale, Mr. Rockefeller played the role of Solomon arbitrating a dispute between rivals.

The family told a different story decades after the fact, a simpler one: John 3rd was chairman of the board but his father was still boss. As the son became increasingly interested in education and international projects, the older conservative simply dug in his heels. John 3rd was entitled and even expected to pursue his own interests; having inculcated a sense of public service in all his boys, the senior Rockefeller had not meant to raise any slouches. But he believed his firstborn son could walk to his own drummer on his own turf and that Williamsburg should stick to its steady course. According to relatives, it was not Chorley who clashed finally with young John but Mr. Rockefeller himself. His preference had been to let the staff pursue de facto educational projects when they were thinly disguised as "interpretation." This was not a matter of a wise judge settling a dispute, it was a contretemps between father and son that ended in the son's resignation.

In any event there was nothing very final about John 3rd's departure in 1953. Becoming chairman of the Rockefeller Foundation and turning to international matters, he remained a devoted Williamsburg visitor for twenty-five years. His mother had died in 1948 and his stepmother, Martha Baird Rockefeller, refurnished Bassett Hall to her liking. After Mr. Rockefeller's death in 1960—and a memorial service under the old oak—John 3rd inherited the house. Blanchette remembers that "All the boys wanted it kept as their mother had it." So with the help of a Williamsburg maid who had served the first Mrs. Rockefeller for decades, they put back every hooked rug, ladderback chair, mourning picture and porcelain figurine in its original place. The house, then bequeathed to Colonial Williamsburg after John 3rd's death in 1978, became a popular exhibition building that reveals the elder Rockefellers' personal tastes.

John D. Rockefeller, Jr. ("Mr. Junior") and all his sons in 1937 (from left): David, who as a boy enchanted Dr. Goodwin, will head Chase Manhattan Bank; Nelson, later champion of his mother's folk art collection, will be vice president of the United States; Winthrop will chair Colonial Williamsburg's governing board and serve two terms as governor of Arkansas; Laurance will sit on the Williamsburg board, then become an avid conservationist and philanthropist; John 3rd will win distinction in international affairs after directing this, America's first outdoor history museum.

Brother Winthrop succeeded John 3rd as chairman and held the post for twenty years. Perhaps because his home was distant Arkansas, where he served two terms as governor, he is remembered as an almost model chairman. He didn't hover. "Win" came often enough to chair board meetings and oversee general policy. One of his notable accomplishments was to acquire Carter's Grove, the downriver plantation owned by the McCreas who decades earlier had sought Dr. Goodwin's advice on restoration and then entertained the thirsty congressmen who had come to study the idea for a colonial park. The Restoration was "incomplete" without an associated plantation; the original city had received its sustenance and economic lifeblood from country plantations. Thus, there was a need for a restorable plantation to act as a modern adjunct to the Historic Area.

Shirley Plantation had been actively sought in vain and some closer-in estates were ruled out because they had been subdivided and developed. Laurance, who was then a member of the board, remembers that when Carter's Grove became available Mr. Rockefeller, his new wife and Chorley all thought it "inappropriate"—especially Chorley, who felt it would be a financial millstone around the Restoration's neck. Others on the staff and the interested brothers thought they had best not let it slip through their hands. Thus, at Winthrop's behest it was acquired by one of the family trusts, which retained title until Colonial Williamsburg demonstrated it could be operated as an exhibition annex without running up crippling deficits.

The change in chairmen in 1953—and the nearly simultaneous arrival of a new administration—had been a kind of omen. Colonial Williamsburg was about to experience an identity crisis regardless of who wielded the gavel at board meetings. It now seemed soundly established; but then so the dinosaurs had been. Colonial Williamsburg's future—whether or not it had a future—really depended on its continued appeal, its meaning to people outside its pale. Mr. Rockefeller would doubtless continue to support his creation. But if it became simply his expensive recreation and semiannual retreat it could be as perverse a place as Citizen Kane's reconstructed castle, an oddity, a theme park with roller coasters only in the mind. The benefactor would die eventually and his heirs turn to other interests (as indeed they did). Then Williamsburg might simply go the way of Ozymandias's city of stone. Quite obviously that didn't happen.

Instead the restored colonial capital continued to grow internally and to remake itself. Broadening its appeal to the American public, it became an international spa of sorts and embarked on courses even more "radical" than those John 3rd had suggested, albeit with the sympathy and consent of new directors—including members of the family. In a word, Colonial Williamsburg changed to meet changing circumstances. The proximate reason for its first metamorphosis was the arrival of an ebullient printer's son from the unlikely burg of Hagerstown, Maryland.

For many people World War II offered stepping stones to the stars; Carlisle H. Humelsine took them two at a time. A junior university administrator when he joined the Army, through a chance encounter at a football game he found himself assigned to General George C. Marshall's communications center, and was soon the man in charge. He was a genius at handling details, a necessity when setting up communications for General Dwight D. Eisenhower in London. He had a way of finding things, like a typewriter in Newfoundland during a refueling stop and a colonel who could type a general's speech. In Potsdam for the historic conference, he could provide the secretary of state with his preferred bourbon and branch water before being asked. He impressed Kenneth Chorley when the Joint Chiefs of Staff met at the Williamsburg Inn (opened especially for the occasion), and when he mustered out at the war's end, Chorley lured him into becoming his personnel director, a job Humelsine held for scant months before realizing he had made a mistake and returned to the fast track at the State Department. With President Eisenhower's new team coming aboard,

Intentionally good neighbors in their part-time hometown, Mr. and Mrs. Rockefeller supported many charitable causes in the neighborhood. During World War II they funded a USO canteen and at its opening in 1943 cheerfully posed with enlisted men.

Deputy Under Secretary Humelsine prepared to leave Foggy Bottom; Chorley invited him back as his executive officer and heir apparent. Hardly needing time to consider, he told his Virginia-born wife the news and returned in 1953 as executive vice president and resident governor of Colonial Williamsburg. Five years later he succeeded to the presidency.

A matter requiring early attention was pure business—how to attract more of it. Humelsine left Washington knowing the State Department had a chronic problem: what to do with visiting dignitaries. His friend, Deputy Chief of Protocol Clement Conger, was sick of holding foreign visitors' hands while leading them around places like automobile plants in Detroit. The visitors were neither impressed nor put in a receptive mood for whatever diplomatic business awaited them in Washington. Humelsine offered a superb alternative, one that served both his old department and the institution he now led.

Williamsburg was unique and uniquely American, a place unlike anywhere abroad. It offered comfortable guest facilities, rides in carriages, and glimpses of the national genesis. Once the State Department discovered it—with Humelsine beckoning like a Siren—it became a prerequisite for every visiting head of state bound for an Oval Office meeting. It was appealing, entertaining, diverting, interesting and its cuisine didn't disturb foreign stomachs once the staff learned to inquire into dignitaries' tastes in advance. (That policy was initiated after a local delicacy was returned to the kitchen untouched, and a memo reported hotly that "neither the Lord Mayor [of London] nor the Lady Mayoress had ever eaten an oyster and had no intention of doing so.") The Inn could handle a state visit on short notice, the bellmen didn't lose luggage and, Conger would remember, he got bargain rates. Removed from cities and hotbeds of dissidents, the Inn offered good security, while enabling the distinguished visitor to recover from jet lag less than 150 miles from the White House. Almost every administration from Eisenhower's time onward made use of it by scheduling a stop en route to Washington for reigning dignitaries. And as one hand washes the other, Williamsburg profited from the business, which enhanced its image in the eyes of American travelers.

Some heads of state came early and often, Marshal Tito of Yugoslavia, for example. When demonstrations threatened to disrupt his scheduled trip to San Francisco, he got "sick" between Washington meetings and "recuperated" here. (Tito spoke idiomatic English in private, such as when the mayor escorted him around the town. Astonished to learn their carriage cost $35,000 to build, the independent Communist retorted, "I can buy five Cadillacs for that.") When the king of Morocco checked in at the Inn, an attending satrap demanded to see a floor plan. Though Eisenhower's old room was reserved for the king, only the suite where the Queen of England had slept would do. It was reserved for a couple who came every year but the Moroccans commandeered it. Then a bodyguard lay down across the doorsill where he remained for the duration of the visit, to the astonishment of passing guests. State visitors from certain Third World nations nearly tested Williamsburg's capacity. It became axiomatic that the less stable a government, the larger its delegation because the man in charge brought along every potential rival who might get ambitious if he were left at home alone.

Managing a state visit required an exquisite attention to detail via the "Operations Plan," a man-by-man, minute-by-minute program, which is still routinely prepared for every special event of any size. (Inches thick, these directories assign a person to every task down to the delivery of firewood for cressets and who locks up the milliner's shop door after a Lanthorn Tour.) Sometimes overly meticulous planning backfired, as when a team of horses was tranquilized before being hitched to a carriage; they fell asleep while awaiting their royal passengers at the Wythe House, so that Queen Elizabeth II, a superb horsewoman herself, and Prince Philip had to finish their tour on foot. And

In the powder room of the Palace, two new wigs await the governor for whom they were made to order. In practicing 18th-century trades through its exhibitions, Colonial Williamsburg has actually encouraged the renaissance of crafts, one of them being wigmaking.

Foreign leaders flock to Williamsburg, a Mecca of democracy for decades. In 1946 British Prime Minister Winston Churchill and America's commanding general, Dwight Eisenhower (top left), drink each other's health in the Raleigh Tavern, as their predecessors never did 170 years earlier. In 1985 (top right) Japan's Crown Prince Naruhito tried out a new violin in the musical instrument maker's shop. In 1957 (middle left) Queen Elizabeth II and Prince Philip rode in a blue phaeton with board chairman Winthrop Rockefeller. In 1997 the President of the People's Republic of China Jiang Zemin and his wife Wang Yeping donned Virginia hats. Bottom: President Ronald Reagan hosted the ninth Economic Summit of Industrialized Nations in 1983, welcoming six other heads of state to Williamsburg. Left to right: Prime Minister Pierre Trudeau of Canada, Gaston Thorn, president of the European Economic Community, Federal Chancellor Helmut Kohl of Germany, President François Mitterrand of France, Reagan, Prime Minister Yasuhiro Nakasone of Japan, Prime Minister Margaret Thatcher of the United Kingdom and Prime Minister Amintore Fanfani of the Republic of Italy.

if everything was planned in advance there was still room for improvising. As the president of Romania toured the town, he mentioned a passion for volleyball, so while he visited the Palace, a volleyball net was erected beside his official guesthouse before he returned.

Some years only one head of state might visit, in other years one came every other month as Williamsburg welcomed the presidents of an alphabet of nations from Argentina to Zambia. Over time there were dozens of prime ministers, reigning monarchs, dictators, heirs apparent, cabinet ministers and the like: King Hussein of Jordan, King Baudouin of Belgium, the crown prince of Libya, Burma's Revolutionary Council chairman, King Olav of Norway, King Faisal of Saudi Arabia, the Shah of Iran, the Emperor of Japan, Dame Te Atairangikaahu Queen of the Maori, and so on. In addition a parade of American presidents (or would-be presidents) followed Roosevelt's example: Harry S. Truman, Lyndon Johnson, Richard Nixon, Gerald Ford, Jimmy Carter (as a candidate), Ronald Reagan, George H. W. Bush, and Bill Clinton (while staying at Williamsburg for a television debate with Bush *père*). Plain old Ike came, wearing his famous Eisenhower jacket and escorting his old ally Winston Churchill, who uttered a memorable *bon mot*. Introduced to Board Chairman John 3rd, he noted that in England "we number our Georges; here you number your Rockefellers."

~

While Mr. Rockefeller, Jr., lived, there was no need to solicit financial support on the open market, so to speak. But Humelsine was swift to accept gifts of art and antiques from serious collectors, many of whom visited regularly and attended the annual Antiques Forum (an event adroitly held in late winter when attendance was otherwise slow and hotel rooms empty). He cultivated the wealthy and influential, such as Philadelphia publisher (and later ambassador to Great Britain) Walter Annenberg, who first visited Williamsburg unannounced and gave an unsolicited $50. Humelsine wrote a personal letter of thanks, which prompted a six-digit donation by return mail; Annenberg would become a truly substantial Williamsburg contributor, as did DeWitt and Lila Wallace, founders of *The Reader's Digest*. But his giving began with fifty bucks.

Another couple who became generous friends were antiques collectors whose names were legend within antiquarian circles as the owners and residents of West St. Mary's Manor, a grand old house near Maryland's first colonial capital. Elizabeth and Miodrag Blagojevich had missed the first annual Antiques Forum in 1949 but came to all the rest as long as they lived. (For many of those remaining years they would live within walking distance of the Forum, which often featured their furniture and objects.) Their home near St. Mary's City was celebrated not only for its seventeenth-century origin, but for their inspired restoration of the house and its ancient furnishings. Now starting to feel their years, they wanted to sell the estate overlooking the St. Mary's River, a tributary of the Potomac, and find a less removed place to live, but they could not find a buyer who could pay their price other than developers who would desecrate the site. The brass got wind of their predicament and devised a plan that benefited everyone.

Under the complex arrangement, Colonial Williamsburg acquired the riverside land along with the promised gift of the Blagojeviches' fabulous antiques collection for a relative pittance, plus the guarantee of an annuity and life tenancy on Duke of Gloucester Street (where the couple would become popular fixtures). This arrangement was designed to serve the sellers, yet it would aid Williamsburg even more. To save the pristine and historic St. Mary's River from development, the state of Maryland agreed to pay handsomely for a scenic easement that protected the rural tract in perpetuity. (Thus the land could never be developed; thus in theory its resale value was reduced by the state's official act; and thus all this justified the expenditure of public funds to secure long-term

Today's gardens run the gamut
from a most formal arrangement
of brick walk and topiary (left) to a
vegetable patch guarded by a scare-
crow in colonial garb (opposite).

public benefits and compensate the owner for the loss of its development potential.) So Colonial Williamsburg, having bought the land cheap and sold its future value dear, now possessed this uniquely beautiful and historic property, which was now additionally unique as its pristine state was assured forever. Might it have special appeal for a discriminating individual who would appreciate the site's combination of assets, indeed its inestimable aesthetic worth? Williamsburg found such a person, who bought it for an exceptional price, i.e., a small fortune, and Williamsburg profited again.

Humelsine paid close attention to the board of directors, a slowly changing group of men and women who enhanced the institution with their names, their connections and their expertise. During his years as president and later chairman of the board, this roster included Richmond attorney Lewis F. Powell, Jr., who became a Supreme Court justice and served briefly as chairman after Winthrop Rockefeller's death. At one time or another it included former Secretary of State Dean Rusk, the author Ralph Ellison, television journalists David Brinkley and Jim Lehrer, Librarian of Congress Daniel J. Boorstin, Supreme Court Justice Sandra Day O'Connor, and AT&T Chairman Charles L. Brown, who would succeed Humelsine as chairman in 1985. It was also Humelsine's inspiration to bring new Rockefeller blood to the board. In 1966 Abby Milton O'Neill, daughter of the founder's only daughter, began an association with Williamsburg that has not ended yet, as she served as a trustee until 1994, then became a senior trustee and special advisor. Steven Rockefeller, another "grandchild," served on the board from 1995 to 1999.

During these years—and sometimes to its president's chagrin—Williamsburg honored its legacy of free speech. For example, there had been a tradition at the College of William and Mary for some sons of the Confederacy to muster around the solemn effigy of Dixie's coffin. Bearing the Stars and Bars, they would march down Duke of Gloucester Street to the Wren Building, go in the front door and then disperse out the back. In the 1960s, a time of civil rights activism in the land, a group of black students decided to protest this atavistic rite and lined up before the hallowed steps. The Confederates marched, and reaching the edifice, sang "Dixie." The protestors stood their ground, responded with "We Shall Overcome," then parted ranks and let the marchers pass—a fitting accommodation in a place famous for honoring the right of dissent.

Far more spectacular was the row that followed a sermon in Bruton Parish Church during America's bloody and tragic war in Vietnam. The Reverend Cotesworth Pinkney Lewis, thirty-first rector, mounted to the pulpit and respectfully questioned the foreign policy that would cost the lives of 60,000 U.S. combatants and millions of Asians: "Since there is a rather general consensus that what we are doing in Vietnam is wrong . . . while pledging our loyalty, we ask respectfully, why?" The sermon, a model of restrained rhetoric, was delivered before a de facto national congregation because the White House press corps was in church that Sunday and President Lyndon B. Johnson was sitting in the first pew (the one with George Washington's name on it), having concluded a national tour of military bases where he urged Asia-bound GIs onward. As he listened to the sermon, he seemed the soul of composure, except that he kept a white-knuckle grip on the railing. At the door as the first family left, his wife Lady Byrd managed to compliment the rector on the choir and it first appeared that Johnson would not shake the priest's hand. But he did, and said, "Thank you."

Colonial Williamsburg hastily announced that Bruton was not the institution's "official church" (whatever that meant), and Humelsine called the sermon in "exquisite bad taste." After the gist of it echoed from coast to coast—it made the front page of just about every paper in the land and the network news—the Reverend Lewis responded that he had not intended to be critical and regretted if the president had taken offense. He had only meant to make a point as ancient as Isaiah's hopeful prophesy about beating swords into plowshares. Still, it marked yet one more occasion when

Made in the 1720s by a skilled cabinetmaker, this high chest had become hopelessly outdated by the 1770s, the era to which the Thomas Everard House has been interpreted. Thus it is consigned to a modest bedchamber under the eaves and has a spice storage box stowed on top to save space.

historic Williamsburg heard a dissenting voice and survived—even long enough to see the dissenter proven to be more prescient than the government in power. At other moments in that era Colonial Williamsburg itself rose to the tradition too, if with reluctance, as when antiwar demonstrators scheduled a march down Duke of Gloucester Street to the Capitol. Some CW officers argued that the march should be prevented by the simple expedient of closing the Historic Area. But more democratic heads prevailed, and the protestors had their day unaware that security forces were posted inside the building—on the premise that whatever a demonstration's motive, the museum's treasures must be protected.

~

If Colonial Williamsburg could not have survived its infancy without Chorley, it would not have weathered its adolescence without Humelsine. After Mr. Rockefeller's death in 1960, Colonial Williamsburg was on its own in a way it had never been before. The challenge was to direct its evolution from one man's favorite philanthropy and consuming hobby to an independent nonprofit institution that could hold its own in a competitive world. Now it would have to begin getting major financial support from strangers, both to augment its endowment and to pay for special projects. A development officer came aboard as a vice president with new ideas—new to Williamsburg if old hat elsewhere. For example, he chartered a major donor's club, the Raleigh Tavern Society, whose members pledge substantial gifts in objects, securities or money. Roger Thaler instituted various levels of personal affiliation with the institution and, in general, made Williamsburg a player in the nonprofit arena.

By the time the nation celebrated its bicentennial, Colonial Williamsburg was firmly established as a free and independent institution, one that enjoyed a substantial degree of corporate, financial and physical security. A governor of Virginia had been persuaded to provide easy access from new superhighways, which were routed far enough away to not encroach. Buffer properties had been acquired around the Historic Area, and buses disgorged their loads of schoolchildren and tourists at a spanking-new Information Center, a little distance away from Duke of Gloucester Street, which was now closed to daytime traffic. Kingsmill, the estate lying between Williamsburg and Carter's Grove, was bought, then sold after it provided a right-of-way, the Country Road, between the two colonial venues, the capital city and the plantation that provided it sustenance.

These middle years saw the growth of collections and the birth of various programs. The year after the bicentennial, Humelsine named a committee of "junior faculty" members to review Williamsburg's "educational missions" during its first half-century in an attempt to answer the salient question: "What should its future mission be?" The committee report laid the groundwork for significant changes in philosophy and direction by Colonial Williamsburg under its next president, Charles Longsworth, a man recruited for his experience in an unusual combination of fields: education, business and development.

Longsworth came aboard in 1977, as chief operating officer, then two years later took over as chief executive officer. Possessing impressive academic and administrative credentials (as well as a pilot's license), he had a broad range of experience. A Phi Beta Kappa graduate at Amherst College, he went on to Harvard Business School, then worked for Campbell's Soup and in advertising before returning to Amherst as development officer, then becoming a founder of neighboring Hampshire College and its second president.

Adapting many new business practices, Longsworth established "management goals," then delegated responsibility to his executives, many of them recruits from a variety of museums and business corporations. Key department heads came not only from the Smithsonian's National Portrait Gallery and Boston's Museum of Fine Arts, but from Lever Brothers, Gillette, Harvard and Citibank

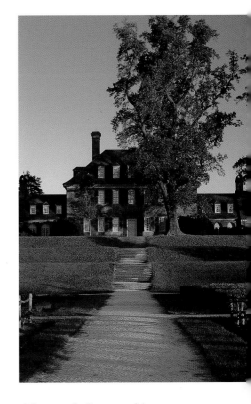

The staunch silhouette of the great house at Carter's Grove, once a 1,400-acre plantation owned by the colonies' Midas-rich planter Robert "King" Carter, stands against the twilit sky. Its resemblance to the house built in the 1750s is imperfect, because it was substantially altered in the 1930s by its moneyed and well-intentioned owners. Still, it commands its heights above the James River as the old house did and it has an honored place in the history of the Colonial Revival movement.

to address the challenges that this not-for-profit enclave offered.

In his first years Longsworth oversaw completion of many projects begun by his predecessor. The renamed Visitor Center was remodeled, the Public Hospital built, the DeWitt Wallace Decorative Arts Gallery opened. In addition, the Williamsburg corporations were reorganized, the institution's financial posture strengthened and hotel management restructured. The new administration also expanded its efforts in the Balkan realm of "grantsmanship," the solicitation of support for specific research projects. At the same time, new administrators updated everything from personnel management to accounting procedures in the craft shops.

Longsworth was willing to take risks, witness his decision to host the 1983 Economic Summit of Industrialized Nations, which brought President Reagan, French President Mitterrand, British Prime Minister Thatcher and five other heads of state to town along with three thousand reporters. The event required closing Williamsburg to the public for several days and losing significant ticket revenue. It further cost two hundred eighteenth-century panes, which cracked when howitzers boomed salutes and helicopters landed behind the colonial Courthouse—all over the objections of the Resident Architect. But "the Summit" also raised morale, in part by showing some of Colonial Williamsburg's staffers just how good they really were. (In contrast to CW's insistence on historical accuracy, when the U.S. Army's crack "colonial" marching band appeared, said a knowing staffer, "their uniforms were wrong and they played nineteenth-century tunes.") Preparing for the Summit nearly cost some officers their sanity, as when the contract with the State Department arrived by Trailways bus only the night before the conference began. But the marathon event reasserted Williamsburg's status as an international way station and conference center of major repute. It also raised the patriotic profile again, and attracted new numbers of American vacationers for a time.

In general, under the guidance of Longsworth's Senior Vice President Robert C. Birney, Williamsburg began to explore new territory in scholarly research, interpretive activities in the Historic Area, educational programs, restoration projects, archaeology and a host of other cerebral fields. Conventional scholarship had been performed here since the early 1930s, when Kenneth Chorley insisted on it to save Rockefeller possible embarrassment lest the Restoration err in its building and rebuilding programs. Early efforts, reflecting historical disciplines of the time, depended on conventional archives and the unearthing of written documents. The "great man theory of history"—the notion that events turn on personalities who thrust themselves to the forefront of their time—was popular then. In recent years, the emphasis has been more on "social history," which assumes that conditions of any era push individuals to the fore. To overstate for the sake of example: If Patrick Henry had not risen to the occasion of championing a cause that led to revolution, Patrick Doe would have.

Social historians examine the past with special reference to ordinary people in a manner that reflects another shift in emphasis around Williamsburg. The first restorers set out to commemorate the founding of the Republic and the great events leading to the Revolution. By contrast, scholars in the 1980s consciously chose "Becoming Americans" as the long-term theme and centerpiece for research and interpretation, a theme of remarkable flexibility and fertility. This theme focuses on the evolution of American society and the life of all its people; it was picked by a younger generation of scholars, historians, curators and administrators.

～

The result was the landmark York County Project, brainchild of then research director and later vice president for research Cary Carson, holder of parchments from Harvard and Winterthur, and former factotum at Historic St. Mary's City, the tiny history museum that oversees Maryland's oldest set-

OPPOSITE: The main bedchamber in the George Wythe House boasts a bed dressed in a heroic copperplate textile that shows George Washington being crowned with laurels—a bit of neoclassical iconography.

tlement of West St. Mary's Manor fame. This investigation twice received major funding from the National Endowment for the Humanities. It involved the transcription, analysis, and correlation of all surviving court, land, and church records for the county in which half of Williamsburg was originally located. (Records for the other half of the city, namely the part lying in James City County, were removed to Richmond for safekeeping during the Civil War. But the clerk of York County never took his records as ordered to Richmond, so when the capital of the Confederacy was torched, York County's records survived.)

Over two hundred years worth of records wound up in files of index cards that eventually filled three hundred boxes, each with a capacity of one thousand cards. A card was made out for every name, whether recorded as a plaintiff, witness, juror, dependent, defendant, landowner, tenant, bride, communicant, convict, voter, slave, servant, or whatever. Then the corps of researchers tentatively assigned people to families, households and locations. Using land records, they even programmed a computer to map homesteads on the basis of recorded acreages and known stretches of common boundaries. Cybernetic graphics aside, Carson's project revealed so much about the eighteenth-century York County and Williamsburg communities that it continues today to inform interpretation and programming at Colonial Williamsburg. It is often the first resource that Historic Area interpreters consult when creating a new character to impersonate, a new persona. It is a mother lode that historians mine when planning new events to stage and themes to present to school tours and general visitors alike. And beyond Williamsburg boundaries, the project is highly regarded too. It has provided the raw material for several master's theses and doctoral dissertations, according to Linda Rowe, one of the staff historians who contributed to it.

One segment of the community noticeably absent from the early Restoration's interpretation was the black population. In its first several decades Colonial Williamsburg simply overlooked the diverse roles of eighteenth-century blacks, both slaves and freemen. The only blacks in colonial dress punched admission tickets and, with a very few notable exceptions, demonstrated "domestic" crafts, though in the colonial era many blacks—slaves, indentured servants and free men alike—had highly skilled occupations. The oversight was not exclusively the fault of short-sighted management. On one hand, by the 1960s, many blacks who worked for Colonial Williamsburg were solidly middle class. When tentatively invited to interpret colonial black life for the visitors, they declined; some had come too far to be willingly associated with slavery in any way, shape or form. Other older blacks declined because these new opportunities were seen as arising out of the civil rights movement, which they considered as rabble-rousing. Others looked down on the liberalizing effort by Colonial Williamsburg as an early form of what would be called "political correctness." Simultaneously young blacks were simply uninterested in Williamsburg as irrelevant to their lives in every way. Some local men who were recruited to work there in the 1980s remember that the Historic Area was not a place they visited or knew as children growing up nearby. It wasn't that they were barred—to the contrary, the Restoration quietly flouted many of Virginia's segregation laws and welcomed all comers. But as Rex Ellis, a local man who became the first black program director, recalled in 1984, "There just wasn't anything here for us." In large part the onus for this lay in the fact that the institution stressed Williamsburg's role as a seat of government and hotbed of dissidence. Since government and revolution were the business of gentlemen, blacks simply didn't have featured roles. It was at least as much a case of historical emphasis as discrimination.

The new generation of Colonial Williamsburg executives under Longsworth's administration would address this imbalance out of their desire for historical accuracy and a commitment to progressive social change. Dennis A. O'Toole, who came from the Smithsonian's National Portrait

African-Americans in colonial Virginia had their own society, their own culture and their own economy—to a degree. Here in the slave quarter at Carter's Grove plantation an entrepreneur offers a prime chicken for sale or barter.

The slave quarter stands out of sight from the main house at Carter's Grove. The cabin and other habitations here were built in 1989 (with traditional tools and techniques) on the discovered site of the 18th-century compound, a dependency of the old plantation. Here lived the African-Americans of the neighborhood—and here they raised a few garden crops and kept a few animals.

Gallery to head up Historic Area Programs and Operations, took the lead. As part of his intention to accurately represent eighteenth-century life in its intriguing and instructive diversity, he recruited blacks as interpreters, supervisors, craftsmen and program presenters. Most obviously so far as visitors were concerned, the demographics of eighteenth-century Virginia began to be more accurately perceived and encountered.

Now a visitor might hear impersonators of dead white Anglo-American males in the chamber of the House of Burgesses debate Colonial grievance against King and Parliament, and then moments later come upon a free black evangelist preaching on the emancipation of heavenly salvation, or three African-American women taking their ease among the outbuildings behind a tavern. There they gossiped about their masters' foibles, revealing their own importance as the actual working people who kept households functioning, and reflected on the relative merits of British rule or some unknown form of government that would come with this unknown thing called independence. Would it make any difference to a slave? Some said yes, some said no. In any case, the irony was no longer overlooked or simply ignored that while the nominal "Founding Fathers" engaged in lofty debate and then open rebellion against hereditary royal authority, they themselves required chattel slaves to cook their food, wash their linen and care for their children. However, lest the gentle reader infer that all such backyard chat involved abstruse political issues, be assured that the servant population often seemed to be having more fun than the gentry—at least to judge by the incidence of humor. Humor became a survival technique.

Not that black characters offered vaudeville entertainment, not by a long shot. The accommodation of an historically honest black presence in the reconstruction of eighteenth-century society involved heightened awareness, sensitivity and daring in many respects by living interpreters and historians alike. Costumed interpreters of African-American descent entered into their roles as aggressively and faithfully as any other and, like dedicated theatrical actors—which indeed all costumed interpreters prove to be essentially—they kept pushing the envelope. Finally, in 1994 the time came to stage an event that would have been unthinkable a decade before, a slave auction. Some black staffers shook their heads and asked, "How can you participate?" because the event must perforce be unspeakably degrading. Other African-Americans asked, "How can we ignore this any longer?" Their argument was that such auctions were without doubt a real and undeniably important part of the American experience, and therefore deserved to be presented—in an appropriate context. (The chosen scenario presented the sale of a deceased planter's estate, which property included slaves.)

In terms of public reaction, the event was a mixed success, as some witnesses found it revealing and educational to see the ugly historical truth of humans being sold like goods to the highest bidder. Other visitors and observers were shocked or horrified by the spectacle, which they found humiliating and obscene. While no one who saw it went away unmoved, the slave auction was so offensive to some that it will not be repeated anytime soon.

More amenable to most people, regardless of race, was the construction of the slave quarter at Carter's Grove plantation, on which enslaved blacks owned by the Burwell family lived. Barely a cluster of log buildings and post-in-ground wooden dwellings clad in rough clapboards and crudely fenced pens for fowl and small animals, the site was first excavated by archaeologists, then reconstructed using traditional materials, tools and techniques. African-American interpretation at the slave quarter explored the fractured integrity of colonial black experience. Here lived people who themselves or whose parents had been stolen from homes in Africa (like as not by other black Africans), then traded as chattel for goods or gold, and eventually shipped by white slavers as cargo to the New World.

This slave house at Carter's Grove would have been occupied by a man, his wife, two teenaged sons and an infant girl. The beds had mattresses filled with cornhusks or straw; the mortar and pestle stand ready to grind the ration of corn issued weekly to make hominy, a staple that slaves supplemented by hunting, fishing and tending small garden plots.

Those who survived these horrible ordeals brought their culture(s) with them, and, as inevitably as the people of any European or Mediterranean diaspora—if more clandestinely—transplanted and adopted their ways and lives to the new circumstances. Thus another group of newcomers to this continent started the process of becoming Americans as they perpetuated parts of their heritage, adjusted whichever conditions they could, and affected the strangers they encountered as new neighbors.

As Colonial Williamsburg came to recognize its blind spots and correct them, it encouraged depictions of many historical realities that had been considered taboo. Thus, time was that Colonial Williamsburg's eighteenth-century ladies were seen as practicing gentle arts and occupations exclusively, when in fact colonial women did every sort of work. Thus, just as more blacks appeared in real eighteenth-century roles, lectured on black history and performed African-American music, women began to appear as shepherdesses, coachmen and apprentices—even in the blacksmith's shop. In fact, female smiths were known in the eighteenth century, particularly in cases where a male blacksmith died and his wife took over the business. By the late 1990s, women marched as soldiers, i.e., as cannoneers in militia units. They wielded sponge and worm to clean a cannon's bore; they rammed home the powder charge and wad; they touched the slow match to the priming and felt the ground shake to the roar of the field guns. In doing this they wore men's uniforms, taking as their model at least one Massachusetts woman in the Revolution, Deborah Samson, who masqueraded as a man and fought with a cannon company, was wounded and recovered to fight again, then fell ill with brain fever whereupon her secret was discovered—and she was persuaded to leave the service, though eventually she was granted a pension!

Without much ado, girls were admitted to the Fife and Drum Corps, and a woman was named to the staff post of drum major.

~

In 1992, Charles Longsworth stepped aside as president (while becoming chairman of the board). His successor was Robert C. Wilburn, who came to Williamsburg from the presidency of the Carnegie Institute and Carnegie Library of Pittsburgh. A graduate of the Air Force Academy, and armed with a doctorate from Princeton, he was an economist who worked in the Pentagon and the White House before becoming a vice president at Chase Manhattan Bank, then president of Indiana University of Pennsylvania and a member of Governor Richard Thornburgh's cabinet.

Starting his seven-year tenure in the Goodwin Building, Wilburn inherited some major projects and saw them to fruition: the building of the Bruton Heights School Education Center, the start of the new Visitor Center renovation, the reinterpretation of the Peyton Randolph House. At heart Wilburn was an educator, and his most important initiatives were in the pedagogical realm. Wilburn would be remembered for encouraging Historic Area personnel to behave more like docents—i.e., teachers. It was on his watch that two de facto museums within the museum were renamed to more accurately identify the buildings, their contents and missions. The Abby Aldrich Rockefeller Folk Art Center became the Abby Aldrich Rockefeller Folk Art Museum, and the DeWitt Wallace Decorative Arts Gallery became the DeWitt Wallace Decorative Arts Museum.

In was in the 1990s too that Williamsburg joined the Internet age with its website and electronic classrooms, which are state-of-the-ever-changing-art. If Colonial Williamsburg has not always been a cutting-edge kind of place—credit cards were first accepted only in 1981; servers in restaurants were exclusively male until 1982—it has blazed trails in outreach education through technology. Shortly after World War II, Williamsburg led the way in the distribution of history and civics lessons via the "film strip"—a series of still pictures arranged in a cogent sequence with narrative supplied.

The windmill grinds grain of all sorts when the outreached arms are fitted with canvas sails that catch the wind to drive the mechanism. Here it appears the miller has taken his sails out of the wind.

The Courthouse of 1770 again echoes with cries of "Oyez, oyez . . ." The Courthouse served the city of Williamsburg during the first week of the month and James City County the second week. Civil suits, criminal misdemeanors and slave felonies were heard here; in addition this court handled a host of administrative matters. As the local justices in this court typically lacked formal legal training—they came from the ranks of the local squirearchy—when hearing cases they often discussed the issues with each other. They also consulted manuals such as *This Virginia Justice* by George Webb, the 1736 edition if you please, a book written by one colonial judge specifically to advise his peers elsewhere.

Their dialogue based on colonial court records and other surviving documents, today costumed interpreters prepare to decide the destiny of the newly orphaned boy who bows to them upon being introduced. Acting *in loco parentis,* the court will place him in an apprenticeship where he will earn his keep and learn a trade.

In the 1990s, the pioneer media employed here were compact disks and narrow-cast television via cable and satellite transmission.

While the dramatic leap forward seemed to be the use of high-tech hardware, let it be said that the new media were primarily the means of delivery, the vehicle. Witness the "Electronic Field Trip," an event whose didactic purpose remained the same as the conventional pedestrian field trip. In each case, schoolchildren experience the Historic Area as a place where great events of history happened, and also as a place where ordinary people lived ordinary lives that were very different from ours today. Obviously, the children stay in their schools for the electronic field trip, which brings Williamsburg within the financial and temporal reach of many more schools than before. The electronic visit requires only a modest service fee, not the commitment of serious money for the trip itself and the nightmare of travel and logistics. And while the electronic version lacks the adventure of travel, it compensates by providing more in terms of some experience than an in-the-flesh visit— or if not more, then different. For example, when an "Electronic Field Trip" happens, it is offered to schools nationwide, simultaneously, in real time. In Williamsburg studios, panels of historians and other experts are on hand to discuss the video presentation and answer questions via satellite, so that the participating children are able to truly participate. And given the economies of scale, Williamsburg is able to host many more children via electronics than bus and minivan. At this writing, some two million schoolchildren will visit via "the Electronic Field Trip," or nearly twice the total number of visitors in the busiest year on record.

In an associated program, Williamsburg hosts Teachers Institutes each summer, which bring a few hundred professional teachers from around the country to weeks-long study programs. In all of this, Mr. Rockefeller's baby is doing its utmost to teach more basic American history to American kids.

Robert Wilburn's term was followed by an interregnum ably chaired by Frederick C. Nahm, who served as acting president for nine months before returning to his post as senior vice president.

The penultimate winter of the millennium arrived with unprecedented fury. (Winters can be harsh on the peninsula: Between summers that brought temperatures spiking over 100 humid degrees, Christmas of 1983 saw the mercury plummet to zero, causing a variety of small crises that the staff handled with aplomb.) Christmas Eve 1998 brought an ice storm of perilous strength, downing power lines throughout the region, and making walkways treacherous and roads impassable. The weight of the ice crushed the ancient boxwood bushes beside the St. George Tucker House that had made glorious hide-and-seek territory for generations of children. The crystal weight broke tree limbs without warning, bringing hundreds of pounds of wood and ice crashing to the ground. Just walking around outside had become unsafe on several counts. Responding to recommendations of the managers in charge of security, facilities and the Historic Area, the Historic Area was closed for a day—the first unscheduled closing in history. Presciently, a staff photographer was sent to take one last picture of the grand old oak behind Bassett Hall, the tree Mr. Rockefeller and Reverend Goodwin loved, before it crashed in huge splinters. Now the oak is gone.

In 2000, Colin G. Campbell, the chairman of the Colonial Williamsburg board of trustees and president of the Rockefeller Brothers Fund, was named president of CW. Briefly a practicing lawyer and then assistant to the president and later vice president of the American Stock Exchange, he was president of Wesleyan University in Connecticut for eighteen years, board chairman of the Public Broadcasting System and vice chairman of the New-York Historical Society. A graduate of Cornell and Columbia University Law School, Campbell moved to Williamsburg with an undeniable asset at his side; his wife, Nancy Campbell, arrived as chairman emerita of the National Trust for Historic Preservation, a member of the White House Millennium Committee to Save America's Treasures, a trustee of Historic Hudson Valley and a director of the Gateway Visitors Corporation of Philadelphia.

Perhaps the best prepared individual to step into the presidency, Colin Campbell knew Colonial Williamsburg and had a vision for it that involved making the complex institution more of what it is and better, to boot: a more active museum with a higher profile; a more effective educational institution that will be more accessible to its constituents through technology; a more veracious sanctuary for the American past; a more productive historical research center; and in general a better place to visit.

He was well aware that he would be the first chief executive to take over in the post-Cold War Era, a time that presents Williamsburg with new challenges and purposes. In the 1930s, when America suffered in the grip of the Great Depression, citizens hungered for a new validation of the nation's hopeful founding, a symbol, if you will. With the coming of World War II, the Restoration's beacon brightened with noble purpose; patriotism was a sacred matter for the challenged people of the "Greatest Generation" who had fought Fascism to the death. Then, with the start of the Cold War and through its long duration, Williamsburg became a shrine to the rightness of democratic Capitalism. Cherished ideal images of our nation's founding—particularly notions of noble patriots' sacrifices—gave many people a sense of righteous destiny at a time when it was quite possible that the two superpowers might blow us all up. Then with the fall of the Soviet Union, the implied victory of Capitalism and the untreatied end of the Cold War, Williamsburg subtly shifted its sights and its purpose.

A returning visitor would note new activity in the Historic Area year after year it seemed, and new agendas everywhere. In part what happened was a function of economic reality. After peaking in the 1980s, attendance (or "visitation") declined, which meant declines in the revenue generated by ticket sales, meals in Historic Area taverns and patronage at three hotels. When this occurred, the response by the programmatic side of Colonial Williamsburg seemed almost biological: The organism was threatened, and it would fight to survive. Whether or not any sense of an organic phenomenon was discussed, interpretive programs were vitalized to attract and appeal to Americans through new motives and sentiments.

There was the simple response of doing more and doing it better. There were qualitative as well as quantitative changes that appealed to visitors, and there were changes in the visitors themselves. Time was when nearly every non-official visitor was of Northern European descent—people whose heritage was either identical to or highly resonant with Virginians of the eighteenth century. These people could think like and identify with the colonists who became patriots; the Americans' escalating conflicts with King and Parliament made at least intuitive sense. But new visitors—the new numbers of Hispanics, Asians, Africans, Eastern Europeans—found it puzzling. In these peoples' historical experience, it has been the "have-nots" who rebel when social, political or economic equality has been denied. Contrary to what often passes as "common sense" (with a nod to Thomas Paine), the American Revolution was fomented and fought by gentlemen, by the "haves." Thus one of Colin Campbell's tasks would be to see that his Colonial Williamsburg explains itself to newer Americans, people of other cultural traditions and political origins. Having to its credit dropped its color bar and its gender bar, it must leave the nationalistic bar behind, too, if it hopes to explain the elements of the American Revolution that have special implications for America's wider range of citizens today.

Clearly our own changing times mean new and changing challenges to Colonial Williamsburg. Most of the personnel—from the clerk in the Raleigh Tavern Bake Shop to the costumed interpreter armed with both a master's degree and an archaic craft, and from the ticket seller in the Visitor Center booth to Colin Campbell in the President's Suite of the Goodwin Building—would not have it any other way.

DIGGING THE PAST AND MINDING THE FLOCK: ASPECTS OF PRESENTING HISTORICAL REALITY

Worried about his increasingly fractious mother, a graying man from Williamsburg took her to a specialist, who talked with the old lady and then wisely told the son, "The older we get, the more we become ourselves." So be it with Colonial Williamsburg, which as time passes becomes more closely what it was—one and one-half centuries ago, and two centuries past, and three and even four centuries before our time.

If those counts seem extreme, consider: Mr. Rockefeller sent his "David's Father" telegraph to Reverend Goodwin in 1926, which was one hundred fifty years after the signing of the Declaration of Independence (and seventy-five years before the publication of this edition). The nation's two-hundredth anniversary was celebrated here with pomp and fireworks. Now, even as you read, staff archaeologists are sorting artifacts that date from the era of the founding of Williamsburg as the new capital of Virginia in 1699 and the settlement of Middle Plantation decades earlier. Nearby, at Jamestown, other scientists have found traces and belongings of the intrepid Englishmen who first set foot on this peninsula in 1607. Given Mr. Rockefeller's mandate "that the future may learn from the past," and given seventy-five years of this institution's complex activity, a proven purpose of Colonial Williamsburg is to make these environs resemble their earlier states during the times of America's colonial gestation and republican birth. (Each generation does it a little better, in part because the first restorers didn't do it so very well, because they were content to make the city look as they thought it *ought* to look. Subsequent generations have set themselves a tougher task: to discover by direct and indirect means really how it appeared, then make it look that way again with the purpose of enabling people—scholars, adult visitors and children alike—a better understanding and appreciation of this nation's beginnings.)

In reconstructing and re-creating the past, the Colonial Williamsburg Foundation has accepted a better mission than riding a time machine back to one day or year and snapping a freeze-frame picture. Williamsburg is "the museum of the idea of America," in the casual words of Richard L. McCluney, CW's executive publisher of both traditional and electronic material. The fact is that the very "facts" change when they involve the discovery of events and styles of life in the distant past. Another fact: The very "facts" change with time. History, after all, is the progression of events, conditions, people and ideas; or, to put a finer point on it, colonial Virginia's population on July 3, 1776, was not the same as the Commonwealth's population on July 5, 1776.

Thus at its own distinct pace, this museum must change as, say, archaeologists recover more real data from the seventeenth and eighteenth centuries and as historians examine anew what has been learned—and is being learned—and as they then offer new interpretations in the context of their own times and world. Still, cultural and intellectual relativism notwithstanding, these investigators and inquirers seek truth, and the abiding question to be answered is simple enough: What was here, truly, in and around such landmark years as 1607, and 1676, and 1699, and 1765 and 1776? The answers vary and change.

Pigeons perch on the ledge of the dovecote where they nest in the gable of an outbuilding on the Peyton Randolph property. Through a false wall inside the building, a servant would collect eggs—and the occasional squab —for Mr. Randolph's table.

Another complexity arises, as McCluney may know better than most: This museum's mission is magnificently double sighted. Half its work, conducted by the historians, archaeologists and other intellectual investigators, aims at uncovering the past, piece by piece (or the *pasts,* year by year). The other half of its work, carried out by the docents, costumed interpreters, writers of study guides, video producers, et al., involves presenting emergent fact and interpretation to the many audiences for American history who come here: schoolchildren, scholars, veterans, retirees, honeymooners, collectors, re-enactors—all the plain folks who come for a casual visit once and then come again and again. Admirably, all Williamsburg's museum professionals accept an ambiguous absolute that is as essential to the study of history as the uncertainty principal is to the science of physics. The absolute, or the perfect dichotomy, is this: What occurred in history is as fixed in the past as an insect in amber, yet every act of historical discovery affects our perception and alters our understanding. In plainer words, the past is over and unchangeable, while the present view of it is always changing.

Next question: How are these images of the past discovered? Answer: By scholarship, archaeology and other methods of scientific research. And the next: How are they shown, revealed, exhibited? By interpretation, publishing, electronic media, and by sheep on the hoof and mares in the traces. But, first things first.

Conventional book work, which occupies a corps of staff historians in the Department of Historical Research, provides copious information, and adds to the body of understanding of the past each year. Intellectual understanding contributes to the *mise en scène* of Williamsburg, yet another source of information is contributed by the Department of Architectural Research. Most immediately involved in discovering the physical precedence of the past, staff archaeologists have played a major role at Williamsburg almost from the beginning, and through their efforts Williamsburg has played a seminal role in the development and evolution of a subspecialty in their discipline, historical archaeology—the use of archaeological method and investigation to illuminate the recent, i.e., historical past. (By academic definition, "historical" refers to an era or culture whose goings-on were recorded in decipherable writing. Thus the historical period in Mexico began around 1500 with the invasion of the Spanish, while the historical period in Virginia opened about 1607. Anything before those dates in those places is regarded as prehistoric.)

The earliest and most physically ambitious work was supervised by Prentice Duell, a classically trained archaeologist. A decade later, James Knight, an architectural draftsman who found himself in another line of work during the Depression, came on the scene. He received orders in 1938 to excavate the entire Historic Area by digging innumerable trenches one shovel head wide and a handle's length apart. His method was crude by any standard, his assigned purpose practical and shortsighted: to locate the remains of every old building that left a stone upon a stone or two bricks mortared together. When Knight struck something hard, he uncovered and mapped it. When he found nothing but potsherds and bits of metal, his laborers shoveled them back in the ground with the fill, and in so doing destroyed whatever meaning they might have had for later archaeologists. He was not doing archaeology, he was looking for the remains of old buildings so that they could be reconstructed. If there was substantial error here, it was a matter of nomenclature. This was a treasure hunt for old foundations, not archaeology, since the latter involves scientific method, systematic procedure and objective inquiry.

By the 1950s, thanks in part to the pioneering work done by Minor Wine Thomas and Jamestown historical archaeologists J.C. Harrington and John Cotter, Williamsburg set its sights higher and looked to the Old World to see if rigorous investigation could accomplish something more. Ivor Noël Hume proved it could. Born in London, where he learned classical archaeology by excavating

ABOVE: An astonishingly ambitious restoration of Peyton Randolph's house over the last two decades of the 20th century employed virtually every manual skill and intellectual discipline found in Colonial Williamsburg. Architectural sleuths learned that the dwelling's front had been shifted from North England Street to face Market Square and Nicholson Street, a much tonier address.

BELOW: Archaeological sleuths uncovered foundations of a two-story kitchen connected to the main house by a covered walk—the better for servants to fetch food to the master's table. They also found artifacts that proved the uses and dates of outbuildings in the yard of this plantation-in-miniature, domain of one of Virginia's most affluent and distinguished men in the pre-Revolutionary period.

Roman sites, he transplanted its proven techniques to this erstwhile colony. Here he set out to learn from the ground whatever it could teach him of the past—not just about building sizes and locations, but about the habits of the passing generations of people who erected them. In so doing, he expanded our view of old Virginia. Until Noël Hume arrived, many American historians assumed that the recent past spoke only through written materials, while archaeologists confined their work to prehistory, the uncovering of natives' relics from periods before Columbus and the tides of European invasion. Practicing the distinct discipline of historical archaeology, Noël Hume broke new ground, much to the chagrin of members of both groups who resented his intruding on their academic territories. Hell hath no contempt like a scholar challenged.

In truth, neither conventional historical study nor archaeology alone could have done the job. The historical record has too many gaps and voids; official papers and the diaries of statesmen may record great events, but often tell too little about commonplace things and everyday life, matters of growing interest to many scholars and laymen and of growing importance to Colonial Williamsburg. So, too, the archaeological record without the written one is similarly flawed and frustratingly incomplete. (Just think what an archaeologist of the future would make of a contemporary family room without an owner's manual.)

Almost single-handedly (at first) Noël Hume proved the worth of historical archaeology as a hybrid discipline with roots in two fields. The history fraternity came to recognize that archaeology unearths objects containing information that was never written down and thus eluded conventional scholarship—such things as what sorts of implements people actually used, and even what diseases carried them away. The archaeology community begrudgingly learned that excavating historical sites could provide the means to test techniques and theories relating to prehistoric investigation.

In his search for the artifacts of colonial Williamsburg, Noël Hume used the time-honored methods of classical archaeology: marking out ten-foot-square plots without regard for topography, for one example, stratigraphy for another. Soils build up in layers through natural processes and humanly induced ones. The archaeologist depends on common sense within a rigorously systematic approach; he spends much of his energy plotting distinguishable layers before assessing everything found in each one: artifacts, chemicals, seeds, etc. Find a dated coin or, more often, a bit of glazed porcelain known to have been first made in, say, 1740, and it follows that the layer in which it lies must have been deposited that year or later. Thus every layer below the find must be older than 1740, and every layer above it later, newer, younger. What about a coin that was buried for safekeeping in the days before banks—buried deep, several strata below the topsoil? Careful excavation would reveal a telltale difference between the dirt in the hole and the earth of the surrounding soil so that the hole would be seen as an intrusion to be studied and its cause described. Needless to say, there is little room for poor technique, because the process of even careful excavation destroys the ground along with any original evidence.

Assisted by his wife, Audrey, Noël Hume painstakingly excavated scores of Williamsburg sites and revealed special particulars about the city's past. In the shafts of short-lived wells, which were typically filled with trash when they went dry, he found virtual inventories of well-worn household goods. A corner cupboard in the Middle Room at Wetherburn's Tavern now often contains serving wares of the exact types used there in colonial days; shards found by excavators enabled curators to identify specific china patterns. Artifacts found in the cellar brickwork of Wetherburn's provided dates for the additions to the building, so that it could be accurately restored to its eighteenth-century state. Corroded implements discovered in the old Public Hospital site proved the methods used to treat the insane.

Shavings curling like wisps of frozen smoke, a skilled carpenter planes a "bead" along the lower edge of a clapboard. Why did 18th-century builders bead their clapboards? Beading may have made rainwater drip off faster, or perhaps it retarded splitting as the wood weathered or perhaps colonial builders just liked the look of it.

Most spectacularly, the Noël Humes struck archaeological gold in an exploratory dig on the grounds of Carter's Grove, where traces and clues led to the full-fledged excavation of Wolstenholme Towne, one of the James River outposts overrun by Indians in 1622. Among Noël Hume's most prized artifacts are two "closed helmets," the first ones ever found *in situ* in North America, military headgear previously thought to have been obsolete by this era of settlement. All these objects and more provided new knowledge about colonial life. Further, they enabled Noël Hume to write widely (and popularly) about the discipline he championed and his chosen corner of the historical period, thus contributing to knowledge of colonial America generally. Specifically, his *Guide to Artifacts of Colonial America* became the standard reference, a work of inestimable value to academics and amateurs alike. An honorary research associate at the Smithsonian, Noël Hume augmented and amended the historical record through the discovery and analysis of physical artifacts. His contributions were so significant that Queen Elizabeth conferred on him the Order of the British Empire.

In 1980, Noël Hume stepped aside as boss of day-to-day operations in order to devote his time to writing and planning the archaeological museum at Carter's Grove, which is, appropriately, entirely underground. His successor, Marley Brown III, brought even newer techniques to bear. For example, when his crews excavated the yard behind Peyton Randolph's house, they catalogued every artifact using a system that can be manipulated by computer to answer future questions phrased in numerical terms. In time, Brown hopes to excavate the Custis site, where John Custis, Martha Washington's first father-in-law, tended his gardens, which were famous throughout the colonies. Using sophisticated archaeobotanical and biochemical techniques, the archaeologist at this dig could provide unprecedented information about colonial horticulture—not just as the gentlemen gardeners wrote journals about its practice, but as their farmhands actually performed it.

Alas, while electron-microscope analysis of buried pollen and other space-age techniques could add chapters to Colonial Williamsburg's achievements, the ways of bureaucratic communications

Beside a new/old shed in the Randolph yard, a white-shirted carpenter hews a beam while his helper minds the cart that makes transporting timbers easier. In the background the windmill, used to grind grains of all sorts, faces west. When the wind changes it can be rotated on its supporting post.

remained a mystery. In the mid-1980s, at the same time that Colonial Williamsburg's Department of Archaeology and Conservation was applying for a National Science Foundation grant to date old brick, the Buildings and Maintenance Department bulldozed a new parking lot just outside the Historic Area. A dismayed archaeologist looked out his window just in time to see an earthmover scrape away the last of the archaeologically virgin ground, destroying its stratigraphy, artifacts and all. Likewise, when a new golf course was created and approved, plans for a sand trap or bunker were adjusted here and there, so that a bulldozer's blade sliced through more than one identified prehistoric archaeological site. Complaints about these ad hoc destructions led to an archaeological policy that future innovators will disregard at their peril.

One would think that Williamsburg, which has seemingly been studied and probed within an inch of its life in the past seventy-five years, would have no secrets left. Presumably every promising site would at least have been identified, like the Custis site, which lies patiently beneath a meadow of grass, doing nothing more than nourishing the occasional oxen or sheep put out to pasture there. Yet exciting and important sites come to light frequently, certainly often enough to keep a staff of archaeologists busy, along with teams of field school students, people who pay for the privilege of doing the down-on-your-knees-and-dirty work of real archaeology. In recent years the number of sites has been almost as notable as the variety of means by which they were discovered.

Consider: Rich Neck Plantation was uncovered absolutely by accident a mile west of the Historic Area when earthmovers began clearing woodland for another of Williamsburg's upscale suburban developments. Established in 1636 by Richard Kemp, Secretary of the Colony, this plantation was one of the first settlements in the area that became Middle Plantation. Kemp built an extravagant dwelling for the time, a house of brick with two rooms downstairs separated by a central fireplace. There was a separate kitchen/quarter building, and outbuildings on the 4,000-acre spread. After Kemp died Thomas Ludwell, another Secretary of the Colony, acquired the property in 1668 and doubled the size of the house, adding more outbuildings as well. On Ludwell's death the plantation passed to his brother Philip. Excavations in the 1990s have provided significant new information to the still-fragmentary mosaic of knowledge about Virginia's development and social life in the early seventeenth century.

The Douglass/Hallam Theater was as tantalizing as the grail from the beginning of the Restoration. Any number of documents mention the playhouse near the Capitol in the late colonial period, when a visiting company performed such plays there as Shakespeare's *The Merchant of Venice* and John Gay's *The Beggar's Opera*. As in English theaters of the period, an evening's entertainment would open with a long serious work, and close with a light diversion, the hall lit by candles, the middling audience seated hip-by-thigh on benches crowded in the pit, an area well below stage level. Wealthier patrons were seated more comfortably in boxes, and the hoi polloi was crammed into galleries around and behind them.

The Douglass/Hallam was the third theater built in the capital, a city that cherished entertainment and welcomed the itinerant troupes that came from England to tour the colonies. It was erected by a group that first found favor in Williamsburg in the 1750s as Lewis Hallam's London Company of Comedians. The company was well received, but some of its members had money problems, and so they moved on under a bit of a cloud to tour the Caribbean. After Lewis Hallam died in Jamaica, his widow married another actor, David Douglass, who led the group thereafter. In 1760 the company was back in Williamsburg, and now received permission to raise a brick and wood theater near the Capitol, where the actors performed with memorable success for several seasons—in October's and April's "Publick Times."

The Palace's gardens, like the building they surround, were intended to be the grandest gardens in the colony as they symbolized the wealth, power and style of the British crown. Thus such outdoor accessories as a stone plinth bearing a lead urn which had to be imported from England at great effort and expense.

The troupe was a family business featuring several Hallams, including the fair Nancy, who probably made her debut as a teenager; in due course it changed its name to the American Company. George Washington attended its plays here; Thomas Jefferson apparently went to the playhouse almost every evening in October of 1770. But theater was not to thrive as revolutionary fervor grew, and colonial leaders held such dour events as the celebrated "Day of Fasting and Humiliation" in Bruton Parish Church. In 1774 the Continental Congress passed a resolution calling for the avoidance of frivolous pastimes. The theater fell into disuse, and apparently it was dismantled, its timbers and planking recycled in other buildings elsewhere. In 1780, a deed recorded the sale of a parcel of land at the east end of town "whereon the Old Play House lately stood." The footprint of the theater itself vanished in soil that was planted in farm crops and would be turned by the plow as late as the twentieth century.

When James Knight's trenches reached the east end of town, he located the remains of a few promising brick foundations, but nothing well enough defined to permit reconstruction; the theater could have been just about anywhere in the vicinity. In the 1990s, an investigation was begun that involved a systematic series of test holes dug over the course of several years. This revealed a confusing mix of archaeological features, including more than 150 post holes of various sizes. The holes were studied, plotted and analyzed, then examined again when it appeared that one row of shallow post holes, the remains of a fence, led into a line of larger, deeper holes—ten of them, that spanned a distance of 72 feet. It was the one side of the theater. At this writing the full excavation has begun, and it will take another two digging seasons. Then, if a dream scenario plays out, the funds may be found to reconstruct the city's brightest entertainment center, perhaps as a working playhouse where classical plays may again inspire and amuse live audiences in pit, boxes and galleries. But until that comes to pass, mark this: The discovery of the Douglass/Hallam Theater site resulted from no stroke of serendipity but from plain, dogged, systematic archaeological work.

Another site was identified but left undug for half a century for practical reasons. For at least five decades after Colonial Williamsburg defined the Historic Area and the city fathers protected it with special zoning, two aging Armistead sisters continued to operate a tourist home in their clapboard house on Duke of Gloucester Street closest to the Capitol. Indeed, it was the closest to the Capitol of any private building—only the Secretary's Office is closer—and however handsome this tall Victorian dwelling was, it stuck out like a grande dame transported from the wrong century. After the last lady's demise, her heirs agreed to lease the site to Colonial Williamsburg and to allow the house to be moved a mile away to Henry Street in 1995. As the house had stood where it was for well over a century, its cellars and the ground beneath were a time capsule that CW's archaeologists were eager to examine. James Knight had not lanced this ground with his ubiquitous shovels.

The Armistead house proved to be standing on earlier brick foundations in English bond (alternating courses of bricks laid end-to-end and side-to side), and it provided more than a virgin dig. The structure itself held evidence of a previous life. Architectural historians Willie Graham and Mark R. Wenger examined the interior framing, the lower tier of which contained more than ninety pieces of frame or trim that had been used in an earlier building on the site, an eighteenth-century structure used for more than a decade as a coffeehouse. Analyzing the dimensions, nail holes and other construction scars of these recycled pieces, the architectural historians matched up pieces of wood into a kind of three-dimensional jigsaw puzzle, which thus presented the size and design features of the building. Analysis of the annual growth rings in the antique timbers revealed that the trees from which they were sawed had all been felled in the autumn of 1749.

In the slave quarter at Carter's Grove, reconstructed dwellings—built as they would have been thrown together in the 18th century—reveal the no-frills approach to the homes of people in the lowest estate.

The first building was erected as a storehouse in 1751, according to written records produced by staff historian Pat Gibbs, who compiled a paper trail for the property. By 1767 Richard Charlton, an immigrant from England, had acquired the nearly square structure and had turned it into a coffeehouse, using as his model the shops that had been the rage in London, where they served as semi-official gathering places of merchants and businessmen. (One of these, Lloyd's Coffeehouse, became the haunt of ship owners, and eventually a place where individuals bought shares of the risks in each other's vessels and cargoes; thus it became the center of the British insurance market, Lloyd's of London.) While some coffeehouses served food, wine, beer and spirits, their character was distinctly different from that of taverns, which were boisterous places made all the more so by the intoxicants. Coffeehouses favored nonalcoholic beverages; they encouraged more sober intercourse, and thus more serious business.

In Williamsburg, archaeology proved further that Charlton's Coffeehouse catered to an elite clientele. Located near the outdoor Exchange, the market for wholesale agricultural products, it became the place where dealers, major merchants and shippers met, as well as certain politicians, such as members of the Governor's Council. In 1765, as the Stamp Act crisis was coming to a head, Governor Fauquier was taking refreshment on the porch of Charlton's with his councilors when they saw an angry crowd surround the crown's tax collector, George Mercer, and threaten him. Fauquier, one of the ablest and most popular of governors, wrote that he waded into the mob and escorted Mercer to the Palace unharmed. This incident suggests that Charlton's was the drinking place where gentlemen and Tories met; by contrast, when Fauquier's successor, Lord Dunmore, disbanded the House of Burgesses, those rowdier fellows reconvened just a few hundred yards down Duke of Gloucester Street in the Raleigh Tavern, having perforce passed Charlton's. The Raleigh was frequented by more liberal men, at least the ones who led Virginia's dissenters and later became rebels.

Artifacts found by the systematic excavation of the coffeehouse lot—especially when compared with data from earlier digs of similar establishments—proved that Charlton's was indeed frequented by gentlemen of a higher economic order. We know that they drank from finer china than customers at taverns nearby, for better wares were broken here and left their shards in the earth. Charlton's patrons lost brass buttons from their clothes, and several dropped the handsome little keys used to wind their pocket watches, which were still accessories that only the wealthy could afford. (Such watches as these prompted Adam Smith's great discovery: At first rare and expensive objects owned only by the very rich, pocket watches were widely admired and coveted by persons of lesser means, which created a popular market, which in turn prompted more tradesmen to make more watches, thus meeting the higher "demand" with greater "supply," which lowered the price of a watch until in time almost anyone could own one. Today this classic law of supply and demand governs the falling prices of computers and other electronic widgets.) As the staff archaeologists wrote, Charlton's uniquely "yielded hundreds of clothing-related objects, including buttons, hooks and eyes, sleeve- and cufflinks, watch parts, rings, earrings and shoe buckles"—not items from the wardrobes of the poor or working classes.

Through the several scholarly disciplines that studied this virgin site, Colonial Williamsburg deduced new knowledge and insights into colonial culture. As the report continues, "When combined, this research led to the discovery of a previously unknown facet of the eighteenth-century town's social, economic and political stage. The evidence suggests that the coffeehouse acted as an extension of the Exchange, the open area adjacent to the Capitol, where merchants met to decide the prices of agricultural products. It appears to have served the same function for the men who worked in government, as witnessed by . . . the presence of the Governor and several council members . . . during the Stamp Act protest. The coffeehouse also provided entertainment and edification to some of Williamsburg's most prominent citizens as the setting for lectures, curiosities and social clubs."

Here was the case of a site that was known to be of prime importance for years, but all the while lay beyond the reach of the archaeologists—by virtue of the fact that people were living on it. When the lot finally was cleared and the site excavated, it held artifacts and information that the excavators could not have anticipated.

Another important archaeological site was a not-quite-accidental discovery—a tract of land that James Knight had glimpsed just outside of the Historic Area. When a trench was being dug for a storm sewer, before it was backfilled Knight had seen what appeared to be the substantial remains of brick foundations dating from the colonial era. Later this area was covered over by the building and amenities of Bruton Heights School, the black school that Mr. and Mrs. Rockefeller had so generously aided more than fifty years earlier. When the school was closed in the late 1980s, news was bruited that a developer might buy the site from the city, or that Colonial Williamsburg might acquire it. Knight got in touch with the Restoration, and as staff archaeologist David F. Muraca later remembered, "he sought to acquaint me with the archaeological potential of the tract." Knight could only attest to what he had seen. To assess the site, CW archaeologists systematically dug 1,000 test holes and found enough artifacts to make the site appear very interesting. When heavy equipment arrived to clear the area, the first backhoe to start removing a parking lot uncovered the foundations again: This was the house that John Page had built.

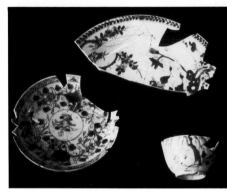

Recovered from datable layers of earth around Wetherburn's Tavern, broken glassware (top) and fragments of Chinese export porcelain reveal that innkeeper Henry Wetherburn provided utensils of notable quality for the time. The ceramic cup and saucer could well be part of a set of six listed in the 1760 room-by-room inventory of Wetherburn's estate.

Born to a good family in England, John Page came to Virginia in 1650 at the age of 23 and began making his mark. Within four years he was a member of the House of Burgesses for York County, the owner of land at Middle Plantation, a man of affairs and political influence. When Nathaniel Bacon led his rebellion in 1676, he took as hostages the "prime mens wives, whose Husbands were with the Governour"; one was Alice Page. John himself signed a pledge supporting Bacon, perhaps understandably under a husband's duress, or because like others he feared Governor Berkeley could not restore order. When Bacon's cause failed, Page (among others) sought the governor's pardon and became "high sherriffee of Yorke County" briefly. He would be a member of the Bruton Parish vestry, and donor of the land on which Virginia's first brick church was built. He was a sometime "colonel," a physician (at least to the people of his extensive household), and in 1680 he was named to the *ne plus ultra* Council of State. He also was very prosperous from very early on, and he remained so to the end.

In 1662 Page built the grandest house in Middle Plantation near the palisade that stretched across the peninsula to keep Indians out and livestock in. Above the door he placed a cartouche in carved brick comprising the date, his wife's and his own initial and a simple heart. Shaped like ones on a modern valentine, in those times it represented religious piety and a notion of centrality. (The heart was the center of the human body, and God's love the center of universal existence; the house that Page adorned with this symbol was the center of his estate and perhaps he meant to imply it was the center of the colony as well.) The house was cross-shaped in plan, containing two rooms on the ground floor, a porch tower and a stair tower front and back, and cellars beneath. In overall design and detail it resembled contemporary grand houses raised in Bermuda, Ireland, Virginia (such as the ineptly named "Bacon's Castle," which had nothing to do with Bacon), and in England itself.

Virginians in the third quarter of the seventeenth century were frightfully aware of their mortality: Life was short, disease widespread, famine possible; families were often fractured by early deaths—or so historians had surmised. Many Virginians gambled on the quick profits tobacco could earn, building short-lived wooden dwellings without foundations, until their initial investment panned out. Page staked his claim in Virginia and was one of the first to build for the ages, in brick. While it is barely possible that he was unique in his thinking, more likely we should read his history as an example, and see his implied viewpoint as representative of others.

He laid his foundations in the brick-intensive Flemish bond, and scored the mortar for visual finish—even in the utilitarian cellar where he stored wine bottles for his entertaining. He contoured the basement floor so that it crowned in the center, cleverly using shaped tiles to channel seepage and ground water into two sumps where it drained away through the sandy clay. He covered his interior walls with plaster, and glazed his windows with leaded panes.

This house, it now appears, was the center of a thriving plantation, one that bespoke a degree of social stability that historians had previously thought would not arrive in Virginia until a generation or two later. In fact, John Page invested in a kiln for the making of good bricks and tiles, building materials that would last decades or centuries rather than brief years as inferior products did. Not only did the installation of the kiln require time and some capital, brickmaking was a difficult craft and tile making nearly an art; thus the gentleman who owned a kiln must have the resources to employ skilled artisans to operate it, whether itinerant journeymen or permanent workers who might be independent souls, indentured servants or even slaves.

Such a man would have his portrait painted and establish something of a dynasty of Virginia leaders. As one of the first to live in Middle Plantation, he undoubtedly had a hand in bringing the capital there, and was credited as being a prime mover of the college as well. By the time of those events, his once grand home would have been regarded as dated; in any case, it was destroyed in a fire around 1730, a quick, relatively cool fire that started in the ground floor fireplace and tumbled the whole house into the cellar hole where its contents would remain undisturbed for nearly three hundred years.

Outbuildings in the complex (nay the gilded hamlet) that is the Governor's Palace include a substantial laundry and the "bagnio," his lordship's bath house.

~

As moving forward in modern Williamsburg has always meant looking more closely into the past, the longer historians have looked, read and dug, the more they have seen. Research proceeds, as projects such as promising archaeological digs are prioritized or deferred (for reasons of ownership or other practicalities). In some respects research broadens as resident investigators and visiting scholars pose new questions, many of them purely practical ones, such as how to grow and process wool according to a manual published by a Williamsburg planter in the 1770s. Rarely, however, do searches for verisimilitude in crafts and agriculture create the kind of uproar that followed on the heels of a seemingly innocuous experiment.

Conventional wisdom holds that Europeans from the late Renaisance to the Enlightenment were steadfast in seeing the New World as a boundless trove of botanical and mineral treasure. When Virginia was discovered to lack cities paved with gold, English adventurers settled for baser riches, starting with ships' spars and tobacco. Briefly they tried glassblowing and iron mining in this colony, and even tried to start a silk industry though, alas, the worms did not cotton to the paper mulberry trees used rather than the real McCoy mulberry. A plant that performed better in Virginia was hemp, source of an important maritime staple, rope, and a Colonial Williamsburg weaver proposed to revive the historically prosperous trade of ropemaking.

It seemed a natural addition to the exhibition repertoire: Costumed interpreters possessing (or developing) the requisite range of skills would grow hemp, harvest it, process the fiber and turn it into cordage as colonists had done—all right before visitors' eyes. Scholarly research uncovered the historical facts of hemp growing. More research of a practical nature—i.e., doing it—would discover techniques.

The weaver was a Scotsman remembered decades later as being as so nimble-fingered that he could spin woolen thread one-handed from a ball of fluff cradled in his palm. He didn't need a spinning wheel to make yarn while discoursing on all kinds of lore in a brogue thick as tweed. A kind of manual genius with a sense of history and the gift of gab, he asked the Purchasing Department to get him the seeds he needed, which were duly ordered from a garden catalogue in the Midwest. The seeds thrived in Virginia soil. Come harvesttime the weaver and his crew brought in a surprising crop. Using antique tools, they beat the hemp and extracted fibers to spin into thread to twist into rope. The first year they let the plants grow to full height, then learned that it was better to harvest sooner before the plants branched and produced tangled fibers. At any rate, when they cut the plants they stored them in a barn to dry and paid no mind when birds swooped in to snatch the seeds, and then swooped out again with markedly less agility. The birds seemed more flighty, more gay; they flew a little higher, to borrow a phrase. This delighted certain savvy visitors who giggled at the idea of growing this plant for rope.

Years later a staffer who helped grow the hemp said he and his colleagues *really* had not known that a rope by any other name could cause such heat. They learned otherwise when detectives descended in high dudgeon and raided the joint. "Hemp?" they frowned. "That's marijuana, pot, herb, Mary Jane and you all are under arrest." The charge, possession of a controlled substance, threatened to become a federal case with international implications. The Scottish weaver, a guest in the Commonwealth, was alarmed and threatened to call his embassy before things got out of hand. Needless to say the colonial precinct's overseers were concerned about the possibility of a public scandal. Some may have had nightmares about seeing headlines reading something like "Colonial Williamsburg Grows 'Grass.'"

Decorative planting is raised to a fine art in the Prentis House garden and elsewhere. Here a pomegranate tree glows golden in the autumn sun among trimmed yaupon holly hedges which border the garden's parterres.

Eventually all was put right, and all is nearly forgotten, grist perhaps for some archaeologist to discover anew generations hence—if such things as modern scrapbooks stand the test of time. One erstwhile suspect's keepsakes contains, among many nobler mementos of a life spent plying colonial crafts, a yellowed clipping from the local press. It reports that a grand jury, that honored panel born of English common law, weighed the evidence and instructed the prosecution to drop its case. There was no malicious intent on the several craftsmen's part; they had simply planted what had been ordered from a reputable seed catalogue to grow hemp—for rope, not dope. And that was simply that. It was understood by all, moreover, that the stuff that filled the barn and addled the sparrows' pates was forfeit; it should not be grown again. A panel of their peers set the tradesmen free, their names and records as clean as Colonial Williamsburg's abiding reputation in the world at large.

Other domestic trades—weaving, basketmaking, coopering—were all essential to eighteenth-century life, and thus to Colonial Williamsburg's presentation. For a time the interpreters who practiced these arts were clustered together behind the Peyton Randolph House, while the miller's kin kept chickens and raised tobacco near the Windmill.

If a museum's mission is to preserve objects and nurture knowledge within its chosen realm, and if Colonial Williamsburg's ken is life as t'was lived in eighteenth-century Virginia, how does an outstanding living feature—namely, the livestock—fit in? Given that eighteenth-century economies were firmly rooted in agriculture, the sights and sounds of domestic animals should be part and parcel of this place today. So have they been for decades; and so they are now, to even redoubled purpose. James Sampson and his oxen were part of the scene for many years, hauling a farm cart with passels of children aboard. There have been rides around the Historic Area for decades in horse-drawn carriages, wagons and chairs. There have also been a few cattle in a meadow, and a regular flock of common sheep, that are sheared every year. Year in and year out pigeons have roosted in the cote behind George Wythe's house, and on at least one memorable occasion around 1984, horses raced down Palace Green in a match race. All this was part of the Coach and Livestock Department's domain, and all part of the charm of Williamsburg. Yet in recent years the presence of animals has taken on a newer importance and served a distinctly museological purpose, namely, to contribute to the preservation of the exhibits themselves, to wit, now-uncommon historically correct animals—or as correct as may be ascertained. The domestic animals found here now are the kinds that could or would have been here centuries ago.

In the mid-1980s, a new talent came to Williamsburg. Like many of the specially gifted people whose names still command respect—Fife & Drum Corps leader John Moon, first cooper George Pettengell and a certain innocent weaver—he was a Briton. The son of an English surgeon, Richard Nicoll came to America and managed a stable and its stock. He worked for several individuals who helped keep alive a waning tradition, call it the carriage trade: the driving of horses harnessed to carriages. They would come to Williamsburg from time to time to stage what amounted to a grand vehicular rally. They brought two- and four-wheeled vehicles drawn by one or two horses, or sometimes, by teams, which were driven by skilled coachmen and women. These are people who know one meaning of the descriptive term "four-in-hand"; they can drive four horses at once, handling four sets of reins. (The term also applies in the Anglican realm of handbell music to the rare individual who can hold four bells at once, ringing only one at a time on cue.) Interested in vanishing breeds of livestock, at Williamsburg Nicoll found a venue where these special breeds of animals might be bred and raised with a particular appropriateness of purpose.

Take the breed of horse known as the Canadian, a strong and hardy beast whose traits made it

Closer to the center of town behind the Davidson Shop, sheep stand in an enclosure.

popular for crossbreeding. Although it was popular and a good crossbreeder, increasing mechanization in the twentieth century caused it to all but disappear. Thus it ranked high on the roster of the American Livestock Breeds Conservancy, one of the two leading organizations in the English-speaking world dedicated to the premise that any true breed of domestic animal possesses a unique genetic heritage and thus deserves to survive, just as a species of warbler, rodent or minnow in the wild does. (The other organization of this type is Britain's Rare Breeds Survival Trust, which like the ALBC keeps tabs on endangered or dwindling breeds of livestock.)

The Canadian horse, be it known, is listed as "critical" by the ALBC, meaning that there are fewer than 200 registered individuals in North America and fewer than 2,000 estimated in the world. Consequently, the Canadian was one that Nicoll brought to Williamsburg—in part to help preserve the breed. Yet that reason alone was not enough. This is also a horse that might have been found in eighteenth-century Virginia. The breed's foundation stock was brought to Acadia and New France in the seventeenth century. The stock in Canada grew tough and sturdy in the face of a harsh climate; in New England, the Canadian was the mainstay of stagecoach lines. A horse of medium build, usually black (though sometimes brown, bay or chestnut), it became known for its versatility. The Canadian could be called upon for riding, for drawing an elegant carriage or drab dray, or for hitching to a plow.

Once again today, it is a riding and a carriage horse around Williamsburg, because in addition to being an inexpensive, intelligent animal, it is even-tempered and reliable around people—a must for a beast that will ply the Historic Area, sharing the streets and byways with people of all ages and degrees of agility. Thus Nicoll swears by the Canadian on two counts, its temperament and its probable historical fidelity, as he swears by the American Cream Draft Horse on one count: perhaps even rarer, it is the only modern American breed of livestock in the rare breed program. Though the demand for work animals was declining, this breed of draft horse arose early in the twentieth century in Iowa through the cream-colored progeny of one mare; then it nearly vanished in the 1950s. Now it is making a slow comeback, thanks in part to a scientific breeding registry that keeps records of all known individual animals of the breed, and in part to participants like Colonial Williamburg.

A kind of cattle deemed "critical" by the ALBC is the Milking Devon, an animal that might well have been described in a 1775 *Virginia Gazette* by the plantation overseer who announced his "red" cow, calf and steer as strayed or stolen and advertised for their return. Like the Canadian horse, the Milking Devon was versatile. Milking Devons were raised as diary cows, as beef cattle and as draft animals—that is, they were favored by the farmer who kept only a very few head of stock and consequently required the animals to serve several purposes. In the last century this breed fell out of favor because they gave less milk than Jerseys or Holsteins and matured more slowly than the Hereford or Black Angus, and because few American farms kept animals for toil. Thus they, too, hovered near the brink of extinction. Now, at Williamsburg, they earn their keep as milkers, providing a staple for CW's food demonstrations. Another of their duties here: to prove for the first time to many of the visiting schoolchildren that milk doesn't come from a carton.

For sheep, Nicoll sought the Leicester Longwool, descendant of one of the first varieties of livestock to be designated as a breed. Livestock breeds were a creature of the Enlightenment, after all, the eighteenth-century Age of Reason that saw great innovations in agriculture and industry as well as the strides in political thought that gave rise to the American Revolution. A pioneer sheep breeder was Robert Bakewell of Leicestershire who bred for selected traits and became celebrated throughout the kingdom. George Washington, for one, wrote about Bakewell's methods and imported Leicesters to his flocks at Mount Vernon.

The first sheep of this variety to come to Williamsburg in the twentieth century was a ram bought at auction, Willoughby, who sired some lovely crossbred lambs with Dorset ewes. But in a possibly unique happening for Colonial Williamsburg, Willoughby was found killed in 1988; the public announcement of this tragic event prompted considerable mail and offers of support. The upshot was a breeding program that stretched around the world. An Australian breeder gathered ewes from four different Tasmanian flocks, which were then bred to different rams. After the ordeal of shipment from Australia and then the delay of quarantine in Canada, when the little flock arrived in Williamsburg, there were eight ewes, six lambs and one ram. These sheep in turn have been managed through a scientific breeding program to maximize their genetic diversity. After a couple of seasons in Williamsburg, some individuals were used to establish satellite flocks elsewhere; thus this breed may be making its way back from critical status.

Colonial Williamsburg, said the Secretary of the Smithsonian Institution, is "America's most cherished testament to its past." More concretely, today it is an amalgam of institutions. It is certainly a "destination" in the lexicon of travel agents, a place that has attracted as many as seven thousand visitors on a good day and upward of one million in the banner years of the late 1980s. It is also a conference and convention center for groups as distinct as trade associations, the Southern Governors Conference and the American Livestock Breeders Association. In another of its guises, this is a patriot's mecca, a shrine dedicated to the nation's founding that grizzled veterans seek out on national holidays and commemorative occasions. At Christmas it is a holiday spa, one weekend every fall a colonial fairgrounds, and on Independence Day a place where local folk converge for fireworks. Williamsburg is a perennial garden club, a crafts bazaar, and a hideaway for honeymooners and other lovers. But more than any of these, it is a museum, indeed a complex of museums.

Since the great library in ancient Alexandria first used the term, "museum" has meant a multitude of things. In eighteenth-century London a museum was typically an aristocrat's private collection of objects. Charles Willson Peale opened America's first successful public museum in Philadelphia, which displayed his passion for collecting paintings, dinosaur bones and all manner of curiosities. In living memory, museums have been dusty places, each one a kind of mausoleum featuring ranks of vitrines filled with such things as insects impaled on pins tagged with their names in Latin. But in recent decades museums have come into their own as places that amuse adults and educate children, or, very often, vice versa.

Today a museum is an institution that collects a chosen body of material things because they are valuable—whether intrinsically as in a trophy cup weighing two hundred ounces of gilded silver, or by association, as in a common eighteenth-century man's private diary or an apothecary's ledger that suggests which Virginia gentlemen suffered "the French disease." A museum is a sanctuary for objects, a place whose mission is to hold them in safekeeping for posterity. A museum is also properly a place of exhibition that mounts shows of this or that for public enlightenment and pleasure alike. A museum is a center for the study of its own collections and, by extension, a nexus for the study of all the arts and sciences relating to those objects. In sum, a museum is an institution that collects, protects, displays and reveals its chosen ken.

As a young institution, Colonial Williamsburg became an outdoor museum—America's first—almost accidentally, a historical institution whose purview focused on the historic town that was capital of both a colony and newly independent Commonwealth. By extension that purview soon comprised all of seventeenth- and eighteenth-century Virginia, and in some respects all of European America, for the commonsensical reason that what obtained here did not vanish at the colony's border. Conditions, institutions, traditions and dynamics found in Virginia existed elsewhere contemporaneously.

Almost inevitably this museum's curators and scholars concerned themselves with everything they found within the boundaries defined by time and place: with antiques, with art and ideas,

OPPOSITE: That such fragile fretwork in the pediment from a double chest first owned by John Deas and his wife, Elizabeth Allen Deas, of Charleston, South Carolina, survived over two hundred years is a miracle. When similar fragile pieces come to a museum such as Colonial Williamsburg their new stewards willingly accept the duty to assure perpetual survival.

with historic guns and historical theories, with artifacts as base as leg irons and hypotheses as lofty as St. George Tucker's belief in emancipation four score years before Abraham Lincoln proclaimed it. But it is more than a museum of pots, art, furniture or folklore. It grew into its many roles in one because it is a museum of history.

Williamsburg's purpose is to reveal its chosen site and era according to lights that vary from generation to generation. For decades the emphasis was on the town as the best preserved of the many "cradles" of the Revolution. From its opening, through World War II and the subsequent Cold War, Colonial Williamsburg saw itself as the Shrine of Freedom, a place of political genesis in a world threatened (ironically) by proselytes of newer heterodox, if not revolutionary, ideas, namely Marxism, Fascism and Communism. Since the waning of those particular threats on the world stage, there have been changes in interest and focus. Gathering momentum through the 1990s, the emphasis shifted toward examining the lives of our ordinary forebears and to see how it was that they *became* Americans—in their folkways, science, philosophy, economics, jurisprudence, aesthetics, social behavior, politics, business, agriculture—as well as in their very minds. In a way, twenty-first-century Williamsburg is as dynamic and protean as Jefferson hoped his Republic would become. Initiated by scholars, the didactic thrust of the place was to explore the idea that people were "becoming Americans" in eighteenth-century Virginia—both the colony and the commonwealth—and furthermore that the Americans they became were a people unlike their forebears! This people, *e pluribus unum*, emerged from a spectrum of ethnic groups: English who settled in Tidewater Virginia, Germans who drifted down from Pennsylvania to the valleys to the west, Africans brought here in chains, Indians who were deemed and demeaned as aboriginals. As all of these groups and more adapted to what they found here, and as each group affected the place and the other people they encountered, they changed, like as not becoming even *more* American as time went on. Today, we are all changing still, with the coming of newer conditions—the lengthening of life expectancy, the ubiquitous mobility brought by airplanes, the nearly universal communications of the Internet, the influx in the last quarter-century of new immigrants—most of them Asians and Latin Americans—about one for each ten resident citizens.

Colonial Williamsburg qualifies as a museum on many grounds, first as a historic and historical town of 173 acres and more than 400 period buildings, from privies to Palace and including shops, stores, a Courthouse and Capitol. (Eighty-eight are painstaking restorations, the rest well-intentioned and at least careful reconstructions of lost originals.) More than forty major structures—the number varies from year to year—are exhibition buildings. Lest the Historic Area become a ghost town after visiting hours, nearly a hundred dwellings and larger outbuildings such as kitchens were dedicated for use as rental homes for Colonial Williamsburg employees. (Formerly there were also the homes of life tenants, a number that has perforce dwindled from two score to—inevitably—one, as of this writing.) Another dozen buildings are elegant guesthouses, while most of the rest provide offices, storage and facilities for staff. Here the structures themselves are the first objects on display.

The entire town is an exhibit—its gravel streets, its greens and ravines, even its human activities—from the brass founder's casting of brass candlesticks in the Geddy Foundry to the harpsichordist's playing of Handel concerti upon a baroque instrument in the intimacy of the Palace ballroom. As a museum, the whole displays a priceless collection of artisans' rediscovered skills, resources as special as the rare objects that were created by similar workers several lifetimes ago. And of course, Williamsburg is a museum in the intellectual work that goes on here, for this is a place of research, study, convocation and scholarship.

It is also a cluster of museums in the conventional sense. Its larger possessions, the buildings them-

A chest-on-chest made between 1765 and 1780 in the popular style of the period probably never saw Williamsburg for two centuries. It was first owned by John Deas of Charleston and descended through his family to his great-great-grandson Colonel Alston Deas. Acquired by an antiques dealer, it was purchased by Colonial Williamsburg in 1974 as the manifold museum of 18th-century America continued its search for authentic furnishings.

John Collet, a generation younger than the more famous and caustic William Hogarth, painted scenes of everyday life in 18th-century England. In this genre painting *High Life Below Stairs*, he depicts a covey of servants lampooning their social superiors. Paintings like this provide a wealth of visual information about a period's material culture for study by social historians.

selves, contain myriad smaller objects of very special quality and importance: Antique silver hollowware and pitchers, like those James Craig raised from scrap sterling, are now displayed in the Golden Ball; the Speaker's Chair, built for the first Capitol, has been loaned indefinitely by the Commonwealth for display in the reconstructed Capitol; the imposing and imperfect portrait of Reverend James Blair that hangs in the Great Hall of the Wren Building; the Chelsea porcelain figures that grace the mantel in the Palace dining room. From the copper saucepans in Lord Botetourt's kitchen to the coverlet in his bedchamber, all of these are "museum pieces" as the saying goes. Yet many of them are not grand *objets d'art*. Many are as common as chamber pots, since the historic buildings have slowly and controversially evolved to reflect forgotten commonplaces of the eighteenth century.

Two special exhibition buildings are traditional museums as well, structures built for and dedicated to the display of prized antique objects. One of these, originally called the Abby Aldrich Rockefeller Folk Art Center and now the Abby Aldrich Rockefeller Folk Art Museum, came to be by virtue of the founder's fiat; the other, which nearly didn't get built at all, arose out of ingenious design. The change of its name, from high-sounding Gallery to the DeWitt Wallace Decorative Arts Museum, similarly reflects the fact that Williamsburg has grown by intent, and has improved itself in the process. This 1980s addition to Williamsburg's complex was a complex in itself, both the largest reconstruction in fifty years and a pure gallery of absolutely contemporary design, program and mission.

Having been the ward of one benefactor, the historical hamlet did not have much experience in fully managing its own affairs when Mr. Rockefeller's heirs set it loose in the world. Never having had to support itself, Colonial Williamsburg had not ventured far into the competitive world of nonprofit institutions. When the first professional development officer was lured away from Duke University—like every college, an aggressive solicitor of gifts—he was bemused. Looking at a list of regular guests who returned repeatedly and had clearly demonstrated their interest in one way or another, he asked how much money they had been invited to give. "None," was the answer. That would be set right.

One frequent visitor stood tall among those known for generous support of their favorite charities; his name was high on every fund-raiser's wish list. DeWitt Wallace, with his wife, Lila, founded the *Reader's Digest,* arguably the most successful periodical on earth. Their little magazine grew into a publishing empire that hardly knew national boundaries, and their fortune approached the same magnitude. DeWitt Wallace was very wealthy and very patriotic. (He started the 1960s craze of putting little American flag decals and patches on everything.) He also loved Williamsburg. He not only visited several times a year, but he sent a small planeload of employees down from New York about once a month for their recreation and inspiration, all expenses paid.

Eight *Reader's Digest* hands, typically maiden ladies, would arrive on a Friday night, each with a little dividend in her purse for spending money. When they got back to work on Monday, at least one would be interviewed by the boss, who liked to hear about goings-on in the colonial capital. It was always good news, until one year a lady reported that she had not seen *The Story of a Patriot.* Her employer was incredulous. *Not seen "The Patriot"!?* The idea was shocking. She had tried, she said, but they weren't screening it anymore.

The Story of a Patriot is something of a museum piece itself, a fine example of Technicolor filmcraft, if not the cinematic masterpiece that the screenwriter James Agee was contemplating at the time of his early death. Directed by George Seaton, famous for *The Country Girl,* and starring Jack Lord, later a private eye in the television series *Hawaii Five-O, The Patriot* relates a history of Williamsburg on the eve of the Revolution with dated charm and sentimentality. Projected continually at the old Information Center, it prepared visitors for what they would see around town. Made in 1957, the subtly jingoistic film reflected the national mood; it was "dedicated to the principles of liberty wherever and whenever they may be threatened." Withal, it was made with great historical care; Thad Tate, then a member of the Research Department and later director of the Institute for Early American History and Culture, now the Omohundro Institute, spent two years assuring the accuracy of its content. (Still, there were some inside jokes. When a change in the script required instantaneously a fictitious name that "sounded colonial," the burgess-elect who made an entrance was one "Thaddeus Tate." Similarly, a barrel of goods imported from England bears the name of the long-time architect Ed Kendrew.) Almost every visitor has seen the film, and none more delightedly than Wallace and his favored employees.

But that year Williamsburg was gearing up for the Bicentennial and had come to believe that thirteen million modern patriots would be making the pilgrimage to the town's hallowed halls. A shorter film had been made in order to better accommodate the throngs, and *The Patriot* had been shelved pro tem. In a flash, Wallace was on the phone offering to build a new and enlarged Visitor Center with three theaters capable of screening his favorite movie for each and every arrival. In a manner of speaking, he offered to endow *The Patriot* in perpetuity.

Williamsburg was loath to look this gift horse in the mouth and nearly took the offer without a second glance, but cooler heads prevailed. Early plans called for Wallace's building to handle several million people a year, even though few more than one million have ever showed up. The donor offered a gift of $4 million, but the price tag would have been more. When Bicentennial Year attendance fell short of the grandiose expectations and rising gasoline prices caused several lean years, Colonial Williamsburg seriously reconsidered. In 1975 the board of trustees had endorsed a new gallery in principle, but had not yet found the money to fund it; meanwhile a major reconstruction project had been postponed for decades, that of the last (presumably) major public building within the Historic Area, the mental hospital. Having demonstrated his willingness to help Williamsburg, Wallace was invited to consider funding a decorative arts gallery and the Public

Pure fancy led a cabinetmaker—
possibly in New Hampshire
around 1920—to build a chair
that looks like a banjo, complete
with inlaid strings, tuning pegs and
head brackets. A rarity, it resides in
Williamsburg's folk art collections.

King George III, displaying the hauteur and extravagance worthy of a monarch, wears his coronation robes in 1762. Allan Ramsay painted many copies of this state portrait and one hung in the Governor's Palace by 1768. This original copy adorned Knole, the seat of the Dukes of Dorset, whence it came to Williamsburg —two centuries after its creation—where it came to rest in the Wallace Museum.

General George Washington strikes a pose similar to the king he opposed. Charles Willson Peale painted this monumental picture, complete with a glimpse of the pivotal 1777 Battle of Princeton in the background, on bedticking in 1780. The painting hung in Virginia at nearby Shirley plantation until Mr. Rockefeller bought it in 1928, making it the first of many pictures to be acquired by the Restoration. While Peale probably saw King George's portrait either in Williamsburg or London where he studied with Benjamin West, it is unlikely that he meant his portrait to be a parody. Rather, scholars believe, he meant to show the nascent nation's commander in chief in the classical hero's pose.

Hospital. Would he be willing to complete work that Mr. John D. Rockefeller, Jr., had not been able to finish? Yes, he would consider it.

Thus the reconstruction of the Public Hospital became conceptually and financially linked to the DeWitt Wallace Decorative Arts Gallery, which opened in 1985. Indeed, Wallace contributed $14,000,000 to the project and established a fund to defray the gallery's annual expenses. Kevin Roche, the celebrated architect who designed it, recalled that the first part of the assignment was straightforward enough: to reconstruct the old Public Hospital's shell on its original site with a couple of underground levels for exhibition galleries. But as the Collections Department spelled out its space requirements, it soon appeared that the whole building must resemble a huge submarine sunk in earth with the old hospital rising above the sod like a conning tower. Impractically expensive, it was, in a word, ludicrous as well.

The more Roche visited the site, the more he was troubled by the city's functional courthouse and jail building. Located outside the Restored Area, this modern brick structure lay behind the hospital site like a sleeping ogre, an eyesore in brick and concrete. People wandering through the old town often found themselves pleasantly lost in time, transported back two centuries—until this sorry sight jolted them back into modernity. A self-styled "unreconstructed modernist," Roche was more offended than an antiquarian architect. This courthouse not only clashed with its carefully restored surroundings, but in his opinion it was a shoddy example of modern design to boot.

After pondering for many months and visiting the site several times, the architect pressed a new specification on his client: The project must somehow screen the courthouse from view. Plantings or landscaping seemed a likely answer. But no one could come up with a plan that would serve year-round short of an earthworks mightier than Yorktown's battlefield, which clearly would have violated the notion of restoring the town as it had been. Roche found a solution in one of the causes of the two-fold dilemma, namely the Historic Area's boundary. That line lay just sixty feet beyond the hospital's rear foundation.

Roche suggested reconstructing the little hospital on its old site and building a modern gallery sixty-five feet away, just outside the Historic Area's limits. He would make its exterior serve more purposes than simply to contain the museum: It would conceal the offending lockup and resemble a structure often encountered in the eighteenth century, a brick garden wall. It would be laid in a variation of the familiar Flemish bond not surprisingly called garden wall bond. (Alas, the thin wall, constructed on a cement block core, required expansion joints that break up the brickwork's serene visual rhythms.) The hospital building, detached and insular as ever, would provide access to the gallery building by way of an underground tunnel.

This complex of reconstructed asylum and modern gallery is unique in its combination of elements, a singular mix of old and new. The rebuilt hospital's exterior appears to be as faithful a copy of the original building as scholarship and technology could make it, while all that appears of the sixty-two-thousand-square-foot gallery building is the brick wall. Though magnified, it looks as modest as the brick fences that surround the little family cemeteries and some gardens hereabouts. If it lacked an imposing front of columns to announce itself as a museum, that was fine with Roche, who intended it as an unobtrusive "frame for objects which mirror history."

The hospital's facade was fairly easy to ascertain because several pictures of the original building survived, including nineteenth-century photographs showing it with an added story and several wings shortly before it burned in 1885. The elements used to create the new facade were hard to find. In the 1930s the Restoration could afford the luxury of making its own bricks; clearly it would use so many that fashioning them by hand after arduously learning how by trial and error made a

ABOVE: The unique Tompion clock stands as a horological masterpiece that combines inspired design, superior materials, royal provenance and exceptional workmanship. The works are by London clockmaker Thomas Tompion, and it was made about 1699 for King William III whose monogram it bears. A small dial on the face counts seconds; two calendar apertures show the current month, its number of days and the current date. Standing just over ten feet tall it features Minerva, goddess of arts and trades, on top.

BELOW: The spiderlike orrery, which can be set up in a variety of configurations, demonstrates celestial objects circling in their orbits and rotating on their axes. Made in London by William and Samuel Jones circa 1800, this was the sort of instrument that a gentleman with scientific interests would proudly possess—assuming he was endowed both financially and intellectually—a man like George Wythe perhaps. The two large globes, one terrestrial and one celestial, made in London in the early 1780s had practical as well as decorative uses. The globe representing earth was fitted with a paper disk that enabled gentlemen of the Enlightenment to tell what time it was anywhere on earth. The celestial globe illustrated the position of the constellations—useful knowledge for both the astrologist and the navigator.

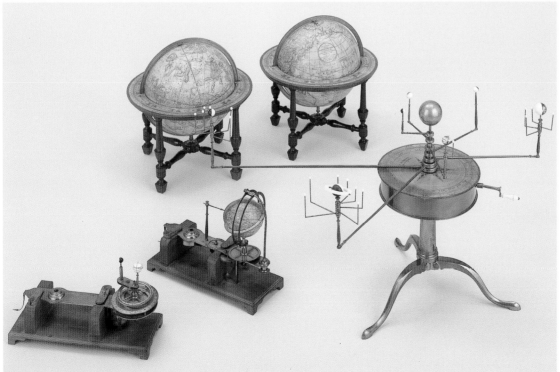

A silver-gilt horse-racing trophy, the Richmond Cup was commissioned by an English profiteer who made a fortune provisioning English armies for the Seven Years' War and then dedicated himself to buying social prominence. One of a series wrought annually for several consecutive years by Britain's finest silversmith, the cup represents monumental silverwork of the highest order—a paradigm against which all other pieces may be judged. It is also a most dramatic expression of early neoclassical design. Though this one did not reach Virginia until 1980, commemorative cups were cherished by colonial aristocrats about the time it was made, namely 1776.

certain kind of fiscal sense. But no longer, and indeed, the art of making usable brick had been lost again. Colonial Williamsburg's architectural historians combed the East for a supplier who would make bricks that looked like, well, "Williamsburg brick," their color that rare rich salmon hue, their shapes showing slight variations, their composition spiced with inclusions of lighter material added to the wet clay before firing, like raisins in rice pudding. Then every brick destined to lie exposed was selected by two architectural historians who picked over seven railroad cars of bricks by hand.

Next on the agenda was the roof, known to have been cypress-shingled in the original building. While it wasn't impossible to buy cypress logs, it was harder to turn them into sixty thousand shingles. After several false starts, a Yankee woodsman was found who could do the work by hand. Douglas Wilson had not made shingles before, but he had done every other sort of work with wood, including living off the pine forests of his native Maine, and he was willing to have a go at it. Taking eighteen-inch-long sections of log, he split them with a froe and carved each section into scores of shingles with a drawknife. Each shingle was then shaved to a slight taper toward the top and rounded at its lower end. The operation might almost have been a craft demonstration, except that Wilson worked in a garage off the beaten track and wore modern clothes. His Down East accent might have jarred aurally sensitive visitors; more important, a Colonial Williamsburg tradesman who explains what he is doing while he works gets less real work done and, as it was, Wilson spent nearly a year at his task.

The weathervane atop the cupola also took considerable work and required an odd compromise before it was installed. Silversmiths James Curtis and George Cloyed raised flat disks of copper into two halves of a sphere as big as a medicine ball, which was then gilded. Blacksmith Peter Ross made the armature and the vane itself, discovering tricks of construction as he worked. (In order to turn in the wind the slender arrow must be almost perfectly balanced. Thus antique weathervanes often have a bit of extra metal welded to one end.) For visual accuracy, Ross also forged a lightning rod, a single bar of three-quarter-inch iron that rose four stories to the top of the cupola. This is where one of the compromises came in, because modern building codes require a "lightning arrestor" in the form of an oddly shaped disk fixed at the very top of the armature. (From the ground the disk resembles a squashed version of the coronet atop the cupola of the Capitol.)

The cup's details—handles, swags, gadrooning (ornamental bands) and surmounting Angel of Victory—were cast, then heightened with punch and hammer. The whole piece was painted with powdered gold mixed in mercury and then heated; the mercury vaporized, leaving the gold in place and the gilders reeling from toxic fumes.

As for the hospital's interior, the second floor is devoted to offices while the first contains two patient's cells furnished as they would have been in the eighteenth and nineteenth centuries respectively, along with an explanatory exhibit. The rest of the first floor provides access to the basement level "tunnel"—actually an introductory exhibit hall—leading to the decorative arts museum. What are the decorative arts? One of the museum's purposes is to answer that question and to educate an interested but often daunted public. The decorative arts include painting and sculpture but go far beyond these two disciplines. They also embrace furniture, textiles, ceramics, silver, tableware and the like, homely objects and useful amenities that people chose to embellish for the simple sake of beauty. The term can be widely encompassing, an even broader concept than "interior design" in its many manifestations today.

Roche expected the visitor to lose his bearings underground; thus he had the tunnel lead to a bright two-story atrium with plantings and a forest of concrete pillars that serves as the gallery's entrance court. Ideally, art galleries have only artificial light that lacks ultraviolet rays (the part of the spectrum that bleaches natural colors), but Colonial Williamsburg's curators wanted some natural light. Roche, too, who also designed the new American Wing at the Metropolitan Museum of Art in New York, insisted that his galleries serve human visitors as well as objects—"and people need natural light." He provided it in this entrance space, which features a split staircase curving up to the Masterworks Gallery on the upper floor.

The real heroes of the Wallace Gallery are the exhibition spaces and the collections they contain. Here some eight thousand objects represent the spectrum of British and American furniture, paintings, arms, ceramics, silver and pewter, prints, textiles, clothing and more. Many were acquired decades ago during the Restoration's acquisitive heyday, but languished in storage because their dates or styles did not suit the Historic Area. One of the pieces on display, for example, is an English tall case clock of such unique splendor that it would never have found its way to any colony and could not even be legally exported from Britain today; its works were built by Thomas Tompion of London about 1699 for the newly crowned King William III. Here also is Peale's remarkable portrait of Benjamin Harrison, there Lord Dunmore's suite of hunting arms. Furniture in the Miodrag and Elizabeth Ridgely Blagojevich Gallery—much of it from the donors' collection—displays relationships between English and American regional designs. The ceramics gallery and metals gallery present definitive arrays of serving wares in stunning diversity. These exhibits in particular are works of art themselves.

In addition there are examining rooms and study alcoves, for this museum is designed to serve both casual visitors and serious students of several disciplines. Collectively and separately, the galleries within the Wallace serve as "libraries" of British and American objects. The place also contains storage ranges, a café and a 240-seat auditorium with state-of-the-art audio and video systems donated by Joseph H. and June S. Hennage, a couple from Washington who soon built a residence in Williamsburg for their retirement.

Since the gallery must preserve the objects it displays, the heating and air-conditioning systems are so finely tuned that the interior temperature may not vary more than five degrees throughout the year. It also bears mention that the passing seasons do not present the worst problems; people do. In any gallery the patron is as destructive an organism as foxing on an old print; we constantly exude moisture by the simple act of breathing; we radiate heat just by being warm-blooded; we sluff off dead skin cells, which attract tiny vermin. Surprisingly, perhaps, even in winter the central air-conditioning will do more work than the steam boilers to counteract the thousand-odd lightbulbs and people emitting 450 BTUs of heat an hour.

Williamsburg's older museum building is the Abby Aldrich Rockefeller Folk Art Museum, a memorial and monument to the doyenne of folk art appreciation in America. When Mr. Rockefeller was walking near the Inn after Abby's death in 1948, he pointed to a spot and said "I want it here!" That was that. In this rare instance he did not seek the staff's advice, nor carefully weigh their recommendations. He knew what he wanted and where he wanted it. Having found the site, he made a special gift—above and beyond his others—and separately endowed the memorial to his first wife. Though the little Georgian Revival building turned out to be awkwardly located between the Inn, swimming pool and Lodge, it has become a mecca in its own right, a destination for devotees of folk art, a panoply of painting, sculpture, metalwork and textiles created by unschooled artists of memorable creativity and skill.

During the city of Williamsburg's eclipse in the nineteenth century, American folk art flourished; early in the twentieth century Abby Rockefeller became one of the rare individuals to recognize its aesthetic and educational value. A genuine tastemaker, she began collecting this intriguing material, by definition the oeuvre of artists who lacked academic training or technique. In the end, her collection was nonpareil. (She also collected contemporary art, including work by Georgia O'Keeffe. When she learned that the painter had lived in Williamsburg as a child and was returning to receive an honorary degree at William and Mary, Mrs. Rockefeller gave an important flower painting by O'Keeffe to the College.)

ABOVE: Graphic arts in the Abby Aldrich Rockefeller Folk Art Museum—much of it collected personally by the lady herself—include works by unschooled yet gifted artists who commemorated benchmark events in the lives of rural Americans. So-called "mourning pictures" were so popular in the 19th century that Mark Twain had Huckleberry Finn remark on them satirically. Most mourning pictures were sacred to the memory of a particular person. This example commemorates Mr. Richard Waldron and expresses loving emotions with what we moderns deem as excessive sentimentality; yet this painting seems a bridge between previous conventions of folk art and expressionistic forms of modern art.

BELOW: Calligraphic creations in the *fraktur* tradition similarly documented events such as births and marriages, often offering, in German, a *curriculum vitae* of sorts as in this one that describes the course of Catharina Deibler's life.

Mrs. Rockefeller's folk art collection's undeniable merits notwithstanding, the question was discussed at length as to whether Colonial Williamsburg should pursue the lady's passion. No less a light than Kenneth Chorley broached the matter with Mr. Rockefeller when the art was on display in the Ludwell-Paradise House. It seemed clearly anachronistic within the Historic Area and Chorley suggested that if the works had been bequeathed by a "Mrs. Smith" they would have been consigned to a repository elsewhere. Troubled by the simple logic of that position, Mr. Rockefeller agreed that something would have to be done eventually. If the situation were left unresolved until he left the scene, the collection would inevitably be jettisoned one way or another. So it was up to him to devise a better solution. He seized on the idea of locating the collection outside the colonial enclave and with that established the Abby Aldrich Rockefeller Folk Art Museum in its own handsome quarters. Here, the building and its collection are no more anachronistic than the Regency-style Inn or the modern-functional Lodge.

Mr. Rockefeller's solution turns out to have been a reasonable one, since expertise in the decorative arts generally has become a forte of Colonial Williamsburg. One might even argue that to exclude folk art here would be contrary to good sense. In any event, the folk art museum has become a perennial favorite, especially at Christmastime, when its collection of nineteenth-century dollhouses and toys goes on display. Perhaps more significant, folk art has gained recognition, even respectability, by virtue of its having received the Williamsburg imprimatur. Published reports that the museum purchased a fruit vendor's charming advertisement, a watermelon rustically carved from a log and colored with house paint, made wooden melons the rage in some circles for a time. Since 1939, thousands of objects have been added to the collection, and special exhibitions are mounted each year. In the last analysis, Colonial Williamsburg owns a folk art collection of the first magnitude and has made substantial contributions to the serious appreciation of great native traditions, even though they are not completely in accord with Colonial Williamsburg's chosen period. The institution and the town proved big enough to accommodate nineteenth-century art as well as earlier pieces.

If there was something tentative in the genesis of the Abby Aldrich Rockefeller Folk Art Museum, and something museologically utilitarian in the planning of the DeWitt Wallace Decorative Arts Museum, the crown jewel of latter-day Williamsburg is visionary and atavistic, memorializing and declarative, antique and futuristic. Quite simply, it is a compound: the Bruton Heights School Education Center, a 30-acre campus comprising a central quadrangle of four buildings containing more than 150,000 square feet of interior space dedicated to the manifold tasks and pursuits of a modern museum. Funded by donations from Ambassador Walter H. and Leonore Annenberg, Jean and Bill Lane, Abby and George O'Neill, Franklin W. and Gladys Clark, the National Endowment for the Humanities, and the DeWitt Wallace Fund for Colonial Williamsburg, it stands as a kind of contemporary satellite community adjacent to and supportive of the antique village.

This campus is visionary in its architecture and its specifics: The two new buildings in the complex, the John D. Rockefeller, Jr., Library and the DeWitt Wallace Collections and Conservation Building, display post-modern exteriors. Inside, they contain state-of-the-art equipment of all kinds from the library's archival-standard environmental controls—for temperature, humidity and light levels—to the Velcro-sealed storage frames that hold old fabrics flat (to avoid physical stress) and nearly dust-free.

The complex is a throwback in the new buildings' use of brick, and more especially in the restored Bruton Heights School building itself. This is the school that Abby Rockefeller herself took such an interest in. Opened in September, 1940 to replace the dilapidated school that had served

OPPOSITE: An institution of parts, Colonial Williamsburg became a repository of splendid objects, a museum first of Virginiana, then of Americana, then of folk art and decorative arts as a whole. Many possessions that did not suit the Historic Area in terms of geography or time now may be displayed in two special museums. The gilded Indian-on-horseback weather vane, a unique piece made of pine and sheet iron late in the 19th century, stands in the Abby Aldrich Rockefeller Folk Art Museum, which broadened CW's ken as has the DeWitt Wallace Decorative Arts Museum.

the city's African-American children as best it could, Bruton Heights School became a model school and community center for blacks in Williamsburg and surrounding rural areas until it was desegregated along with other public schools in Williamsburg in the late 1960s.

It is a memorial, as a derelict school building that was declared obsolete and too expensive for renovation by the school board, and then rescued by a new owner and given a new lease on life. That building was restored, first by having superfluous additions removed; then its original central physical plant was renovated so that part of it contains classrooms again, albeit mostly for Colonial Williamsburg employees. The school's auditorium, returned as nearly as possible to its original look, is equipped with state-of-the-art sound and video for meetings, lectures and theatical presentations. A permanent exhibition area was installed off the foyer to display photographs and artifacts from the school's thirty-odd years as an integral part of the local black community.

In sum, this is the study center of a history museum, after all. While its scholars, librarians, and curators focus on the past, its purpose is forward-looking: to serve Colonial Williamsburg in perpetuating Mr. Rockefeller's original chosen mission, "That the Future May Learn from the Past."

The Bruton Heights School building itself may be the most ordinary and easily comprehended structure of the four within the campus. This is a multipurpose building, with the auditorium, the classrooms, seminar rooms and meeting rooms for the Foundation and public groups. Here are generous office suites for such departments as Archaeological Research, Architectural Research, and Historical Research, and a drafting room for Architecture and Engineering. Here, too, is the media center for Williamsburg in the electronic age. The old gym now contains a Colonial Williamsburg Productions video studio, with a digital sound lab and satellite link for the electronic field trips that bring schoolchildren via television from all over America. A new addition to the old building was built to serve a photography studio large enough to accommodate virtually any object in need of an archival portrait likely to come its way—the lining of General Washington's dining tent, for example.

The John D. Rockefeller, Jr., Library is a sublime home for scholars, and perhaps the building for which there was the most crying need: Before it opened, there was a library for the Foundation, to be sure, but every department in Colonial Williamsburg also had a little library of sorts, and they were scattered all over town. Now there is one central library, manned by a professional staff, who provide the last word in on-line cataloging, networking, visual storage and rare book facilities. The only edifice in Williamsburg that bears the founder's name—he was averse to anything that approached self-aggrandizement—it was designed by Perry Dean Rogers and Partners of Boston, the descendant firm of Perry, Shaw and Hepburn, the group that did the first architectural work for Mr. Rockefeller.

As Samuel Johnson once said "The Library is the Heart of the University," this is the heart of Williamsburg scholarship. It contains 72,000 volumes, 12,500 rare books, 150 manuscript collections comprising 50,000 manuscript pages dating largely from the eighteenth century. There are 50,000 architectural drawings, 6,000 reels of microfilm, 10,000 microfiches, and 500,000 images, most of them photographs. Its general collections provide comprehensive coverage of pertinent fields of learning: architecture, archaeology, decorative arts, eighteenth-century history, enlightenment economics, politics, social life, historic trades and more.

The book collections in particular contain treasures: a copy of the first cookbook printed in America, E. Smith's *The Compleat Housewife,* published in 1742 by William Parks, one of Williamsburg's celebrated printers. There is also the first history published in America, William Stith's *The History of the First Discovery and Settlement of Virginia,* also printed by Parks. A rare copy of George Washington's *Journal* is here, along with Patrick Henry's original manuscript of his resolves against the Stamp Act of 1765. There is also a Bible, the gift of William Perry of Perry,

ABOVE: Published in 1755 as Britain girded for the French and Indian War, this six-foot map played a major role in history: diplomats used a copy of it when writing the Treaty of Paris, which formalized American Independence. It was drawn by John Mitchell, a native-born physician and botanist who fled Virginia's climate for London's scientific circles and who sponsored Mark Catesby as a member of the Royal Society.

Psittacus Carolinensis.
The Parrot of Carolina

BELOW: Mark Catesby, America's first artist-naturalist and the painter of this "Parrot of Carolina," spent much of the 1710s and 1720s studying New World wildlife (He gave John Custis, the town's most famous gardener, the cutting for his rare pink dogwood.) He devoted eighteen years to etching the plates for his magnum opus on natural history, all of which, like the Mitchell map, were colored by hand. These superb prints are now in the Wallace Museum prints and maps collection.

Shaw and Hepburn, which was printed by the eighteenth-century English printer and type-founder, John Baskerville, whose namesake typeface is a standard among American designers and publishers. While many of these documents are pored over frequently by Williamsburg staff, CW proudly makes its facilities available to visiting scholars from virtually anywhere.

Designed as a state-of-the-art library building, it, too, was erected with the future in mind. Its load-bearing capacity, for example, is more than enough to handle the weight of conventional stacks; if compact shelving is installed in the future, the building will be able to take the added weight. Also, it contains sufficient space to accommodate normal collection growth for fifteen years, and the building was designed for easy expansion thereafter.

Next door, the DeWitt Wallace Collections and Conservation Building, the largest structure in the complex, is a paradigm as well, a facility built with lengthy and detailed input from the curators and conservators who would work there. Indeed, it seems to manifest a model of collaboration between the professionals who study, care for and explain the thousands upon thousands of objects: paintings, textiles, arms, chests, chairs, goblets, spoons, testers, chamber pots, harness brasses and Lord knows whatever else, including the largest collection of English pewter outside of Britain.

For decades, the conservation, curatorial and storage facilities had been as awkwardly evolved as they were highly dispersed; they were the height of the Rube Goldberg tradition. Textiles were conserved in a converted motel on floors that sagged. Curators performed research at stand-up work stations for lack of space. With the prospect of a new building or buildings on the spacious Bruton Heights site, the participants were encouraged to think out their needs and ideals from the ground up. In the end they agreed that the benefits of consolidating storage, conservation and curation far outweighed the merits of independence. John O. Sands, former director of administration in the Collections and Museums Division, explained the process in the Foundation's quarterly journal:

What had been somewhat inchoate expressions of need began to take on very tangible form. Curators and conservators measured and counted artifacts, learned once more to compute in cubic feet and make them mean something, and thought about how much space was enough without being unrealistic. They called colleagues around the country to learn what the latest thinking was on the design of curatorial storage equipment and conservation laboratories. They researched environmental systems, including the currently acceptable limits of temperature and humidity variation. . . .

A lot of thought was given to what the implications of what activities needed to be in adjacent areas and what the implications might be of putting them together. Did we want storage and labs intermingled, for instance with the associated potential for increased risk of damage by fumes, fire or other mishaps? What about storage and curators?

We met. We talked. We generated notebooks about five inches thick with all the specifications and requirements . . . We talked some more. Schematic designs went back and forth and we couldn't seem to get anywhere. Wallace Gusler, then director of conservation, and I both wrestled with the problem without seeming to come to a resolution. And then Wallace decided to go off and play with blocks.

He had the furniture conservation lab cut wooden blocks to scale, each representing the floor space and height required to accomplish a specific function. The result was a crazy quilt of pieces that looked as though they had fallen off a truck full of scrap lumber. Wallace stacked them up to solve the bulk of the problems for the conservators and went away happy. I came into the playpen, took it all apart and stacked it to solve the problems of curators and their collections. I went away equally happy and then equally dismayed to find that Wallace had reconfigured the pile again. No video game could possibly have offered the challenge or the frustration of this three-dimensional jigsaw puzzle, as we deconstructed our old ideas and rebuilt them over and over. After about two weeks however, Wallace and I found that each was making fewer and fewer changes to the other's scheme. At that point we drew the whole design out on paper and sent it with some trepidation to Massachusetts. To our surprise that basic layout turned out to be pretty much what we ended up building.

In essence it was a single building designed from the inside out. In the center are storage ranges, some of them rooms as big as airplane hangars, and all of them fitted with useful gadgetry: huge floor-to-ceiling automated doors, and shelves nine by eleven feet square to store fabrics flat (thus saving them the strains of folding or hanging), fitted with curtains with Velcro seals to keep out dust. For paintings, there are vertical screens of heavy wire mesh set a foot apart and mounted on wheels to slide in and out singly for easy access. Arms and weapons are hung on suitable racks; furniture is stored on two-level carts and dollies to minimize handling.

One reason to put the storage ranges in the middle of the building was for optimum security; another was to let the support spaces—offices, laboratories and such—serve as insulating buffers against Virginia's unamenable climate extremes. The building proved to be so efficient in terms of atmospheric stability that when the infamous ice storm of 1998 brought two days of power outage along with bitter cold, the storage spaces were barely affected and the temperature varied by only a couple of degrees. Locating storage in the building's core also allowed offices to be placed on the sunny sides of the building, and laboratories to be on the north side where conservators have the advantage of steady northern light.

The roof was designed to shed water in every direction from above the storage areas. Below, the storage ranges lacked ceilings, so that any roof leaks would be noticed immediately. No water systems or pipes go anywhere near the storage areas for fear of some accidental damage; the emergency sprinkler system's pipes are normally empty, lest they eventually leak or misfunction. As for the laboratories, they are up-to-the-minute, with high-efficiency ventilation hoods to remove chemical fumes, vacuum chambers, x-ray machines, tubs for washing textiles in de-ionized water, and a host of other space-age amenities.

The fourth building in the complex, a small cottage, originally served Bruton Heights as the home economics center, including domestic spaces where students practised theories learned in now-missing classrooms, and a demonstration kitchen and laundry. Moved a little distance and refurbished, it now serves as a guest house for visting scholars, a fitting facility that restates Williamsburg's hospitality to experts from elsewhere who will benefit from the extraordinary collections and resources of Mr. Rockefeller's contrivance.

The heart of any museum lies in its collections, the objects which it has come to possess. In Williamsburg that means roughly 5,000 pieces of furniture, 10,000 ceramic and glass objects, 1,500 firearms, 10,000 machines and tools, 1,500 paintings, 5,000 prints and maps, 7,000 examples of textiles, 7,000 rare books, 126 musical instruments, 6,000 pieces of metalware, 3,500 costumes and accessories, a dozen period vehicles from handcarts to a blue landau, 60 million archaeological artifacts, and much more. In short, Williamsburg's collections represent the entirety—the chaos in the microcosm, if you will—of an eighteenth-century town and then some.

During the early years the Restoration acquired art and furnishings in a positively prodigal manner. Mr. Rockefeller himself was a masterful acquisitor, corralling such icons as Gilbert Stuart's portraits of Washington, Jefferson and Madison with typical dispatch. He bought the first, then saw the second over a friend's mantel and asked her to bequeath it to his patriotic cause, where it would be cared for and appreciated in perpetuity. The third portrait was in the Metropolitan Museum of Art in New York, one of his family's annual beneficiaries. In a letter to the director, he wrote that the portrait could be displayed proudly in Williamsburg's colonial Capitol building, adding simply that Mrs. Rockefeller joined him in hoping they could continue to support the Metropolitan as generously in the future as they had in the past. His tactic worked.

Along with Dr. Goodwin, two people, more than any others, were responsible for laying the foundation of today's collections: William Perry, who acquired the first furnishings, and Susan Nash, who supervised their use in the exhibition buildings. Together they traveled to England where they scouted out great antiques. Rockefeller and his wife then joined them to assay the best pieces of art, furniture and furnishings that could be had in London. Collecting according to criteria that would have made a pack rat proud, they came back with enough to furnish a Governor's Palace, and more (albeit not in a fashion that would stand the test of time, as we shall see).

When James L. Cogar became the first curator in 1931, the motive for collecting was simple enough. Once the first phase of restoration and reconstruction had begun, Colonial Williamsburg was compelled to either furnish the buildings or settle for a village of empty shells. The early method was understandable too: Perry and Nash bought eighteenth-century objects of English, French and American origins, delighting in acquiring especially fine pieces regardless of whether these might ever have found their way to colonial Virginia. The result was a fabulous, if somewhat diffuse, selection, according to later generations of collectors and curators who refined the Restoration's purposes. Advances in scholarship and a clearer sense of what Williamsburg should be eventually led Colonial Williamsburg to cull from the exhibition buildings furnishings that were either out-of-place or out-of-time. Only those objects that could have been made in Williamsburg or brought there sometime during the eighteenth century would remain in period buildings by the last quarter of the twentieth.

OPPOSITE: The entrance hall of Governor Botetourt's Palace was decorated to impress the visitor with his wealth and power as symbolized by the royal coat of arms over the hearth, the unfurled flags and the huge number of sabers, pistols and flintlock rifles abundantly displayed. For years, CW's scholars wondered how it was possible to display as many weapons as contemporary letters and journals mentioned, until the senior curator Graham Hood found telltale brackets in the hall of the Botetourt family seat in England. These were replicated, the Palace was "reinterpreted" and once again the entrance hall is a place of mighty display.

Thus, over the years, much of what had formerly been in various period rooms became consigned to storage. The result was an embarrassment of warehoused riches that led Williamsburg's fathers to make a choice: Either they could dispose of myriad objects or find a rationale for keeping them without violating the integrity of the Historic Area buildings. The dilemma was finally resolved with the decision to build an exhibition building whose displays need not be confined to one time or style, namely the Wallace Museum.

In the meantime, Williamsburg had amassed diverse and superb holdings and become celebrated for them, thanks in large part to John Graham II, curatorial mastermind for two decades starting in 1950. Working in broad strokes (and sometimes buying in large lots), he is remembered for building the collections to a state of excellence. Graham also enhanced the institution's standing by augmenting the staff and hiring the first of its curators to specialize in given areas—metalworks expert John Davis, and John C. Austin, who found himself charged with the enviable task of refining the broad-ranging ceramics collection. For the most part this meant filling in the gaps, occasionally paying the freight by deaccessioning redundant material. To accomplish this required an encyclopedic knowledge of the field and a reputation for knowledge, discrimination and integrity in the eyes of private collectors, dealers and competitors. By the time Colonial Williamsburg published Austin's catalogue of its Chelsea material, it had only one rival in this type of porcelain in the world, the British Museum. Further, Williamsburg could boast of possessing "one of the finest collections of English seventeenth and eighteenth century pottery and porcelain ever assembled."

Curator John Austin, now retired, gathered one of the world's great collections of 18th-century porcelains for Williamsburg. Thus the mantel in the Palace's front parlor can display birds like the set of "11 Chelsea china Figures" mentioned in the 1770 inventory of Governor Botetourt's possessions.

~

What makes a collection great? Dollar values aside, the worth of a group of objects derives from its status as a collection per se. To be simpleminded about it, an art or history museum's collection can be said to resemble a mechanic's toolbox: If it lacks sufficient breadth it will be as limited as a toolbox that contains only wrenches of one size. But the collection that includes the full spectrum of objects in a chosen medium can reveal the history of an entire form of human endeavor. Held in a museum, it becomes a resource for the serious student, for the historian investigating an ancillary question and for the layman curious enough to be moved by the variety of utilitarian and creative expressions found within that medium.

At Williamsburg, all the various collections contribute to an understanding of this place in colonial times. Take, for example, the ceramics collection and the way in which it helps Williamsburg to fulfill its evolved function as a comprehensive history museum. First it provides objects for the period buildings, thus supplying the specific means to furnish the Palace bedchambers and reception halls as they would have appeared during Lord Botetourt's years here. Similarly, the breadth of the collection allows for the display of seasonal settings at different times of year. It also permits the representative furnishing of lesser houses, from that of gentleman-and-scholar George Wythe to those of entrepreneur Benjamin Powell and artisan James Geddy. Decorated accessories and serving ware were part and parcel of eighteenth-century life among the gentry.

The posset pot, china basket, three-tiered centerpiece, animal-shaped soup tureen and decorative figurines graced aristocratic houses, and such amenities were aspired to by every middling family in an age of rising consumerism and, for some, leisure. Further, surviving examples of these fragile objects reflect their owners' taste and the period's aesthetic sense. Porcelain objects reveal aspects of their time.

Other disciplines often complicate matters for curators working with collections and exhibitions. Our awareness today of the danger presented by lead poisoning raises questions about the possible deleterious effects that may be associated with the chemical constituents of everyday objects. Both pewter and ceramic tablewares made in the eighteenth century contained significant quantities of lead in the formulas. Comparative bio-chemical studies of human remains elsewhere reveal that pros-perous or middling colonists who ate off pewter and some types of glazed ceramics were poisoned by lead absorbed from the vessels. People at the bottom of the economic ladder ate from wooden vessels. They may have lived longer as a result.

Scholars of "material culture," who study the past through objects, fondly speak of corroded tools, chipped pots and even shards as "documents" that may be "read" just as one might read handwritten drafts of the Declaration of Independence. For example, the varied plates and bowls known as "Chinese export" demonstrate the stages of cross-fertilization that occurred between the Orient and Occident over the course of centuries. Wares first imported to Europe in any quantity were exotic and popular; English potters, predictably, copied them to provide the growing market with cheaper items in the same

style. As trade continued and grew, Oriental potters then invented their own methods of serving a larger clientele. They adorned platters and dinnerware with images of European country scenes; their hunters riding to hounds had Oriental features since that was how the Chinese porcelain painters knew to make faces. Artisans in England's Chelsea and Holland's Delft districts in turn copied these stylized decorations, variously in porcelain and earthenware, sometimes with a coun-terfeiter's intent, sometimes just to offer a cheaper line of goods to less affluent buyers.

In another venue of elegance, namely needlework, a crewel stag leaps among verdant mounds in an 18th-century English bedcover that was once part of a larger set of bed hangings.

For the collector today the subtle difference between Oriental export porcelain and a contem-porary English copy of this Chinese ware is difficult to learn unless the objects can be seen simul-taneously—in other words, in a collection. Thus some people visit museums to increase their dis-crimination, understanding and appreciation. To the economic historian studying commerce in the 1750s, discovering where a given Chinese style was copied can indicate the direction and extent of trade routes. To test a thesis, the scholar examines a good collection and consults a curator like John Austin, a specialist with perhaps only a dozen peers, who can pinpoint the origin of specific objects by virtue of his experience and on the basis of objects in his museum.

To the schoolchild or undergraduate, experiencing objects from far away in space or time is a fun-damental part of education. To the visitor who is not a serious student of history or artifacts but who

Made for a Masonic lodge in Williamsburg this unique chair rests once again in the city after a two-century absence. During the Revolution it was removed for safekeeping to a lodge in Edenton, North Carolina, and remained there until 1983. One of the few pieces signed by a Williamsburg master, it was made by Benjamin Bucktrout, who worked with Anthony Hay. Monumental in the extreme, the chair was designed for ceremonial use, not comfort. It features a bust of poet-diplomat Matthew Prior (a hero among Masons) as well as a veritable toolkit of Masonic heraldry.

just likes beautiful things, examining an array of like objects is an aesthetic experience well worth the cost in time or money. To understand the value of a collection to laymen, consider a parallel between the figurines made in the factories of eighteenth-century Chelsea and modern athletes across the Thames at Wimbledon. To watch the goings-on in center court is to see tennis perfected beyond the realm of simple exercise; it is to witness the best. So it is with these finest examples of soft-paste porcelain, the most advanced plastic medium of its time. Chelsea figures were molded, then painted with certain glazes and fired. They were then glazed and fired again and again, each time with colors that cured at lower temperatures, so as not to disturb the previous ones. These objects possess special beauty and a kind of intrigue. Colonial Williamsburg's array of masquerade figures displays the acme of a whimsical and antique art form at its most expressive.

By a similar token, to use a vacuum pump that George Wythe might have owned lets the scholar of science replicate the old investigator's work. To view spittle under an eighteenth-century microscope is to see the "animacules" that electrified members of the Royal Society and marked the beginning of a whole new realm of "natural philosophy." Some collections exist to serve a specific intellectual, scientific or quasi-practical purpose, others to delight the mind. Some collections have several reasons to be.

The notion that a collection has a particular purpose cuts several surprising ways and could eventually be responsible for deaccessioning some possessions as celebrated as the Gilbert Stuart portraits that Rockefeller adroitly acquired. Were Colonial Williamsburg solely a museum of early American art, these paintings of three early presidents might be sacrosanct. Were it simply a museum of the eighteenth century, it might proudly display them along with chamber pots from Maine and artifacts from recently salvaged Spanish treasure galleons. But this is a very special museum. Its specialty came to be defined in two dimensions, space and time. It was interested first in Virginia's capital before 1780, then by extension in American art and history at large. For decades those of its possessions that did not suit the primary locus were consigned to storage. The addition of the Wallace Museum allowed the display of these wider interests and foretold the broadening of Colonial Williamsburg's purview.

Nonetheless, one day, hypothetically, Williamsburg might consider selling the Stuarts which, after all, were painted long after the town's late eighteenth-century eclipse. While it seems apt to display the "founding fathers," these pictures really relate to the post-Revolutionary period. Remaining very valuable, under possible circumstances, they could be sold to pay for some as yet undiscovered treasures that might suit this museum even more perfectly: a portrait of Jefferson the law student in George Wythe's study with his mentor say, or a group of burgesses that includes Henry and Washington.

What are the chances of such a discovery? Put it this way: Stranger things have happened, and the possibility that they will again is part of the lure of this business. Building collections is a byzantine affair, requiring the eye of a connoisseur, the nose of a bloodhound and the sang-froid of a horse trader. English-born Graham Hood, who succeeded John Graham as chief curator and vice president in charge of the collections in 1971, approached it all with a certain calm: "I'm not one of the Grand Acquisitors," he said. Nonetheless, he made some grand acquisitions of singular importance to this specialized museum, finding prizes variously by strokes of luck, inspired sleuthing and plain old "coppering"—working the turf like a bobby his beat in his native England. Some of these feats happened quickly and simply; others took ages. While some acquisitions have been outright purchases and others gifts, almost all the transactions have been made with an eye to the Internal Revenue Code.

Long before Colonial Williamsburg found its stride, virtually every substantial gift to nonprofit

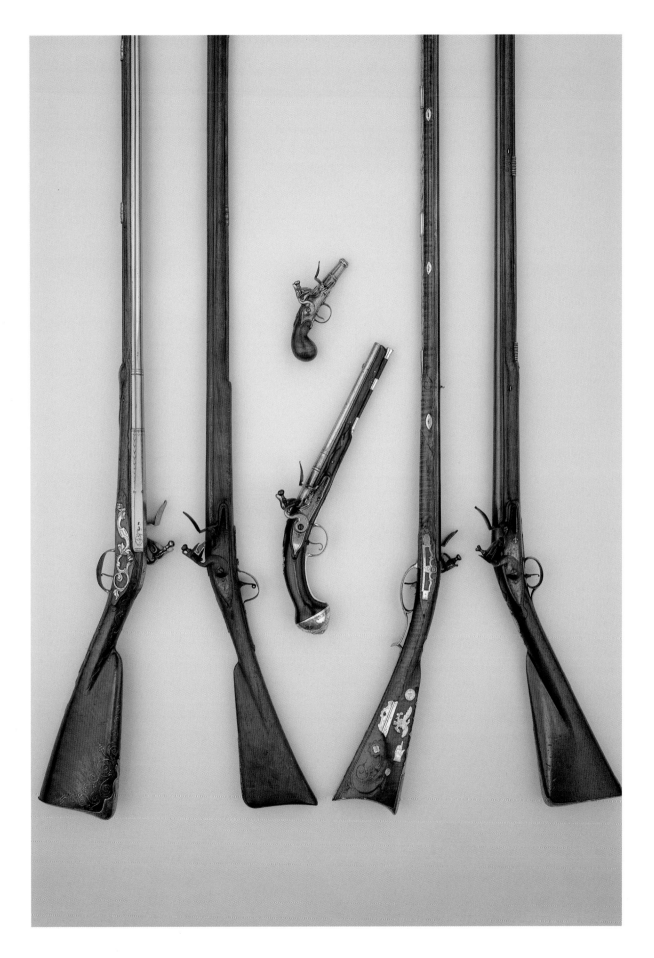

As 18th-century weapons often embodied high fashion (as well as sophisticated technology), they have their place in the Masterworks Gallery of the Decorative Arts Museum. Left to right: 1 An elaborate English fowling piece or shotgun; 2 An Indian trade gun by London maker John Bumford; 3 (above) A small pocket pistol made in London around 1700 by John Brush who later moved to Williamsburg; 4 (below) An early 18th-century silver-mounted English pistol; 5 A Virginia long rifle of diminutive size made for a boy or woman ca. 1810; and 6 A London fowling piece of the "middling sort" also made by John Bumford.

To judge from sales of reproductions, *Baby in Red Chair* is one of the most popular objects d'art in the collection that Abby Aldrich Rockefeller amassed. Possessing an ineffably native charm, its painter remains a mystery. Despite much research, nothing has been learned about its origins; the best educated guesses assign it to Pennsylvania between 1810 and 1830.

institutions in America meant a tax break for the donor. The framers of the Internal Revenue Act intended this when it was enacted back in 1913. They encouraged people to support bona fide educational and charitable institutions by declaring that the value of their gifts (in cash or property) was deductible from gross income. Thus the donor reduces his taxable receipts, and perhaps finding himself in a lower bracket, may even be taxed at a lower percentage rate. Churches, colleges, charity groups and performing arts companies as well as museums have received many gifts in part because donors saved money overall through the deduction device. The many extraordinary art collections to which the public has access in museums—not the least of them here—owe their existence in large part to what some tax critics periodically and shortsightedly call a loophole. As of this writing, the Internal Revenue Act has achieved a purpose its authors intended in this regard: doubtless starting with Mr. Rockefeller himself, Williamsburg's benefactors have taken advantage of write-offs, as have the benefactors of every other museum.

Some donors have had a one-of-a-kind antique appraised, then sold it to Colonial Williamsburg, for, say, half its appraised value. They were then entitled to deduct the balance as a charitable gift since in fact and effect they gave away that much of its value (or its likely sale price at auction). The mechanics of the deduction are understood by all: donors, institutional recipients, the IRS, even dealers. Witness Colonial Williamsburg's acquisition of a small treasure trove which a dealer felt ought to come here. This array of objects included one of two known copies of an antique map and an almost equally rare print. The centerpiece was the curious portrait of Mary Sabina, a South American girl whose mixed ancestry manifested itself in her pied complexion. It was painted in Cartagena in 1740, the year Governor Gooch led a military expedition to that Spanish stronghold near the apex of South America. The painting, by an unknown Englishman, is a lovely primitive with a crude cartouche framing a caption for the edification of Enlightenment men interested in human genetics, a science of rising interest in the expansionist eighteenth century.

Because of its style, date and socioscientific content, the dealer who had the picture believed it properly belonged in Williamsburg. When Hood saw it he agreed, although the museum could not afford the legitimate asking price. Tax considerations enabled Colonial Williamsburg to get the whole package. Hood met one of the dealer's clients, an industrialist who'd made a killing that year and faced an astonishingly high tax bill. By donating to Colonial Williamsburg the price of the independently appraised prints, maps and portrait, the businessman was entitled to reduce his obligation to the IRS. The same stroke enabled Colonial Williamsburg to buy the objects, while the dealer earned a tidy commission for his trouble. Everybody won, even the IRS, if one assumes that as an instrumentality of the federal government its larger purpose is to advance the well-being of the nation, and one way to do that is by enabling its cultural institutions to grow and thrive.

A longer quest began some years ago when Hood received a letter from a Virginia gentleman who wished to sell a portrait of an English peer known to have been a friend of William Byrd II. The painting had hung at Westover plantation, whence it went to another family's seat through one of those many marriages that made most members of Virginia's gentry cousins of some degree. Mention of the Westover connection piqued Hood's curiosity, but the painting didn't sound as though it was worth a special trip. He arranged to view the portrait the next time he happened to be in Richmond and indeed it turned out to be an "undistinguished portrait of an undistinguished knight." But hanging on the same wall was Charles Willson Peale's portrait of Benjamin Harrison, the unexpected sight of which almost curled Hood's graying hair faster than a wigmaker's iron. Here was an American master's vision of an eminent Virginian, a delegate to the First Continental Congress, Speaker of the General Assembly and more.

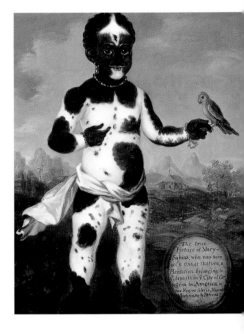

A special find: the "True Picture of Mary-Sabina, who was born oct 12, 1736, at Matuna, a Plantation belonging to the Jesuits in the City of Cartegena in America of two Negroe Slaves." The anonymous portrait was painted in Cartagena about 1740, the year that Governor Gooch led an ill-starred military expedition to that South American port. It is notable for its coincidental link to Virginia history, for its charming naivete of style and for its visual and written information that reflects intellectual interests of the time.

This Harrison portrait had been "lost" to the art world; its whereabouts unknown—although one obscure catalogue had ironically and inaccurately listed it among the Williamsburg Restoration's holdings, where it certainly deserved to be. Nonetheless, no one here had laid eyes on the signed and dated canvas before Hood. Though its surface was dimmed by the dirt of two centuries, he recognized it as "a masterpiece of colonial portraiture [that] summarizes perfectly the characteristics of the Virginia gentry."

Covering his excitement, and perhaps stalling for time to collect his wits, Hood learned that his host was descended from a cousin of Benjamin Harrison, who signed the Decleration of Independence. But that was neither here nor there since, after all, W. Gordon Harrison, Jr., was offering for sale a picture of the unrelated and undistinguished Englishman. For that he wanted substantially more than Hood thought it would be worth to Colonial Williamsburg, not that he thought it was worth very much at all. But because he knew the Peale might fetch ten times as much at auction, he felt an obligation to learn more about both pictures for the following reasons: All kinds of people come to own precious antiques, and Hood believed the ethical museum deals with different sorts in different ways. There are idle inheritors who sell off family treasures to support lavish life-styles; and there are those whose only passion in life is buying and selling *objets d'art*. Still others assume that whatever they have inherited is common stuff. Indeed, there are unscrupulous dealers who work the tea-party circuit like sharks. Spotting a great antique in a naive owner's parlor, such a buyer may befriend the gentleman or lady by offering an inflated price for a scrapbook of Currier & Ives scenes clipped from magazines. The grateful owner later parts with a masterpiece for a song when the new "friend" offers to "take it off his hands." Still stunned at seeing Benjamin Harrison's lost portrait, Hood wondered whether the owner was asking an inflated price for the picture of the English peer because he was being set up by a would-be buyer who had offered an absurdly high price for the lesser picture in order to steal the Peale in the bargain. He needn't have worried.

While Mr. Harrison had not made a profession of trading in heirlooms, neither was he a babe in the woods. He knew the Peale was a masterpiece, and he had not planned to sell it. But he had been offered the handsome price for Byrd's friend by an august institution with very special interests; the painting suited their venue and collection in the same way a portrait of Patrick Henry suited Colonial Williamsburg's. It was plainly worth more to that institution than to Williamsburg. (This raises the matter of vagaries in art pricing. The "fair market value" of any precious object depends on such variables as economic conditions and even the circumstances of its sale or purchase. For example, furniture prices can rise or fall with the value of the dollar. Similarly, a library of rare books to be liquidated by a debt-ridden estate brings a fraction of the price the same books would cost someone trying to create the collection from scratch.) Satisfied that the Peale was not going to vanish overnight, Hood asked Mr. Harrison to let him know if he ever wanted to find a permanent home for it.

In due time, the inheritor and his far-flung family decided to sell the portrait, and a series of negotiations began. It proved relatively easy to agree on a price and terms, but the talks ripened just as Colonial Williamsburg entered "one of its poor periods" and the matter was tabled. Reopening the discussion a couple of years later, the principals agreed on a schedule of several annual payments in deference to the tax code, only to have the timetable scotched by their lawyers. Finally, when the acquisitions budget was flush again, Hood reopened the negotiations—casually as an apparent afterthought in a letter about another matter. New terms were proposed and Hood finally got the prize Peale, for more than ten times the asking price of the English peer, nine years after first laying eyes on it.

Other of Hood's acquisitions resulted from the wandering hunt, often with Wallace Gusler, an antiquarian polymath who has served Williamsburg as gunsmith, furniture curator and conservator.

Charles Willson Peale personified the Virginia aristocracy in this portrait of Benjamin Harrison of Brandon, a member of the first Council of the Commonwealth of Virginia and of the House of Delegates which evolved out of the House of Burgesses after Independence. (This Benjamin Harrison was a cousin of Benjamin Harrison of Berkeley, signer of the Declaration of Independence and great-grandfather of the U.S. president of the same name.) A truly great portrait, it combines a sense of the inner man with his clear likeness and graceful accoutrements in a composition of serene elegance.

(They seemed an unlikely team: Gusler was a Virginia mountainman and native genius who with barely a high-school diploma practically wrote the book on antique gunsmiths and literally wrote the first authoritative volume on eastern Virginia's colonial furniture. Hood, an elegant Briton, had attended the same grammar school as Shakespeare, then Oxford and the Courtauld Institute as a protégé of Sir Anthony Blunt, the royal art advisor who was later unmasked as a master spy.)

On one of Hood and Gusler's expeditions the two found themselves following the scent of an "Irish" table of special interest. The hunt was in rural Virginia where xenophobic folk were wont to steer accented Englishmen the wrong way when they ask directions to the farmsteads of widowed neighbors. But Gusler spoke their language in their own accent and idiom, and on this trip he convinced a postmaster of his bona fides and of the fact that a local lady was expecting them. The museum men followed a winding road through the woods as it went from macadam to dirt, then narrowed to nothing but a track across a cornfield. Following it farther, they came to a Federal-era farmhouse that "looked as if it had been cleaved with a cake knife" and half of it removed elsewhere. A flock of chickens scratched in the yard and roosted in the carcasses of cars. Many windows in the house were boarded up and Hood suspected the place was uninhabited save for a tribe of cats coming and going through cellar holes. Then a woman clad in khaki overalls emerged from the ruin and accosted them, directing them inside and ushering them down a hallway blocked by a wheelbarrow and a broken stove.

The collectors knew at a glance that the table was not Irish. It was a genuine Virginia antique, the work of one of the cabinetmakers whose oeuvre Gusler had painstakingly studied for his treatise, *Furniture of Williamsburg and Eastern Virginia, 1710–1790,* which had helped revolutionize appreciation of southern furniture. He went to examine it closely while Hood made conversation with their hostess, who proved to be as kindly as her wardrobe and domicile were rustic. He stepped over to look at a picture on the mantel when she cried out "Stop, Mr. Hood!" and he jumped back wondering "what code of Virginia honor I'd transgressed." She apologized profusely: "That hearth is unsound. Two cats fell through last week."

Saved from bodily harm, Hood was then surprised that Gusler embarked on a conversational tangent about guns and the woman said, yes, she had an old long rifle. She retrieved it from a hiding place, along with an engraved powder horn. Both were treasures in the collectors' eyes, artfully made utilitarian antiques from Virginia. After conferring in the yard among the chickens, the collectors offered the impoverished inheritor generous prices for the table and powder horn. The gentlewoman accepted but wouldn't even discuss a price for the prized rifle. "That's not for sale," she said, shooing a goat off the rickety porch, "That was my Daddy's. Things are going to have to get pretty bad before I part with that."

It is telling that the rumor the collectors chased down involved an "Irish" table that turned out to be as "Virginian" as salty ham. Time was when no quality eighteenth-century furniture was attributed to the South; the experts, most of them Northerners, insisted all the best work came from Europe, typically England, or anywhere north and east of Delaware. Studying ledgers, newspapers and other written records, Gusler realized that Williamsburg had a community of master craftsmen in residence, and further, that people of taste like the Byrds and Jefferson bought entire room suites from them. Studying every stick in the Williamsburg collections, and tracking down Virginia pieces of ironclad provenance elsewhere, the self-taught antiquarian came to recognize the styles of individual shops, such as those of Anthony Hay and Benjamin Bucktrout. In some respects Gusler's analysis involved the more abstruse subtleties of traditional connoisseurship like line and style. Beyond that, he learned to read regional and then local accents in types of woods and construction techniques.

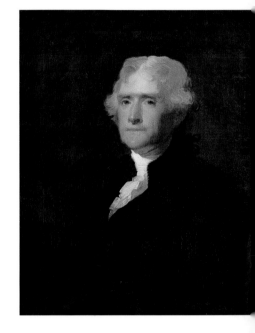

Gilbert Stuart, painter of several presidents, limned Thomas Jefferson's life portrait in 1805. He made several copies of the famous picture and this one, which was owned by President Madison before Colonial Williamsburg acquired it, may be the original. The Foundation also owns Stuart portraits of Washington and Madison.

Recalling how he had learned to recognize the work of different gunshops and then individual smiths in details like patch-box hinges, he looked for similar telltale signs in pieces of furniture. In time he found different makers' "signatures" in how the leg on a chest of drawers was blocked or how a secretary lid was morticed or how a scallop shell on a chair was carved. Thus when Hood unearthed photographs of some "Scottish chairs," Gusler hurried out to take a look at them in Stewart Manor, an eighteenth-century house in Greenbrier County, West Virginia (part of the Commonwealth of Virginia before the Civil War). The owner showed him to the attic where the chairs were stored, some of them broken, all of them uncomfortable, she said. He knew immediately that the suite, which included a settee, had been made in the Tidewater. Well, that confirmed the story she had always heard: They came from the Palace in Williamsburg, according to family lore, and were given to one of her ancestors as a wedding present.

This all made sense to Gusler, but there was scant proof. Having steeped himself in Virginia's history, he knew that in about 1770 a trader named John Stewart had been one of the first to settle on the western frontier near Point Pleasant, scene of the 1774 battle that won Lord Dunmore's war against the Indians. In 1776 Stewart married Agatha Lewis Frogg, for whom he built Stewart Manor. His bride, widow of a man killed at Point Pleasant, was the daughter of Thomas Lewis and kin to Col. Andrew Lewis, one of Dunmore's militia commanders. Gusler had an inspired hunch: that Andrew Lewis had served in Williamsburg after Dunmore fled and bought some of the governor's household goods that were auctioned off to help pay for the Revolution. Hoping to add pieces to the puzzle, Gusler tracked down other members of the family in West Virginia, who provided more than he could have asked for: two antique books with Lord Dunmore's bookplates *and* the signatures of Thomas Lewis and John Stewart. These proved that expensive articles once owned by Dunmore had passed from Lewis hands to Stewart in the distant mountains. Further, the family lore that the settee and chairs had come from the Palace supported Gusler's belief that the stately furniture was made in the Tidewater.

Needless to say, this furniture deserved to be in Williamsburg's museum, indeed restored to the reconstructed building whence family lore said it had come and where the physical evidence pointed. Colonial Williamsburg bought the furniture with the idea of placing it all in the Palace. But it was too rough and not nearly grand enough; it clashed with the gracious pieces that suited everyone's ideas of what should be there—notions in large part supported by what everyone was accustomed to. Yet that is where it was ultimately placed, much to the chagrin of some older Williamsburg hands and fans. The chairs and settee found their place in the ballroom after the "reinterpretation" of the Palace in 1981. That act, viewed as bordering on treason in some circles, demonstrated a significant change in Williamsburg's course and priorities over the years, a change that was a kind of bellwether in the preservation community, which has continued to pursue the new course.

When the Palace was first furnished, it contained grand pieces and won instant acclaim. The Restoration people who worked on it were justifiably proud of their accomplishment. They had read the room-by-room inventory of furnishings compiled by the executors of Governor Botetourt's estate. They had studied other source material as well and, as one participant remembers, decided to equip the edifice as it might have appeared if occupied by a "typical" governor and family man of the Georgian period. No matter that Botetourt was a bachelor; for starters, the scheme was intentionally pleasing to the twentieth-century eye, however hypothetical it might be, even to the point of being invented out of whole cloth. And because of Williamsburg's immense popularity and influence, the Palace came to serve as a model of Georgian grace and elegance.

But Hood and his curatorial generation decided that the original restoration was simply inaccurate. Further, they took to heart the old ambition that Williamsburg should be restored as it actu-

ABOVE: A matter of reinterpretation: A bedchamber in the Governor's Palace seen before its 1981 "reinterpretation."

OPPOSITE: The interpretation of the bedchamber was based on the posthumous inventory of Lord Botetourt's possessions. The room shows new, more vivid colors and notably a carpet called a "bed round"—a U-shaped rug surrounding the bed. (Why waste costly fabric out of sight under the bed?)

ally had been—so far as research could determine—not as some would like to see it. They believed that if anyone is to learn lessons from the past, the data of history ought to be accurate. Herein lies what has been the acknowledged fundamental principle of historical restoration ever since: the intention to discover what *was* and to try to resurrect that; and when new research uncovers more old actualities, to fearlessly alter the restoration to something more faithful to the original.

Considerable knowledge had been compiled since the Palace opened in 1934, even since its decor had evolved under John Graham's stewardship. Hood took it upon himself to perform additional research. He located the ledgers and account books of Botetourt's butler in England, and concluded that the room opening off the front passage had been the butler's office, not the dining room as the first restorers supposed. In an English country house he found an array of arms cunningly hung in a manner that sounded like the display that an eighteenth-century Palace visitor had described, and Hood concluded that Botetourt furnished the entrance hall to reflect his presumed power rather than to be a place where callers would feel comfortable. In this particular, Hood's theory was bolstered by his close reading of socio-political history: The Georgian period was a time when appearances held great importance. (In fact, a governor's most potent weapon was political skill in balancing the interests of crown, councilors, burgesses and citizenry. Things fell apart when an administrator like Lord Dunmore tried to rule by executive whim and threats of force.) Moving from details to the bigger picture, Hood studied the palettes of eighteenth-century prints, fabrics and ceramics, and concluded that the colonists had favored an entirely different set of colors than previously assumed.

His "reinterpretation" brought a whole new look to the once familiar mansion. A bedchamber now sported purple hangings and trim with lime green bamboo chairs in the Chinese style. The entrance hall fairly bowled over the visitor with its arsenal of muskets, pistols and sabers, suggesting that the royal governor was not a man to be trifled with. That the old dining room became a steward's drab lair may have been the crowning blow; even one Williamsburg executive who admitted, "I know better," acknowledged missing the chamber that *"seemed* the perfect Georgian room." A hue and cry went up; friends of the "old Palace" launched letter-writing campaigns against this "desecration." Anti-revisionists even complained that the old decor had, after half a century, become a historical "document" in and of itself. Some aesthetes offered this perplexing and unanswerable argument: Fifty years of scholarship may have advanced knowledge of the eighteenth century, yet the inaccurately furnished old Palace deserved to remain untouched because of its importance to the twentieth-century history of preservation! Saddest, perhaps, a colleague recalls that John Graham "went to his grave a bitter man" because his work—brilliant for its time and of lasting importance in many respects—had been supersceded in this instance. The tragedy there was in the thought that Williamsburg could ever be perfectly finished and immutable—or should be.

Graham Hood's view prevailed, as Colonial Williamsburg came to profit from new knowledge and new talents (while never failing to credit contributions that were state-of-the-art in their day). Its curators would come to believe as an article of faith that they would do the best they could, but that almost inevitably their work would be amended by successors who built on their work using new information and knowledge. They would try to present buildings as they actually were in the chosen period—so far as this could be determined—and always aware of the aim of breathing new life into these historic surroundings, they would increasingly show rooms in a way suggesting that they were inhabited. (The dining room at the Palace, for example, is presented at a chosen moment between courses, as if the governor and his guests had just stepped into the next room.) While Colonial Williamsburg might splendidly display the spectacular fruits of the old Grand Acquisitors in the Wallace Museum or

ABOVE AND OPPOSITE:
Like the bedroom on the preceding pages, the dining room in the Governor's Palace got a new look in the reinterpretation of 1981—with an ornate and costly gilded oval mirror, carefully stenciled floorcloth and, above the mantel, a map of the governor's colonial domain.

The Wallace Museum houses diverse treasures such as these three: The knife box (right), an important dining room accessory by the mid-18th century, held flatware and such on sideboards, in effect proving for guests the fact that the householder owned such lavish accoutrements. This one, made in Wales around 1765, is made of japanned sheet iron, brass hardware, wood, velvet and silver braid. The gown (far right), dating from about 1770 and probably made in France, displays fine silk from China to its best advantage. Adorned with hand-painted designs of leaves and flowers, its motifs are outlined with silver thread now tarnished to gray. Such an elegant garment would have been worn only by a most affluent lady of the era. Ann Holewll stitched, dated and signed this sampler in 1699 (below). It makes manifest the early education—in letters and needlework—of a wellborn young lady in England.

the Folk Art Museum, it would increasingly make the Historic Area more faithful to its actual past. The collections would exist to serve history and historical study—thus to reveal the past to living people, and to posterity just as Colonial Williamsburg's founders had so fervently hoped they would, only with greater fidelity to discoverable fact than those founders could have ever conceived.

In retrospect the Palace reinterpretation appears an inevitable battle justly won—a victory of historical truth over transitory taste. In fact, the Palace reinterpretation would turn out to be a precursor of things to come. This is because the mission of Colonial Williamsburg was increasingly seen as comprising the deeper discovery and broader presentation of what truly *was* in Williamsburg, and by extension, what *was* in colonial America and the eighteenth-century world at large.

Think of it in terms of the cliché that what is past is prologue. The refurnishing of the Raleigh Tavern came first and caused little stir, when, as Graham Hood would remember years later, "We changed this, the first exhibition building, from a place suggestive of an old fashioned club to something more like an eighteenth-century tavern." Then came the decision to redo one downstairs Palace room after it was realized that "the [first] Restoration architects in 1931–1932 had the evidence we did but chose to install a family dining room in what was [actually] a butler's pantry. Everyone . . . examined our evidence and found it indisputable." Even though "all hell broke loose" in a storm of controversy among perennial visitors, the entire Palace would be reinterpreted in the light of hard-won new knowledge of old things. Then, in logical succession, came the decision to completely re-research the Peyton Randolph House, and make its modern manifestation more closely represent what it had been.

As the Raleigh and Palace projects involved progressively more work and produced correspondingly more dramatic results, the Peyton Randolph reinterpretation involved yet another increase in effort—more work by a geometric factor. This reinterpretation took longer—more than a decade at this writing, and as a great baseball broadcaster said of a game tied in the ninth inning, "Like the Civil War, this ain't over yet." It has involved more staffers, more visiting scholars, more departments and even more disciplines than any previous restoration. Its subject was, in a way, larger as well, for if the Palace's resident governors represented royal government in decline, Peyton Randolph exemplified the new leadership of republican America. Here was a man whose intelligence was matched by his stature, wealth and eminence. He was an American paradigm: one of the richest men in town and the preeminent political leader (viz., Speaker of the House of Burgesses and first president of the Continental Congress). In addition he kept the largest number of slaves on his town property, claiming possession of twenty-seven African-Americans.

There is something altogether fitting in the convergence of so many elements in this house, for as Edward A. Chappell, head of the Architectural Research Department, declared, "Circumstances have converged to make the current Randolph [House] work the most important Historic Area project of the decade," nay, of a longer period. Then, as architectural curator Willie Graham and architectural historian Mark R. Wenger wrote when the reinterpretation was unveiled, "it was not sufficient to study features of the site in isolation. Increasingly, relationships among these elements became the focus." It could even be argued that the manifold project was all the more appropriate since Peyton Randolph was the founding father who had been forgotten and deserved rediscovery. How so?

The oldest surviving son of Sir John Randolph, the only colonial American knighted for services to the Crown, Peyton Randolph was born about 1721, studied at William and Mary, then in London's Middle Temple, and was admitted to the bar at twenty-two. Back home a year later, in 1744, he was named attorney general for the colony and four years after that elected Williamsburg's

Artisans at the famous Chelsea Porcelain Manufactory made innumerable series of figures: birds, harlequins, even these anthropomorphic monkeys, dressed in stylish clothing of the period and expressing parodies of human feelings, in the animals' faces and body language.

representative in the House of Burgesses and a year later to the Bruton Parish vestry. He became rector of the board of visitors of the college, grand master of the Masonic Lodge, and speaker of the House of Burgesses. Rising as a leader of the revolutionary cause, he was chosen chairman of Virginia's Committee of Correspondence, then of the first Virginia Convention in 1774, then delegate to the First Continental Congress and by unanimous vote its first president. A year later in 1775 he was elected president of the Second Continental Congress, but shortly after reaching Philadelphia, he was felled by a stroke and died at 53, before the independence he espoused became fact, nay, even before the colonies declared themselves a new nation.

By the time of his death Randolph had been head of the household fronting Market Square for twenty years, and he had made the place his own through a range of changes. Moreover he had made it a property worthy of a man of his resources and importance. Thus the house is large, and while not being the largest in town, it is now one of the most curious in the eyes of architectural historians. The lot it stands on is large as well, and contains many "features" i.e., foundations, cellars, a well and whatnot. Peyton Randolph's possessions are known to have been extensive, for an item-by-item inventory had been made at his death, though the document seemed a hotchpotch. In short, earlier restorers knew that Randolph was a figure to reckon with before they exhibited his house in 1968 as a gentleman/revolutionary's home decorated as they thought it ought to look—a prime example of what came to be called Colonial Revival.

A dozen years later, the complexity and apparent archaeological richness of the yard made it the site chosen for a major excavation and study by the newly organized Office of Excavation and Conservation. It then became square one for the long-term research program of Marley Brown's Department of Archaeological Research. The research methods that had proved so fruitful in the Palace project begged application anew. Thought Ronald Hurst, "What better subject than the mysterious inventory of Randolph's worldly possessions?" Likewise Edward A. Chappell, director of the Department of Architectural Research, saw that the "building long venerated as one of the town's most historic houses" was barely understood in terms of its architectural history, and he set about to correct that oversight. Thus the work began on several fronts, and continues at this writing, more than a decade later.

Starting from the ground up, Marley Brown and his colleagues abandoned the conventional approach, which involves dividing a chosen spot into square-meter sections and excavating more or less independently layer by layer down to the "sterile," or virgin, stratum of undisturbed subsoil. Instead, they borrowed a new "open area" technique developed in Britain, which allows the whole site to be dug one layer at a time so that, for example, the entire site at the Civil War could be viewed and recorded, then that layer excavated away to reveal the whole layer that dated from the 1750s.

In sum, they found that just before Peyton Randolph's time the lot had tenements along North England Street, at least three different kitchens and a number of other service buildings. Documents showed that in 1723 William Robertson sold the lot and tenements to John Grymes, and that John Randolph got it the following year, probably converting the best building for his family. After his death, his son Peyton took the property over in around 1754 and built an addition on the east end of the house. In so doing, he changed its orientation so that it faced Market Square with a façade that was all the more imposing for its new board siding that concealed any difference between the old and new structures. The new front looked nearly symmetrical, in keeping with the newly emerging Georgian taste, though from the rear the house's irregularities were apparent, and a bird's eye view revealed an odd roof on the original house that was covered over. From the ground, it looked like an ordinary hipped roof, one that slanted on all four sides; but the house was too wide

ABOVE: In one of the many changes for which Williamsburg is famous, this house was turned to face Market Square—back before the Revolution when Peyton Randolph made the much smaller original his home. The shift required constructing a wing that connected the old principal house (near end) with a smaller dwelling (far end). Then the joined buildings received a new facade of matching weatherboards so the three would look like one.

OPPOSITE: Peyton Randolph's study must have been this room, researchers decided, partly because it was the one that best accommodated the "book presses" or glass-fronted cabinets. Randolph had a library that was widely admired.

The rear of Peyton Randolph's house shows its piecemeal construction. The original dwelling was joined by a wing with the same roofline to a shorter, dormered house.

to easily span with wood beams, and so the roof was actually shaped like a "W," with two hidden valleys from which interior pipes carried rainwater down to cisterns.

The original building boasted an interior entry with a stairway, three rooms on the ground floor, and three more above. Peyton Randolph's new wing, which nearly doubled the size of the house, added new public spaces downstairs, a grand passage with a new staircase and the largest single room in the house, which the restoration of 1968 treated as a parlor. Upstairs the new wing provided a commodious bedchamber plus a closet for Peyton and his wife, Betty.

Through the physical evidence of layers of paint, tree-ring-dated timbers, nail holes, partition scars, stains and the like, the architectural historians learned that two separate renovations were carried out in the mid-1750s. Prior to the construction of the new wing, Randolph had first plastered ceilings and walls, installed wainscoting, and adorned the window surrounds in the old house with ornamental wooden keystones. When he was done, he had the whole interior and the exterior painted red-brown; later, by 1774, the more formal interior spaces were painted light gray.

Outside in the yard, the archaeologists discovered that he had built a large service building with a vaulted wine cellar below ground and living space for the household slaves on the second story. What once appeared to have been two separate outbuildings were found to have been one long kitchen-and-quarter combined; microscopic examination of the mortar binding the foundations proved that this had all been built at one time—the largest building of its kind in Williamsburg. Thus this outbuilding was a grand structure in its own right, three rooms long, two stories high and containing two chimneys. It was joined to the rear of the main house by a covered passage, the better for servants to bring food to the master's table and for the mistress to check matters in the kitchen. It testifies to the cohesiveness of the complex household and demonstrates the close ties between the domains of the white gentry and the domestic servants.

The most dramatic discovery in the Randolph House's latest restoration came from a careful new reading of Peyton's post mortem inventory, which, as no rooms were designated, appeared to be a random list of worldly possessions. Hurst wrote, "To generations of modern observers, it appeared that the document was little more than an unbroken roster of miscellaneous and unrelated household implements. A 'Mahogony tea Board' and 'Japan'd Waiter' (or tray) were followed in the list by a 'Chariot and 8 harness.' A 'parcel of Sylabub & Jelly Glasses' and '100 lbs.Wt. [white] Sugar' were grouped with quantities of uncut textiles, and all were associated with a series of bedsteads and other chamber furniture." Believing that there must be some order here, Hurst encouraged the curators to compare the inventory with scores of other probate records. One thing they learned when they did this was that Peyton Randolph was a very wealthy man, or at least one who spent several times as much on dining chairs, gilt accessories and such as any of his fellow gentlemen in Virginia. Then, Eureka!

Previously it had been assumed that parlors were the largest rooms in colonial Virginia houses; thus the largest room in the Randolph house had been furnished as a parlor. Yet the Randolph inventory described an array of dining room furnishings (to judge from the other inventories)— two dining tables, two serving tables, a dozen chairs, serving vessels and the like—that could only have been accommodated in the largest room, the supposed parlor in the east wing. Further, this was the only room with enough wall space to accommodate four "looking glasses," i.e., decorative mirrors. The case was closed when two closets turned out to have been "bowfats" or built-in cupboards that would hold quantities of silver, ceramic and glass tableware—objects that were listed in the inventory right after the furniture.

If the dining room furniture and accessories were all listed together, it followed that the contents of other rooms were grouped together too. Backtracking, and armed with the new archaeological proof of the household's layout, the curators tested various hypotheses against the physical evidence and found indeed that the inventory was organized space by space. Thus the appraisers of Mr. Randolph's property had begun in the dining room, then had gone through the passage out the door to the stable, then back into the house and through the downstairs rooms, including Mrs. Randolph's "closet," a term that meant her private working space or possibly "office." Upstairs, another odd juxtaposition of glassware, sugar, textiles and bedsteads pointed to another private space adjoining the bedchamber, this one a secure storage space where Mrs. Randolph kept her fancy glassware, sugar and spare linen.

So it was that the old inventory, known for decades but not fully appreciated, finally revealed some of its secrets to curators, in part because archaeologists had made new discoveries. So it was that new steps were taken in uncovering the past. As Hurst, who succeeded Graham Hood as chief curator and vice president, would write, "With each new iteration, the furnishings shown in our exhibition sites get closer to the truth of eighteenth-century Williamsburg." So it was, and so may it continue.

As Dr. Goodwin unabashedly explained, he knew Williamsburg was inhabited by benevolent spirits of the past. (On an autumn evening when the moon brightens Scotland Path and crickets sing along the Palace wall, one finds oneself gladly listening for the voices he heard.) Yet this place has come to be animated with living spirits day by day: tradespeople plying myriad trades, actors playing people known to have walked these colonial streets, interpreters in period dress explaining erstwhile ways. Not only a collection of buildings and objects, this is a community of people whose skills constitute a vital resource in another sort of collection, if you will, one of constant activity.

They grind corn here and sew wigs and pour pewter. They fill the kitchens at the Palace with the scents of stews and soups and at Benjamin Powell House with meat pies baking in cast-iron vessels set on beds of live coals with more embers blanketing their tight lids. (This works as well as any gas oven or microwave, if at a different pace; as one cook says, "heat is heat" whatever the source.) They tend day-long hardwood fires by the Magazine, turning sides of pigs fit to feed an army. One erstwhile cook meant to test how long it takes to roast a lark within a pigeon within a pullet within a duck within a pheasant within a goose within a turkey within a crust made from a bushel of flour in the shape of the fabled roc, perhaps, a receipt she found in Hannah Glasse's 1747 *Art of Cookery.* Using a basket spit indoors before the hobgrate of the Palace kitchen she also plans to test another of Glasse's recipes—this one for roasting a pig. *Art of Cookery* neglects to say how long it will take; only that a pig is done "when the eyes drop out or you find the crackling hard."

Skilled drivers rein matched teams of horses and a brace of gray mules hitched to coaches, carriages and wagons as they ply the streets carrying visitors or goods. One teamster could steer his oxen by voice alone, as they slowly haul the pale blue cart filled with hay and children around Market Square. In summer the days begin with the sound of martial tunes as the Fife and Drum Corps appears on Botetourt Street, then wheels around the corner onto Duke of Gloucester toward the Magazine, where militiamen raise the colors to the boom of cannon and chatter of musket fire. In one parlor or another, a viola da gamba brightens the air by day; in the Palace ballroom, Handel and Vivaldi rule the night in concert again, while the Apollo Room trembles to the beat of a dozen couples dancing reels and cotillions. The sounds, sights and smells of old abide here because people of our time practice antique occupations. The benefits and fascination of these human activities are legion.

Artisans span the centuries as they produce an array of goods from shoes to silver sauceboats, from forged andirons to spinet harpsichords and lace woven of brass wire plated with silver and gilded for good measure. All year long the shepherdess tends her sheep, then shears them in the spring. The weaver washes homegrown wool, then sorts and cards it, and then spins and weaves it into blankets and such. Iron is wrought into gun barrels with rifled bores. Modern denizens of Colonial Williamsburg make cornmeal and the ovens in which to bake it. They make wagons and harness for the horses, furniture for the houses, candlesticks of brass or pewter, marrow spoons of bronze, mote spoons of pierced sterling, powdered periwigs of human hair, and enough other wares—the

OPPOSITE: An apprentice carpenter deftly carves the back of a chair in the Chippendale style. At Williamsburg artisans earn their way up through the traditional steps from apprentice to journeyman to master.

necessities of old or curiosities of now—to fill a brig bound for Bristol. Many of these things are made for sale, others for use around the colonial town. The blacksmiths wrought all the iron cooking implements, door latches and locks, for the reconstructed Peyton Randolph kitchen, along with 40,000 nails. The silversmith has copied the sterling escutcheon from Lord Botetourt's casket to grace the coffin of a visitor who paid for it with the "ready money" of our time, a plastic card.

The purpose of the so-called trades here is neither modern utility nor artsy creativity. Rather the goal in each of the twenty exhibition shops is to replicate a profession practiced in the eighteenth-century town, to produce a line of goods using eighteenth-century materials, tools and techniques—even conventions of training and employment. If there is a major difference between then and now, it lies in output. Colonial artisans worked as fast and efficiently as possible. Their successors today are eager to explain their work as they perform it; in some shops as much energy goes into discussion as production. Those 40, 000 nails took about 40 man-days of toil in the Anderson forge at about two nails a minute, 120 nails an hour, 960 nails a day; in Adam Smith's time, a nailmaker made 2,300 nails a day—but those were twelve- to fourteen-hour days, depending on the quality of iron and fuel.

Blacksmith Peter Ross insists that "We don't practice crafts" as summer campers use the term. "We work a trade." The day-in-day-out challenge for him is not to make the most exquisite spitjack, a clockwork device used to turn the governor's goose before his reconstructed kitchen's fire. The task is to make a spitjack as close as possible to the one that graced the original kitchen. This requires a range of resources: coal, tools and bar iron, of course, and the blacksmith's considerable skills at handling hammer, and tongs. The work also calls for books, drawings and engravings along with intimate knowledge of the old manuals that describe the techniques of the original eighteenth-century smiths. Finally, it takes antique examples, artifacts that serve as more than just visible models. An antique example not only tells the latter-day tradesman what shape to seek; in addition, its scars and scratches inform the experienced artisan how some long-dead predecessor used his tools and did the work turn by turn, blow by blow, stroke by stroke. Since no one living can show him how to make a spitjack, the new smith must puzzle it out, tempering his own experience with clues found in the antique piece.

Here and now, as long ago, the man who runs the shop is called its "master," though the term has a slightly new meaning. Colonial Williamsburg's master craftsmen are indeed masters of their trade, as well as administrators of small operations within the organization. But in the colony, the title was not conferred by a guild to designate a special level of skill; young America was too short of skilled hands to observe all the Old World's pernickety rules of guilds and such. While he might be as accomplished as silversmith James Craig or cabinetmaker Anthony Hay, the "master" in Virginia was simply the person who owned the place, the widow who inherited a business after fever took her spouse, or a journeyman fresh off the boat who had the cash and initiative to hang out a shingle. (Most newcomers lacked the money or the liberty; many indentured artisans plied their trade for their master's profit.) In any case, if the artisan had fulfilled an apprenticeship in England, or here, for that matter, he was called a journeyman, from the French word *jour* or "day," since he was paid by his day's work. To reach skilled status then, as now, one aspiring to the trade entered a lengthy apprenticeship, which today may last as long as ten years and in colonial times usually took from four to seven. Thus the process of training here today, like the artisans' method, mirrors the colonial model.

The very length of an apprenticeship and the repetition it involves teaches lessons about the binding connections between tools and techniques, materials, methods, purposes and traditions. There are

Woodworking tools used in old Williamsburg bear a striking resemblance to the hand tools used today. By the 18th century woodworkers had refined many of their tools to the point of near perfection.

When completed, these pieces will become treasured examples of the modern cabinetmaker's skill.

ABOVE: Behind the building site of the Peyton Randolph kitchen, the master carpenter and housewright Garland Wood tidies the good old 18th-century way; he burns the debris.

BELOW: The printer inks type for a newspaper to be printed on a wooden press. In the early colonial period printing presses were forbidden by royal authority, lest their proprietors (and other lettered persons) spread dissent among the hoi polloi. Indeed, from the 1750s onward, when newspapers were firmly established, they carried news and opinions from afar, information that often inflamed people and thus contributed to the revolutionary fervor.

lessons in physics to be learned, lessons in the complexities of seemingly simple things, lessons in the purposes of patience. A most striking lesson translates into the rule that just as lost skills can be rediscovered, so too the modern master may reinvent lost tools. Witness an example from the gunshop:

~

The metal parts of old guns are fastened with screws. To fit the screws flush into a gun's butt plate requires cutting some metal away from the plate itself to form a chamfer, a hole with slanting sides to seat the screw head, which must fit snugly and thus have a matching slope. It is certain that colonial gunsmiths had drills to bore and chamfer the holes, but some years ago Colonial Williamsburg's gunsmiths chamfered the screw heads any way they could because there didn't seem to be an old tool for the job. Yet old guns had chamfered screws. Thus an apprentice gunsmith, Gary Brumfield, thought about the problem, and experimented until he contrived a widget that worked. Months later a curator brought over a print of a tool he'd never seen before and asked what it might be. Brumfield recognized the mysterious device that had stumped the experts; he'd just made one remarkably like it, after all. It proved to be an antique chamfer-cutter that confirmed the modern gunsmith's new invention. The lesson here: If a task must be newly done today at Williamsburg and the craftsman knows his stuff vis-à-vis old techniques, technology and materials, he might just reinvent a lost tool.

The reader might now inquire: If chamfer-cutters were so useful, and therefore common, why haven't they turned up by the bushel? The answer: because they wore out and were thrown away or more likely recycled into something else. As it happens, the least useful tools of any trade often last the longest and reach us in rummage sales and roadside antique shops. The more common tool, or a craftsman's favorite, got used up or worn down. The face of a plane that fit the carpenter's hand just right shaved endless boards; it lost its true shape, was planed itself each passing year until too little of the good rock maple remained for any use. When the farrier's file broke off too short to dress horses' hooves, the man ground it down to serve as a knife. The brass skillet damaged beyond repair was tossed into a crucible and melted down to become part of several doorknobs. It didn't survive intact. Neither does a backbreaking technique that has been overtaken by technology.

A stunning example of recovering a lost art at Williamsburg involves not a single object but an entire method. Again it happened in the gunshop under the first master, Wallace Gusler. One of the first goals he set for himself and his crew was to build an eighteenth-century Virginia rifle from scratch, i.e., lock, stock and barrel, to revive an old phrase in its context. The challenge was made all the more worthy because nineteenth-century advances had long since obviated the laborious business of making gun barrels by hand; the old methods had been forgotten. Combing the countryside, Gusler and Brumfield talked to every old-timer they could find. None had made barrels on a forge but some had seen it done when they were boys, and others remembered hearing how, or so they said. Many of the stories proved specious, but the young gunsmiths gleaned and culled enough "oral history" and documentary evidence to have a go at it.

After much trial and error they learned to start with a hammered skelp, a long flat piece of iron. Working after-hours at the Deane Forge, they practiced hammering skelps into long troughs. Heating the iron in a soft coal fire, the trick was to curl the skelp lengthwise around a cold iron rod and weld the edges together into a rough tube. Withdrawing the rod, they heated the skelp in white hot coals each time it cooled. Reinserting the rod, they resumed welding the tube. Once they had beaten the skelp into a four-foot tube, it was relatively easy to bore out the rough hole left by the rod to a chosen diameter. For this they used a long bit and the sort of gunsmith's boring bench that had survived. Another antique wooden tool resembling a huge patent corkscrew then scored the rifling grooves inside the barrel. The outside was then smoothed into an octagonal cylinder by hours and hours of filing.

Handwelding iron is no mean trick; making a weld four feet long is a master's feat in any age. It took several years, but Gusler, Brumfield and company made a barrel in a manner that at least approximated the eighteenth-century way. Was that precisely how they did it then? No one can say for sure, but the experts believe it must be close, because Gusler's new barrels show the same weld patterns as the originals and because other ways he tried did not work. Thus a lost aspect of colonial technology was evidently reborn at Colonial Williamsburg.

The art of barrel making, having been reborn, was then refined, developed, improved and hastened, reported a journeyman gunsmith some two score years later. In 2001, George Suiter, who served his apprenticeship under Brumfield, recalled some of the strides the Gunshop made in the twenty-three years he has worked there to date.

As the gunsmiths made more barrels, they got better at it. They learned how to start with a thinner skelp, which could be bent around the mandrel more easily, and rolled into a tube with less heat and less hammering in less time. Eventually, they found they could make a barrel from start to finish in about 100 man-hours—weeks rather than months or even years for the first one that Gusler and Brumfield made. (In England at the pre-dawn of the Industrial Revolution, four-man teams of specialist smiths could turn out a dozen to two dozen rifle tubes a day.) It was simply a matter of incremental refinements in the process, augmented with the advantage of experience, practice.

Then, says Suiter, bibliographic research led to another great stride. Whereas his predecessors used a late-eighteenth-century written description of a bore reamer as their starting point, Suiter came upon pictures published early in the eighteenth century in a German equivalent of Diderot's famous encyclopedia. He and his peers in the wheelwright's shop built a copy of this two-man device: basically a sliding carriage that holds the unfinished barrel tube, forcing it past (or over) a spinning reamer. As one man urges the carriage forward with the aid of a lever of iron, at the other end of the device his partner turns a four-foot flywheel with a hand crank; this spins the carbon-steel bit that reams out the rifle bore throughout its length as the barrel is pushed forward.

Given improvements in both techniques and tools, the gunsmiths could blaze old armor making paths anew. Thus their latest creation is a hybrid sporting gun of a sort found in Europe and colonial America. This weapon has one flintlock and two over-and-under barrels, one rifled and the other smooth-bore, fitted on a swivel to the stock. This allows a hunter to fire a charge from one barrel, then swivel the barrel assembly on the stock, and fire the second an instant later. The two bores, not incidentally, are identical in size to one-half of one-thousandths of an inch—easily within the tolerances of modern guns and far more exact than necessary in colonial times. "We did it to see what the old technology could do," says Suiter.

Meanwhile, the Gunshop turned its attention to powder horns, then powder flasks—the tidier containers made of cattle horns. As one thing led to another, Suiter and some colleagues helped found both the Contemporary Longrifle Association and the Honorable Companie of Horners. A horner was a tradesman who worked in animal horn, a material that served most of the uses of modern thermoplastics. That is, it can be heated and then shaped into any number of useful items: powder flasks, spoons, cups, eyeglass frames, etc. Five years after its founding, the Companie boasted 400 members worldwide, in what might be a new flowering of antique objects made the antique way—another flowering that began in Williamsburg.

A wagon wheel's integrity depends on physics and geometry. First the wheelwright gets an iron tire forged too small to fit the wooden felloes that make up the rim itself. Placed in a hot fire, the tire expands so it can be slipped onto the spoked wheel. Then doused with water, it quickly shrinks. A little hammering finishes the job of fitting the iron ring, which securely binds wooden parts into a single unit—much in the way hoops bind a barrel's staves.

The gunsmith's art involved
the delicate manipulation of
precise tools—to make a flintlock's mechanism, for instance.
The trade's requirements range
from the strength and endurance
to forge and bore a wrought-iron
barrel three feet long to hours
of wood and metal finishing
accomplished at the bench.

Other colonial skills had not quite died elsewhere before rebirth in the renascent town. Read you now of roundlet, terce, puncheon and tun, of firkin, kilderkin and butt. Each is an almost perfect object: a made-in-heaven marriage of material and design, of white oak, utility and workmanship united daily by one cooper or another. Each is a barrel, a container of exacting complexity. Once common to the point of baseness—the cardboard boxes and plastic bags of their day—these containers were perforce handmade by many men. (A cooper was among the first group to land at Jamestown; his craft was as important to their economy as the smith's.) But when Colonial Williamsburg thought to revive coopering they had to look an ocean away to find a cooper.

George Pettengell's training and experience mirror those of colonial apprentices in many ways. The son and grandson of coopers, he had entered a five-year apprenticeship at Whitbread's, the London brewery, in 1950. There had been no question of his occupation. He had reached fifteen, the "leaving age" from school, and it was time to go to work, a word synonymous with coopering in the family lexicon. Nor was there much question about him staying on in the business in the late 1960s; Whitbread's was one of the last holdouts, but the time had come to abandon wooden barrels for metal ones. Pettengell was recruited to come over to show Colonial Williamsburg how to set up a barrel-making shop, a cooperage; then with his wife and brother he stayed on. Thus Williamsburg's crafts program was doubly blessed. It got a living man with a dying skill, and in him a master who had experienced the long labor of apprenticing.

Pettengell's first wage as a boy in London had been cheap, about enough to pay carfare, and was somewhat analogous to the "meat, drink, cloths, washing and lodging" that Georgian boys received as live-in learners on both sides of the Atlantic. A pittance was considered fair, given laboring traditions that would raise eyebrows today. For starters, the boy was not deemed worth very much because he had no skills. Next, he was paid largely in the coin of knowledge, the specie of a marketable trade. From the master's viewpoint—even in London circa 1950—an apprentice program did not provide cheap labor so much as it assured that skilled workers would be on hand in future. What the employer saved in cash was offset in part by the cost of providing training, of pouring his experience into the vessel of the apprentice's potential.

Not a lifetime ago, the rights and responsibilities were spelled out in a binding contract similar to those signed in eighteenth-century Williamsburg. Pettengell's compact with Whitbread's reads: "The Apprentice of his own free will and with the consent of the Guardian, hereby binds himself to serve the Employer as his Apprentice in the trade of COOPERING." The employer agreed that he "will during the said term to the best of his power, skill and knowledge instruct the Apprentice . . . in everything related to said trade as practiced by him." In return, "The Apprentice shall truly and faithfully . . . serve the Employer as his Apprentice *and his secrets keep.*"

The work was hard and repetitive, too fast for reason as Pettengell at first consciously weighed a thousand decisions while he learned each step of barrel-making: how to wield the broadax; to shave each stave, then round its front and back; to gauge by eye each stave's slightly different width and weight; to distribute intrinsically unequal members around the girth of a barrel to assure uniform strength; to make container after container virtually identical. When he tried to reason out a step or choice, his master told him shortly, "Don't think about it, do as I tell you. It'll work out."

Therein lay one secret of apprenticing: Thou needst not reinvent the wheel, or in this case, the barrel, but instead depend on the experience of uncounted generations. The apprentice learned not only from his own master, but from the work of coopers since time immemorial. Their ways worked; the learner was encouraged—nay, ordered—to simply copy them. If in the process he happened to sort out why and how these ways worked, so much the better.

OPPOSITE: Fresh from their casting molds, silver, pewter and bronze utensils glisten as they cool. Williamsburg silversmiths make and made many different objects for moneyed customers. At the top are the two parts of a pair of grape shears and underneath them a slender marrow spoon for removing the savory contents of beef bones at table.

Through historical research, trial and error and blistering heat, CW is rediscovering an essential industry: making bricks by hand, a process that involves obvious ingredients and forgotten specifics. Mixing clay and water (below) is a "feets on" activity shared with visitors today. It is essential that bricks are thoroughly dried (above) before they are subjected to the intense heat of the kiln.

Learning by rote was a lifesaver for Pettengell—as it is for artisans plying any craft hereabouts—who found after a while that he could perform the endlessly repeated tasks without thinking about each one. "And when you stop trying to think about it, that's when you get out of prison." The trained hand and eye do the work; the brain is freed to think about other things, like "the book I read last night" or the cricket game after work on Market Square. To think only about barrels while producing an endless train of them would make the man a slave, in modern or eighteenth-century Williamsburg. "Of course part of the mind keeps ticking on about the barrel in question," Pettengell said. That's another process "that keeps the cooper sane." The challenge remains to make a barrel that works, which means constantly being alert to the variations in pieces of wood, differences in weight, thickness and density that must be evenly distributed around the circle of staves.

Still and all, a barrel remains a miracle of contained stress, a feat of deftly judged tolerances. Because a barrel is a container, its shape and strength must oppose internal forces that press outward: the weight of ale or pressure of tightly packed Virginia bright. Hoops, the circular bands of riveted iron or split saplings, do most of this work, of course. Then the staves themselves must keep the circumference from collapsing in upon itself. The basic miracle here lies in the irrevocably geometric properties of the circle and its parts. The geometry turns out to be as simple as pie, in that a pie's wedge-shaped pieces cannot be squeezed closer together without being broken, just as the wedge-shaped staves cannot be squeezed into a smaller circle. But bear in mind that the cooper uses no measuring tools, only the eye, as he turns three dozen flat slabs into the tapered, rounded, wedge-sided staves that make a barrel.

One ambiguity of a barrel lies in the fact that it is often used as a wheel, witness the thousand-pound hogsheads that were rolled—often for miles—down rough roads to a wharf for shipment to England. (Hence the frequency below the Mason-Dixon Line of lanes or thoroughfares called "Rolling Road." They began as routes to docks or markets for laborers rolling heavy barrels.) Their shape made them far easier to handle than anything with corners. Roundness also makes a barrel stronger than a box—equally strong all the way around its girth, while the straight sides of a box are weaker in the middle. Stronger and more maneuverable, a kilderkin can be moved by one man who tips it on edge, nudges it into motion, then lets its momentum do the work. Because they are used this way, barrels must resist inward forces. An empty cask also must keep itself from collapsing inward—no mean trick for a few dozen wood slats bound side by side without benefit of glue, nails or pegs.

In making a barrel, the eye and hand must accommodate an extraordinary range of variables: the wood's flexibility, its condition and propensity to expand or shrink, the necessity of compressing the staves yet not applying more force than they can bear. Cut a barrel's thirty-odd staves one-thirty-sixth of an inch too wide, and they will never form the desired circle; cut them that fraction too narrow and the barrel will be too small. Mind you, the capacity of these vessels could not vary with the cooper's whim or ineptitude. Volumes and terminology were mandated by law. A "barrel" of beer contained thirty-six gallons, one of ale, thirty-two. A "barrel" of gunpowder came to hold 100 pounds; by Queen Anne's decree a "barrel" of soap weighed 256 pounds. As for firkin, kilderkin, roundlet, puncheon and terce, each had absolute specifications and uses. (Lest it seem there was absolutely no margin for error, the cooper had compensating tricks. If a vessel-in-the-making appeared too large, he could cut the groove for its head a little farther in, thus reducing its volume and capacity. If he saw a barrel would hold too little, he could shave a little more from the inside of the staves. But again, day in and day out, the measurements were—and are—gauged by the cooper's eye.)

In sum, the lowly barrel and the cooper who made it exemplify the canny talent of preindus-

ABOVE: The industries plied at Colonial Williamsburg today replicate trades practiced in the region more than two centuries ago—though neither the weaver nor the blacksmiths produce as many wares as their predecessors did. First of all, these artisans work shorter hours than their ancestors, and they must explain their work to visitors as they perform it, an activity that slows the pace. Next, their forebears were specialists.

BELOW: Though the smiths at the James Anderson Forge made 15,000 nails by hand for the recent reconstruction of the Peyton Randolph kitchen, they wrought only about half as many each day as the 18th-century specialists. These specialists were frequently located in England where they produced for large markets and arranged their shops and refined their skills for the purpose of making one product more efficiently.

trial artisans and the superb utility of eighteenth-century craft. To visit the cooper's shed today and watch Lew LeCompte (who apprenticed under Pettengell), and George's brother Jim, who was the last Whitebread apprentice, is to encounter a sort of rustic sophistication that rivals in sheer practicality our modern machines and methods.

The most numerous tradesmen in any eighteenth-century city were the tailors, said Mark Hutter, sitting cross-legged on a table in the window of the Milliner's Shop—the better to see by the natural light and to be seen by the passing carriage trade and pedestrian traffic. Before the revolution, the capital boasted six or eight shoemakers' shops along with like numbers of barbers, carpenters and blacksmiths; yet Williamsburg had twice as many tailors' shops, about fifteen of them in 1774. This was by far the most common trade here as in London where tailors were "numerous as locusts and poor as rats." They had a most democratic custom as well; the sole surviving account book of a Virginia tailor shows that William Carlin in Alexandria cut and sewed clothes for everyone from General Washington's "mixt french gray suit" to checked trousers for a local shoemaker, from trimming the livery of servants to mending leather breeches of slaves. A tailor made every sort of men's apparel and ladies' stays and riding habits, Hutter explains, "from mean and course to fine and fashionable, for no tailor could survive on the custom of the better sort alone." It was hard enough to survive with every kind of client; though one colonial tailor left an estate valued at £12,000, another died with chattel worth £24.

Yet if tailoring was a common calling, it was also an anonymous one. For reasons that elude explanation, unlike eighteenth-century cabinetmakers and silversmiths, tailors did not sign their work in any way—except that each one had his own "hand," a distinct manner of wielding shears and needle to cut a fashionlike fit or stitch a fine buttonhole. Cutting and sewing, after all, involve many repetitive actions and resulting motifs that the latter-day researcher can study and compare— the expectation in fit, the angle of a stitch, the placement of seams, and the number of stitches to the inch.

In almost every culture, clothing is one of the most individual and personal accoutrements. Even in a social group that wears a de facto uniform—whether a religious sect or an army—every man's attire is at least a little different from every other man's in distinctions of rank or in size, and in small details like the fold of a cuff or in the pattern of wear. Once it has been worn regularly, every man's garment (especially in the European tradition) flashes clues as to the wearer's occupation, station, age, health, personal style and deportment. Contrarily, clothing is among the most short-lived of cultural artifacts. It tears, wears out, shrinks, gets outgrown, tossed aside, passed on, refitted, altered, downgraded; the gentleman's out-of-fashion coat gets cast off to the house servant; a mother's skirt or gown gets cut apart to make her son's first suit. Almost each change of wearer, each repair, each alteration leaves its scars and signs in the cloth itself, clues about the many hands that have touched it, so that the few garments that survive from the eighteenth century are all diverse documents of social and economic history.

Mark Hutter's sleuthing into clothes combines an extraordinary range of intellectual disciplines, from the practical anatomy of apparel to art history and pure archaeology. Eighteenth-century portraiture, for example, offers a wealth of information about attire and attitudes; ditto all visual relics of the period whether the statue of Lord Botetout or a lampooning cartoon on a political broadside, or the sketch of an Indian in a traveler's journal. Written sources offer collaboration. Even trowel-and-dirt archaeology came into play at the turn of the new millennium, when Hutter was invited to examine grave goods found in an old Susquehannock tribal cemetery in Pennsylvania; what he found embodied a connection in fashion between European immigrants and native Americans.

OPPOSITE: Williamsburg's tailor sits in the traditional posture and place, namely upon his table in rented space in order to work with comfort in good light and be seen by passersby, an advertisement for himself. When the town boasted six or eight carpenters, barbers, shoemakers and such, it had fifteen tailor shops, producing clothing for rich and poor alike. Tailors were the most numerous because they served the entire population; surviving records show that one tailor made or repaired attire for George Washington and his slaves as well as everyone in between.

A bronze kettle—doubtless a prize possession—was buried with a chief's remains about 1750; the kettle's metal oxidized and grew a patina of verdigris, which scoured the ground and deterred the microbes that consume organic materials, like wool. Inside it was stuffed a coat, itself made partly of some metal in the tinsel "lace" that adorned it, a decoration woven of thread wrapped in copper foil plated in silver and gilded, which also oxidized. Thus about one-third of this coat survived some two and a half centuries, the best preserved specimen of its kind. It is a pseudo-military style coat of English cloth, of American cut and construction, that would have been made specially for a chief at the order of some colonial governor as an emblem of authority and perhaps the talisman of a treaty. From these tangled fragments Hutter reproduced the coat as it would have appeared when new, thus resurrecting the garb of a man 250 years dead.

(The find has a bittersweet historical quality because the chief who wore this coat was among the last of his tribe. Chief Pontiac's rebellion in the west in 1763 ignited fear and loathing among colonists, and in Pennsylvania a mob attacked the last autonomous band of Susquehannocks, then living in Conestogatown, killing six of them. The sheriff in nearby Lancaster decided to take the rest of that Indian community into protective custody; yes, he jailed them for their own safety, but not securely enough. A surviving letter from the sheriff reports that the mob stormed the jail that night, seized the remaining fourteen members of that Indian nation, and slew them all in an act of political genocide.)

In his years at Williamsburg, Mark Hutter has portrayed James Slate as he sewed gentlemen's coats overlooking Duke of Gloucester Street and spun yarns that reconstructed the social history of this garment or that. Shortly he will have relocated to a tenant house on the edge of town as Thomas Hansford, a tailor known to have apprenticed in Williamsburg and who then did not prosper enough to leave but little trace of his later life. In this ruder setting, the tailor will carry on the tradition of the trade and sew for all, the better and the lesser sort, as he sits cross-legged on his

Few men of social standing would appear bareheaded in polite company. Wigmaking was a necessary and respected trade in Williamsburg when Virginia gentry modeled their own styles and society (rather slavishly) on the mother country's. Two centuries later, Colonial Williamsburg had to start rediscovering the subtleties of 18th-century wigmaking, a task that requires lots of human hair, and patience.

board, for it has long been known that tailors worked that way from time immemorial.

At the heart of town, silversmith James Curtis, master of the Golden Ball, plied his trade. A full-fledged product of the apprentice tradition here, he was also something of a groundbreaker, being the first African-American to become a Williamsburg tradesman in a non-domestic trade. Raised around the Tidewater, Curtis finished high school and took work where he could find it—in a pawnshop where he learned the value of anything silver that had a sterling stamp or hallmark hammered into it. He married a Williamsburg woman and planned to strike out for California when his new mother-in-law asked them to stay around town a little longer. So he took a stopgap job in the Historic Area. One thing led to another; he had a way with people and was offered an apprenticeship in the Printing Office, though setting type soon bored him. He switched to the old silversmith shop in the Golden Ball.

Curtis enjoyed working silver; he was intrigued by the near-alchemy of raising a dull metal disk into a graceful bowl simply by beating upon it very carefully with different hammers that force the metal into different shapes. In those days it was accepted practice for tradesmen to work on private projects at night. One Christmas the apprentice started making a pair of porringers for his wife, who had just delivered their second daughter. Working on his own time, he was well pleased with the little vessels when the master happened to see them. The next thing he knew, the man who supervised his work announced, "We don't make porringers like this." With that, the apprentice had to put them under the "guillotine," which chopped them into bits of scrap. It was Christmas Eve and the normally amiable Curtis would remember years later that he almost hit the man who made him do it. Returning to work after New Year's, he was assigned to make one porringer after another until they passed muster and he could raise them in his sleep. By then he knew that his first efforts were not up to snuff. He also realized the extreme demands of the apprentice tradition, which he came to believe made him the better tradesman.

In time he graduated to journeyman; the object he made to mark that giant step was a gravy boat that a visitor admired in the making and asked to buy. When he was promoted to master, he made a more difficult piece, and the same visitor bought that, too. Another time, a steady and affluent customer, a doctor who would watch Curtis work for days at a stretch, purchased all the silver on display. The price was about the equal of two master tradesmen's wages for a year.

Curtis excelled in his trade per se, and in his willing ability to explain it, thus providing the interpretation that is a part of every visitor's experience. A moonlighter in the old days, he was waiting tables at a select Colonial Williamsburg banquet when one of the guests asked Carl Humelsine how the candelabra were made; the president introduced the off-duty tradesman. Curtis delivered a brief ad hoc lecture, and when the applause died down, the guest declared that he deserved a raise so he could stop waiting on tables. In time, he got the raise and more: promotion to master, and a certain special status. When dignitaries toured the town, their carriages typically stopped at the Golden Ball to hear the old pawnbroker's especially illuminating talk about almost forgotten skills. When the honored guests retired, he would pick up his work again to raise a sterling cup upon a polished stake or planish a bowl—to gently hammer its surface almost mirror bright with blows so light that it seemed they might not break a looking-glass. Twice around the planisher precisely works the entire surface of the piece in a spiral of overlapping taps leaving marks that likewise overlap so that there are hardly any marks at all. The tempo is *andante,* the tone no louder than a fairy's drum as he beats out the timpani of the Golden Ball.

It is a tattoo that will survive him, for at the turn of the century and of the millennium, when Jimmy Curtis prepared to retire, he was succeeded by three journeymen he trained there, George

Cloyed, Preston Jones, and Gayle Clarke. George Cloyed first came to Williamsburg as a boy in elementary school, a visitor who was intrigued with how men in antique clothes made bright things. He studied metalsmithing at Carnegie-Mellon University, then came back here to work at the Golden Ball, finishing his apprenticeship under Jimmy in 1984. Preston Jones was a native of Williamsburg, and scion of a Colonial Williamsburg family, his mother having worked at the old Motor House cafeteria and his father as a landscaper at Carter's Grove. He hired on with Colonial Williamsburg as an usher in the Information Center, then went off to art school, returning to become an apprentice at the Golden Ball (about the time Cloyed was moving up a notch from apprentice to journeyman) and in due time became a journeyman himself. Gayle Clarke, the first woman to apprentice as a silversmith, started at the Golden Ball in 1978 and advanced to journeyman in 1991. Thus when one enters the silvershop and hears that gentle timpani, it is the sound of a legacy.

Other notably antique musical sounds abound in several quarters here. Twice a week at least, Bruton's nave becomes a sacred concert hall with visiting choirs and solo performers. Playing an antique harpsichord or the modern organ rebuilt in memory of Vernon Geddy, musicians are encouraged to perform music of the eighteenth century. Bruton, a living church first and a visitors' attraction second, is a proud hub of Williamsburg restored. Its dedicated choir presents period music during Sunday services and for special events, while various singers in the group also perform freelance, providing secular song around the town.

In the 1930s, Colonial Williamsburg launched a concert series that may now be the oldest of any American museum's. The Palace ballroom offered a unique opportunity that has been artfully fulfilled: to present what is now called chamber music in the kind of intimate surroundings for which it was written long before the symphony orchestra evolved. This was an art for aristocracy, a genre composed and performed by a small number of court musicians in salons for princely patrons. The instruments were typically smaller then; tuned lower than today, they thus possessed a softer sound. The violins and violas had shorter necks and were held differently than now. All these varied aspects of eighteenth-century music are respected here as modern musicians present an antique repertoire on reproduction instruments of the colonial era in the style that held sway then.

In addition to resident performers, there have been notable guests, according to James S. Darling, a Tidewater boy who grew up to be Bruton's organist and choirmaster for several decades as well as Colonial Williamsburg's consultant in antique musical matters. For one, there was the classical woodwind recital by as skilled an oboist as America then knew, a virtuoso by the name of Mitch Miller, who found broader fame by virtually inventing the sing-along. Ralph Kirkpatrick, then the premier American harpsichordist, was another unforgettable performer. But when he sat down to practice, so the story goes, he startled the staff by requesting that someone go out and shoot a crow at once. His sensitive ear told him that some plectrums used to pluck the ancient instrument's strings were broken; he needed certain quills to replace them.

The quality of Williamsburg's music has a surprising apogee—the shrill sound of martial airs performed by a Fife and Drum Corps whose clarity and precision are rare indeed. Much of the credit must go to the boys and girls themselves, many of whom start marching and piping at the age of eleven. True to eighteenth-century habit, they play the six-hole fife, not the modern eleven-hole instrument, which is fully chromatic and thus can play pieces in any key. (The old instrument is tuned to perform in the keys of G, D, A, and E.) This musical corps, which dates back to its founding in 1958 under George Carroll, found its stride with John Moon, as knowledgeable a drummer of eighteenth-century drum rolls as one could find on this side of the water.

A Canadian by birth, Moon was raised in Scotland and joined the army as a drummer boy at

James Craig is gone yet the Sign of the Golden Ball still beckons. Now its patrons include those who would purchase wares of precious metals and others who wish to watch a deft artisan raise a gravy boat from a lump of silver and cut the bowl of a spoon with a saw blade thin as a whisker.

In the Wythe House parlor the performing musicians would most likely be host and guest, as the social mores of the day required both parties to provide entertainment for each other.

the age of fourteen. Thus when he finally left the Scots Guards, this child of martial music found in Colonial Williamsburg a place to purposefully carry on the tradition—one complex of skills among many others that, were it not for Williamsburg, might have vanished from these shores to our inestimable loss. When John Moon retired, he was succeeded by William White, the first alumnus of the corps to lead it. He was succeeded in turn by Tim Sutphin, who had performed in the corps as a lad under White—and so the beat goes on.

~

Yet another trade is alive and well in Colonial Williamsburg today—that of the thespian—both on the stage and in the streets. Many kinds of conventional theatrical offerings occur on proscenium stages in the Lodge and DeWitt Wallace Decorative Arts Museum and al fresco at the theater near the Governor's Palace. Yet the most captivating acting takes place not when Williamsburg's best actors tread the boards, but when they impersonate persons of history, using trained talent, conventional stage skills and practiced gifts of improvisation. You could say that some of them are born to their parts. One, for example, is descended from a colonial governor; yet another came to play his particular role at Williamsburg by the grace of his genes: He seemed the spit and image of the man whom he first impersonated at various venues in Philadelphia during celebrations of the bicentennial of the Constitution. He was typecast because he looked so very much like surviving portraits and contemporary descriptions of the man, down to the tall stature and red hair, the colonial Virginian who knew this town man and boy, both gentleman and scholar, both revolutionary and governor: Thomas Jefferson.

Bill Barker looks like Jefferson, and to hold a conversation with him is slightly unsettling as he talks his way back and forth through time, now describing how he came here, now quoting his man at length, reciting pages-long passages from Jefferson's writings in a manner that sounds downright rhetorical, as if he were arguing with friends in the Raleigh Tavern or debating in the House of Burgesses. How can Barker justify his Virginia accent? "We know there was a southern accent," he replies, thanks to scholarly research and, among other sources, an early "talking" movie of Civil War veterans on the fiftieth anniversary of Appomattox. How can Barker reiterate Jefferson's lengthy arguments for dissolving the ties between the church in America and the Church of England? Because an act of the Virginia legislature preserves as law the words he wrote, and Barker adapts the legal statement to the context of oration or conversational discourse when circumstances require. How can this actor presume to know such details of Jefferson's private thought as his opinions of his teachers at the College of William and Mary and even the royal governors? Because he has learned much of his paradigm's autobiography by heart:

> It was my great good fortune, and what probably fixed the destinies of my life, that Dr. Wm. Small of Scotland was then professor of Mathematics [at the College], a man profound in most of the useful branches of science, with a happy talent of communication[,]correct and gentlemanly in manners, & an enlarged and liberal mind. He, most happily for me, became soon attached to me & made me his daily companion when not engaged in the school; and from his conversation I got my first views of the expansion of science & of the system of things in which we were placed. Fortunately the Philosophical chair became vacant soon after my arrival at college, and he was appointed to fill it per interim: and he was the first who ever gave in that college regular lectures in Ethics, Rhetoric & Belles lettres. He returned to Europe in 1762, having previously filled up the measure of his goodness to me, by procuring for me, from his most intimate friend G. Wythe, a reception as a student of law, and under his direction, and introduced me to the acquaintance and familiar table of Governor Fauquier, the ablest man who had ever filled that office. With him and at his table, Dr. Small & Mr. Wythe, his amici omnium horarum, & myself, formed a parti quarré, & to the habitual conversations on these occasions I owed much instruction.

OPPOSITE: Thomas Jefferson—in the 21st-century person of one Bill Barker—walks the paths of Williamsburg again. Trained as an actor, Barker played the polymath from Monticello in dialogues and skits during the bicentennial celebrations of the Constitution in Pennsylvania, then brought his persona here. It is fair to say that this magnificent imposter has read nearly all of Jefferson's surviving writings, and learned a fair amount by heart. Thus he can expound on many topics in the paradigm's own rhetoric and words. He may also engage in colloquy and even debate with curious or argumentative visitors—what actors of our time call "improv."

Barker got to Williamsburg almost by accident, but at a moment so right that it seems fated to have "probably fixed the destinies of [his] life." His father was the son of a Carolina tobacco farmer who would not return to farm life after seeing Europe in World War I, and so moved to that "northernmost southern city," Philadelphia. Young Barker, possessed of a southern sense of tradition and a Yankee upbringing, became interested in acting as an undergraduate at Villanova, then enrolled in a history graduate program at the University of Pennsylvania—while working in local theater as an actor and director. Having earned his Actors Equity card, he was hired by agents to play Jefferson in skits and sketches at various patriotic venues—often opposite a Benjamin Franklin impersonator—during the period of the Constitution Bicentennial. There were so many of these staged presentations that he no longer remembers his first gig as Jefferson, only that by 1993 he was touring farther from home as the Founding Father. During an engagement at the Jefferson Hotel in Richmond, the hotel manager suggested he go visit Williamsburg, and so the next day he drove east on a lark, arriving on a Friday afternoon without an appointment, let alone an introduction. Intrigued by what he saw of the place, he sought an interview and found himself facing a Historic Area administrator who had only a few minutes to see him before going to a long-scheduled meeting—on the subject of "who we are going to hire to be Thomas Jefferson." The administrator did not need to look further: He was looking at him.

Seven years later and counting, Bill Barker was still playing Jefferson, again in various settings—in set pieces of dramatic dialogue at the Capitol with other interpreters, on tour as one of Colonial Williamsburg's prime ambassadors, and as a solo act in the Historic Area where he can stand up and engage a crowd of twentieth-century folk on almost any eighteenth-century subject. Barker as Jefferson will discourse against the importation of slaves . . . on the shortcomings of primogeniture and entail . . . on improvements for the curriculum at the College . . . on his idea of instituting three years of compulsory education for every child in Virginia. He will expound on the evils of slavery —though he believed he could not afford financially to flaunt the system while he lived and freed only five of his human possessions upon his death. If asked about the apparent contradiction of morally disapproving slavery yet owning slaves himself and evidently even loving Sally Hemings, he avoids the question by saying it is a private matter. (Nonetheless as Jefferson, Barker knows that a "Mr. Cock," who once dined at Jefferson's table, recorded that the serving girl clearly appeared to be his offspring.)

Barker takes special pleasure in presenting the anti-establishmentarian views of the author of "the Statute of Virginia for religious freedom" (as his epitaph describes him). In part, it is because matters of religion are the most popular subject, to judge by the questions he is asked by visitors. Thus Barker-Jefferson lectures on the "separation *between* church and state," and quotes the aforementioned statute verbatim. It is part of his special magic and, he says, the cause of the most alarming outbursts of opposition he has ever faced from visitors. As he lectured in the Courthouse one day, a fundamentalist couple nearly lost control. "They shouted that I should not speak of religious toleration in front of innocent children," and held newspapers before their faces so as not to see the man they evidently thought was Lucifer; Barker feared they might get violent.

Bill Barker is only the most instantly recognized of the costumed character interpreters strolling through the town. There are others ahorseback, representing the land surveyors who marked the boundaries of the 1760s frontier in the government's vain hope of barring settlers from moving west and clashing with Indians or French. There are slaves taking their leisure behind the Raleigh Tavern and reflecting on the personalities and weaknesses of their masters. There is an evangelical black minister preaching the salvation of Jesus Christ to anyone who will listen. There are gentlemen with

Martha Washington—or a remarkable facsimile thereof—finds a moment's calm to read her prayer book behind a proscenium of boxwood bushes. Her "interpreter" in modern parlance is Mary Wiseman, a veteran of 20-odd years at Williamsburg, where she has played innumerable roles, both in scripted plays on formal stages and in the spontaneous dialogue with visitors who are most often surprised and honored to meet a mother of our country.

their ladies come to the capital for Publick Times. There is a particular lady of gentle mien and prosperous means: Mary Wiseman speaking of her documented life to callers in the words of Martha Custis Washington. Like Barker, she has read widely and deeply about her character—studied biographies and monographs about the period and surviving letters and accounts by acquaintances. She has committed to memory long passages of borrowed prose and original material—all in the first person—to be delivered to a group of visitors as intimately as one's confidences to an old friend.

Thus when a historical personage faces modern visitors, the interpreter has a wealth of material to draw from, whether in monologue or in spontaneous response to a question from the crowd, sometimes even engaging in long conversation or seeming argument. These historical performers are all trained actors, yet all must be historians as well. As they encounter ad hoc audiences in the streets and lanes and parlors, the visitors confront them in many ways. The visitors demand of them all manner of facts and opinions; in response they must be as spontaneous as jugglers and as articulate as lawyers. Thus through training and practice, Ms. Wiseman and the others have become adept at assuming a second skin, appearing as a colonial person and, like as not, even thinking like one.

Thus this other living trade plied at Colonial Williamsburg is a hybrid as native as the mild tobacco that was once this country's pride. It blends historical study, sociological interpretation, cabaret improvisation and, yes, acting as persuasive as on any stage. Its purposes, like that of theatrical acting, are variously to amuse the audience and to entertain, to trouble the auditors and sometimes to move them to tears, to divert and to educate those people present, and to illuminate times past—and all of this in the cause of bringing a foregone century to life before our eyes for our deeper understanding of our origins.

More than three hundred years after its founding—more than four lifetimes ago—Williamsburg blends yore with now: On a winter night the town looks deserted. A pale moon rises behind the Capitol to shine down the frosted empty street. At our end of town almost every house is dark, and even the taverns are closed. Listen to the only sound: my footsteps. Anthony Hay's shop is empty, like the Printing Office, and Peyton Randolph's clapboard home. Then, across the green the mist grows bright and the Courthouse rises like an ark, its fogged windows ablaze. Inside seven men sit on the dais before an audience of peers discussing the rights of men and law—a panel debate for public television.

By winter's day artisans ply their trades before blazing hearths and forges, though few visitors feel the welcome warmth in this slow season. The only person in modern dress may be a convention delegate skipping a session at the Conference Center, until the Antiques Forum brings a flurry of collectors. Then spring steals in with crocuses; the Garden Symposium brings another eager throng by lambing time. The redbud gives way to blizzards of dogwood blooms and the ghostly mantle of shadbush trees.

The days grow bright with birds and endlessly loud with song: cardinals, goldfinches, buntings bluer than any sky, and quick-tailed mockingbirds capable of singing all night long from treetop or chimney pot to claim a place and lure a mate. Pigeons roost in niches between offset chimneys and eighteenth-century walls. Flights of Canada geese follow the rivers north and mallards settle down in the ponds below the Inn, finding spots to brood among the water plants. Two mute swans circle the tiny swamp near Carter's Grove, hissing to defend their young, while herons and egrets dot the marshes. Starlings nest in putlog holes and sparrows in bird bottles. Starlings and sparrows? They played no part in any ancient cycle here! However natural and familiar these speckled birds may seem, they were not in these trees when Nicholson laid out the town or Colonel Washington took his first command. A century ago some New Yorker stocked Central Park with all the birds Shakespeare called by name; every species perished save two that adapted with a vengeance and spread across America. As English immigrants displaced Powhatan's people, so these pests pushed native birds aside. Man was not the only European invader to seize a Tidewater domain.

Honeybees, another immigrant breed, haunt the gardens near the Raleigh by the Ides of April. Their sound dies down over the length of days, and then they come again to make our basswood tree a symphony of humming. To stand beneath its little-blossomed limbs is to be surrounded by a gentle din. Quieter are the flights of native hummingbirds sipping the nectar of trumpet vines suspended in midair. Mark Catesby, who painted them for his volume on natural history, saw them drink so deep they were caught within the crimson blooms.

As summer settles in, people, too, add myriad sounds. The town awakes soon after dawn as cleaning crews make their sweeps. Hear the slap-slap of runners' feet (undergrads jogging from the college like as not); hear shopgirls in long dresses greet each other and the shepherdess drive her bleating flock from the sheepfold to a lea. Once schools let out the martial boys return of a sudden each morning with fifes and drums to pace off along what some irreverently call "D. O. G. Street" or "The Duke." They march down Duke of Gloucester to the rolling thunder of snares and the bright airs

OPPOSITE: Heralding the day, slatted blinds in the stylish Thomas Everard House admit sunlight although they could block it out almost totally. Builders of the 18th century were acutely interested in the practical manipulation of light; thus the invention of the dormer! Whereas a window set in a flat wall admits light straight into the room, a window set in a dormer does that and more. Painted white, the sides of a dormer reflect the incoming light, thereby amplifying it and broadening its reach within the room.

of "Roast Beef" and "The King of Denmark." Visitors collect along the way, and minutes later the militia flies the colors to a cannon's clamor. When morning has officially begun, some fifers disperse to spend the day employed around the town in antique garb, just playing solo airs and brightening the scene with music.

The Golden Ball and the milliner's shop next door to my all-too-brief abode open at nine o'clock to throngs of families, school groups, white-haired couples holding hands, women in shorts, men in mottoed caps. They chatter, of course, and the words drift in through windows that edge the street. The sounds must resemble Publick Times (lacking pigs and geese perhaps) with only the diction changed, the din made livelier by a lad in knee breeches playing his piccolo on the steps of Brick House Tavern and the clop-clop of horse-drawn carriages.

In June the cherries appear, both sweet and sour, brightening the trees behind the Unicorn's Horn like clusters of Christmas treats. They first emerge as little green knobs that harden and grow, then turn full-sized buff yellow in a day. The yellow seems to brighten, then the next day it is red—but only for another day or two. As quickly as it ripens, the fruit begins to rot and squirrels make a feast. Beyond Wythe's garden the flax begins to bloom, its tiny blossoms opening wide at dawn, fringing this ethereal grass with palest blue that fades toward noon as the little flowers fold and close.

The cotton in the field near the old brick kilns raises broad, dark green leaves, another crop for the weavers to think about once they have reaped the flax and shorn the sheep. In July the fireworks draw hordes to gaze at rockets glaring red and white and blue for one brief night. Crepe myrtles color the edge of Market Square and almost every yard with every hue of red. Robertson's Windmill's white canvas sails spin in the wind to grind new grain. Wetherburn's apricots come in rock-hard with velvet skins, and round plump yellow plums in the little orchard opposite the Church beg to be picked, and are. . . .

As evenings fall you must blink to make certain of the century; then a streetlight proves the date.

But the years blur again with the colonial fair, when Market Square becomes a festival and companies of militia from throughout the erstwhile colonies camp upon this green. A few hundred strong—plus complements of families—they muster, march, practice the ancient manual at arms, and display their shooting skills to cloud the autumn air with the rancid smoke of black powder like the stuff that Dunmore stole. Their women cook on open fires; their babies crawl happily about in linen shifts.

Inevitably, in a place as busy as this, the old town's denizens encounter uninvited guests along with expected company. On one occasion, a group failed to observe the discreet sign "Private Residence" because they spoke no English. A local lad left the door unlatched and his mother looked up from housework only to find a score of Japanese tourists photographing her reconstructed hall and parlor. "This is my house!" she exclaimed. They lowered their cameras, made steeples with their fingers and bowed graciously. "This is my kitchen!" she explained as the ladies from the East ran their fingers over the porcelain, wondering at the ancient ways of the mysterious West. After they had toured the entire downstairs, murmuring musically, they all bowed again, expressed their great pleasure at having been so honored and went on their way to lunch.

At a much earlier hour one long ago Sunday, Carl Humelsine fetched the papers and hatched a myth bound to mushroom through the years. As the story is told, he fixed a breakfast tray, complete with a rose in a bud vase, and carried it up to his awakening wife. Relishing their sunny Sabbath peace upstairs they suddenly noticed a family of four at the bedroom door. Humelsine did not get where he got by being slow of foot or tongue. "May I show you this historic house?" he asked bounding out of bed again. "This is the master bedroom, as you can see. And this handsome staircase is original, dating from the eighteenth century." The foursome nodded and gawked as they

ABOVE: Buildings designed to serve as shops were often built with their narrow dimension to the street. Among other things this allowed lot owners to subdivide their properties and develop them more densely. Exposure to the street was money in a merchant's pocket, as a window allowed a display of wares to be found inside—as here in the Milliner's Shop on Duke of Gloucester Street.

OPPOSITE: The ancient town has rhythms of its own in the roll of martial drum and the ringing clash of sabers swung in anger—all only remembered in the peace of a muster by a reenactment regiment come to camp on Palace green.

followed him downstairs, the smallest son testing the balustrade with a drumstick to find it less resonant than a picket fence. "The passage would have seen many a minuet two centuries ago," the instant guide continued. "But as you know, Blackbeard's pirates went to the gallows from the Gaol just down the hill to your right." He opened the door and the boy led his family out into the sunshine, quickened by the prospect of a hanging. The pajamaed president closed the door behind them without another word. This time he locked it.

Perennial residents have fonder tales of visitors, at Christmastimes, for instance, when all Historic Area tenants decorate their doorways on Grand Illumination morning. Some visitors come every year to see the garlands before the colors fade or before the birds peck the wreathes (and, if the weather is warm, get falling-down drunk on fermented fruit). For thirteen years the mistress of one house was attended in her decorating tasks by a Scottish terrier named Flora, who predictably got older and older. Then one year as the lady arranged an apple wreath, she heard herself addressed by a woman about her own middle-age, whom she thought a stranger. "Where's Flora?" the visitor asked, and upon hearing that the dog had died, offered sincere condolences. The news saddened her, for she felt herself a member of Williamsburg's family—if only for one day each year.

The doorway decorating is part of an annual competition in which cash and ribbon prizes are awarded for the most pleasing decorations that reflect eighteenth-century style and taste. Beyond that, there is just one rule: Only materials *available to* colonial Virginians may be used, not that they would decorate this way or waste a precious pineapple on a door. Thus the houses bear garlands of apples, rings of lemons and oranges, clusters of sickle pears. There are pinecones, sprigs of boxwood and fir, sprays of bayberry, ropes of cedar, burst cotton bolls flashing silver linings, rosettes of flowering kale, rainbows of pomegranates, persimmons, kumquats. Some doors boast escutcheons of crab carapaces, oyster shells and wreaths of guinea feathers.

These decorations represent part of a brilliant and necessary compromise for modern Williamsburg, which gives up its insistence on accuracy for the season. Our eighteenth-century cousins did not

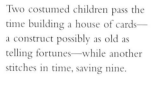

Two costumed children pass the time building a house of cards— a construct possibly as old as telling fortunes—while another stitches in time, saving nine.

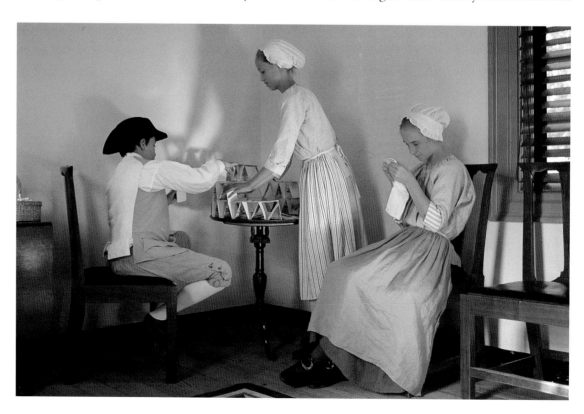

much celebrate the Yuletide; the first Christmas tree was trimmed in 1842 by a professor at the college, a refugee who brought the custom with him from Germany and bedecked the parlor at St. George Tucker's house. Philip Fithian, who tutored Robert Carter's children before the Revolution, recorded that he gave the house boy "half a bit" at Christmas. So much for presents. On the day of the Nativity, George Washington "went to church and home for dinner." So much for special feasts. Less lofty people made a habit of firing guns in noisy witness of the holy birth, according to some antique accounts. But today folk of all faiths (or none) expect to practice contemporary customs.

The holiday season is one of the busiest times of year here and Colonial Williamsburg encourages people to feel at home. Rather than stick to the stoicism of colonial Christmas traditions, the establishment brightens the calendar with extra attractions, many of them the kinds of entertainments that colonists favored on special days at any time of year, such as coronations, royal birthdays or welcomes for new governors. For decades modern visitors marched in torchlit parades, until these became too popular for safety along the uneven cobbles in the dark of night. There are feasts and games, outdoor fairs, concerts in Capitol and Palace, the ways lit with flaming cressets and a "Grand Illumination" in which a white candle (albeit electric) burns in every window. These are "vignettes of colonial activity from other festive times of year," said retired senior executive Peter A. G. Brown, for many years the self-styled overseer of "wreath-making and elf work."

Of course, Bruton Parish Church is a focal point. In living memory, one Christmas Eve service by candlelight was enough for all. But just the local parishioners now number twice the church's capacity; it takes five services Christmas Eve and four on Christmas to accommodate the throngs. A longtime rector felt Bruton satisfied a special need during the season. The flock embraces people who want or need to be away from home for Christmas: couples whose children have left the nest, the recently bereaved, broken families, and whole ones wanting a resort holiday. All are welcome, and Bruton is bedecked for the occasion with garlands, its bright brass gleaming like gold in the candlelight. The choirmaster chooses music of the period: "Adeste Fideles" transcribed in 1740–43, songs from Handel's *Messiah* and such. The texts are older, from King James's Bible, the version published in 1611, the year after "starving time" was done and Virginia seemed likely to survive. "And in the sixth month the angel Gabriel was sent from God unto a city in Galilee named Nazareth to a virgin espoused to a man whose name was Joseph, of the house of David. And the virgin's name was Mary." The gentle words resound; it might be Christmas of any year.

In Bruton Parish Church, the aisle runs straight as a virtue between box pews that bear the names of famous patriots— men who might have prayed therein for all we can tell.

For half of December the Inn is full and every tavern table booked. Around the town bonfires of four-foot logs laid log-cabin style brighten each night and provide the light for caroling, the singing of songs that colonists did not know. There are plays, all sorts of evening goings-on like dances at the Capitol, and at-homes at Carter's Grove. Then by New Year's Day the visitors go home, and the village seems to sleep.

Those privileged to live or linger here find their lives enriched. The first word my little son ever said without prompting was "moon" as he pointed from my arms to the yellow orb rising behind the Magazine's pointed roof. His second word was "boom" at the sound of cannon. For town tots there's nothing strange about kind ladies in long dresses and men in buckled shoes and Sampson's ox cart; nor about scrambling in the perfect playground of Bruton's churchyard with its iconed obstacles of hoary tombs.

Since we lived here, the DeWitt Wallace Decorative Arts Museum has opened, as have the new wing of the Abby Aldrich Rockefeller Folk Art Museum and the Winthrop Rockefeller Archaeology Museum at Carter's Grove, testament to Noël Hume and the struggles of Wolstenholme Towne. Since we left, the St. George Tucker House, lifelong home of Dr. Janet Kimbrough, became,

EPILOGUE: SOJOURN IN AN ANTIQUE PLACE 299

upon her death, a hospitality house for donors to Colonial Williamsburg. And what a chain of history that brings to an end: Janet Kimbrough was the daughter of George P. Coleman, a state highway department functionary and namesake of the Coleman Bridge at Yorktown. He was the son of Cynthia Beverley Tucker Coleman, co-founder of the Association for the Preservation of Virginia Antiquities, which purchased the old Powder Magazine to save it from destruction, and which buried the foundations of the old Capitol building to save its hallowed bricks from scavengers. Cynthia Coleman's father, Nathaniel Tucker, a lawyer and judge, was the son of St. George Tucker, the Bermuda native who succeeded George Wythe at the College of William and Mary; having come to Williamsburg to study law, he bought the house in 1788.

Since my family and I lived here, the Courthouse on Market Square has been thoroughly restored, the old Victorian house close by the Capitol has been moved, and its site excavated to reveal Charlton's Coffeehouse. The footprint of the Hallam Theater has been found at last, east of the Capitol. In coming years—presumably before another revised edition of this book appears—the venerable Williamsburg Inn will be entirely renovated; the Williamsburg Lodge and Conference Center will follow suit. The entire Visitor Center complex, including the Cascades and Woodlands Hotel, will be rebuilt as well. The Hallam Theater site, already under excavation, will be entirely dug to reveal its theatrical and historical secrets. Is it too much to hope that it will be reconstructed as well? Ditto the coffee house?

In the Golden Ball, children still get to hold the hammers that Preston Jones, once an apprentice smith and long since a journeyman, gently wields to turn flat metal into sterling bowls. They still watch with awe as a new apprentice pumps the bellows to turn the coal fire's flames pale green, and clap their hands to see the journeyman pour liquid silver to make a solid sterling ingot in an instant. Yes, the present tense applies; these tasks are plied in an endless chain of time as if then and tomorrow are all todays.

Deft-fingered women taught my wife to stitch sylvan scenes in silken yarns and brighten our home away from Williamsburg with stenciled cloths and handiworks that reflect more patient arts than most folks practice now. Bruton's music master let me join the vested choir in procession down the ancient aisle of well-worn ledger stones that bear the names of those who lived and listened here centuries ago. Music's meaning rings more clearly in a place like this, as if the walls that Nicholson raised and Goodwin restored somehow resonate more truly for their very age. Yet music is art of the moment; you cannot touch its sheen nor hang its motifs upon a parlor wall. It echoes and is gone—until like voices raise its strains again, as we so often sing tunes of the Founding Fathers' time, and read their names on pews and know this place will last beyond our passing.

Like those who come here for just a few brief days, like friends who spend their lives working at manifold tasks in this antique town, we have been changed by the gentle pace; by the evening strolls to the Capitol and back with older neighbors who matched their pace to our toddling boy's; by the shade of live oaks and the shades of folk like Peter Pelham and Christiana Campbell. We have dined by candlelight in the room where addled Lucy Paradise used to sup; we have debated the little issues like "Should the pillory be moved?" and the greater ones such as, "Was the war that started here a revolution—did it make things really change?" We've stood where Patrick Henry walked, and sat beneath the oak adored by Rockefeller, and wondered, amazed, that a country parson was possessed to resurrect a town that was and never was and ever more shall be, in memory of a nation's lost and legendary birth.

In sum, just as when I first came to know this antique place ten and six years ago, so be it still today: I am perplexed and glad that Williamsburg abides.

In colonial times, generations before "the rocket's red glare" became an American icon, fireworks brightened the night over Williamsburg on many festive occasions: to celebrate the births of princes, the coronations of kings, the coming of new governors. Now at the dawning of the new millennium such soaring displays continue— to mark Independence Day, the coming of Christmas and other such events. So as it was, it is, and yet will be again in the bright shining skies at Colonial Williamsburg.

ACKNOWLEDGMENTS

Borrowing a precedent, that the last shall be first, let me thank those at Colonial Williamsburg whose efforts were crucial in bringing out this revised edition at the dawn of the new millennium. Joseph N. Rountree, director of publications, bore an astonishing burden as he provided manifold liaison for both the author and publisher, in particular mustering interpreters, curators, researchers and support staff; arranging endless logistics, and enabling for new photography. Linda Rowe, a senior historian, reread the original edition's text and captions with a critical eye in order to flag statements that had become moot or inaccurate with the passage of time; then she answered my innumerable questions, generously offering the subtlety and sensitivity of her encyclopedic knowledge of Virginia history. Cary Carson, vice president for research and now a CW executive with one of the longest tenures, offered invaluable advice and perspective as well. I thank these three in particular for contributions of incalculable value.

In addition, it was my pleasure to connect again with a number of old friends who abide at Williamsburg or nearby: John and Scottie Austin, Sue Rountree, Barbara Carson, Marley Brown, Charles Driscoll, Jock Darling, and my former neighbors at the Golden Ball, former apprentice Preston Jones (now a journeyman), former journeyman George Cloyed (now a master silversmith), and Doc Hassell, who still carves the runcible spoons with such exquisite delicacy.

Needless to say, the Williamsburg roster had changed considerably in the years between my first sojourn there in 1984 and the several visits I made in 2000. In particular, Ronald Hurst had risen from furniture curator to vice president for Collections and Museums and chief curator, Richard McCluney from a filmmaker to director of Colonial Williamsburg productions. Yet in those years some people who held the same jobs as before had transformed their venues and made Williamsburg a better museum in the process, witness Richard Nicoll, whose Coach and Livestock operation has become a model of national renown.

For the revision, it was reassuring to find some familiar faces in similar roles as they had played before: Mary Wiseman, Lew LeCompte, Jim and Pam Pettengell. I also benefitted from time spent with a number of individuals I had not met before, such as acting director of the Rockefeller Library, Mary Haskell, and the incomparable Bill Barker a.k.a. Tom Jefferson.

To all these Williamsburg folk, I express warm appreciation for their knowledge and assistance. And to my wife, Mary, and son, Tim, I say thanks again and again for their patience during my absences from home.

Finally, I salute new colleagues at the publishing house of Harry N. Abrams, namely the brilliant editors Elaine Stainton and Karyn Gerhard, gifted young designer Brankica Kovrlija, and especially the visionary vice president and managing editor, Margaret Rennolds Chace. Thank you all.

And now that the first may be last, let us recall the debts of gratitude incurred in the making of this book's first edition:

Vice-president Richard A. Schreiber, who championed the idea of cooperating with an outsider, suggested I live in the town and arranged for me to rent the Unicorn's Horn. My first host and frequent facilitator, Dick maintained a shrewd and friendly interest in the project. I thank him for his counsel and for the countless courtesies that he and his wife, Lynn, extended. Colonial Williamsburg's other officers from President Charles R. Longsworth down cooperated unstintingly. Senior vice-president Robert C. Birney, chief curator Graham Hood. Resident architect Nicholas A. Pappas, Historic Area programs and operations executive Dennis A. O'Toole and research director Cary Carson opened their doors—and their departments—whenever I knocked. Former chairman and president emeritus Carlisle H. Humelsine generously shared his deep knowledge, rich recollections and unique experience.

My special tutors in the mysteries of historical re-creation, preservation and administration were ceramics curator John Austin, martial musician John C. Moon, historian Patricia A. Gibbs, picture archivist Patricia Maccubbin, senior executives Roger F. H. Leclere and Peter A. G. Brown, publications boss Joseph Rountree. Others who most generously shared their knowledge include furniture expert Wallace Gusler, tools curator Jay Gaynor, fund-raiser Forrest Williamson, metals curator John D. Davis, historian Linda Rowe, cooper George Pettengell, historical architect Travis McDonald, hotelier James C. Miles, silversmith Jimmy Curtis, wheelwright Dan Stebbins, blacksmith Peter Ross, Lodge factotum Peggy Greene. Retired vice-president of architecture A. Edwin Kendrew's canny recollections of the Restoration's early years added greatly to my view of the recent past.

Other Colonial Williamsburg employees who helped in memorable ways, large and small, include media manager Denise Adams, secretary Sally Barnes, editor Wayne Barrett, textiles curator Linda Baumgarten, vice-president Norman Beatty, metals founder Dan Berg and his wife, librarian Susan Berg, archivist Bland Blackford, cooking mistress Rosemary Brandau, publicist Susan Bruno, gunsmith Gary Brumfield, reproductions creator Gail Burger, upholsterer Gene Burleson, archival sleuth Pat Butler, bookstore manager Delois Campas, architectural historian Edward Chappell, horticulturist Gordon Chappell, journeyman silversmith George Cloyed, Wallace Gallery director Wendy Cooper, marketing master Hugh DeSamper, leather-crafter Irvin Diehl, wizard secretary Fredericka Dooley, archaeological field boss Andrew Edwards, executive D. Stephen Elliott, folk dramatist Rex Ellis, designer Diana Freedman, facilities and property management director William Gardiner, second-generation board member Vernon Geddy Jr., trades historian Harold Gill, retired executive Donald Gonzales, associate ceramics curator Leslie Grigsby, library director Pearce Grove, engineer Will Gwilliam, drama director John Hamant, Inn manager Bruce Hearn, wigmaker Joyce Hedgepeth, Lodge manager James Hisle, furniture curator Ronald Hurst, special collections curator John Ingram, apprentice silversmith Preston Jones, architectural librarian Mary Keeling, historian Kevin Kelly, master of many trades Lew LeCompte, our neighbors Tom and Louise Limerick, buildings historian Carl Lounsbury, Folk Art Center curator Barbara Luck, horticulturist Richard Mahone, filmmaker Richard McCluney, secretary Margaret Miller, special events troubleshooter Trudy Moyles, secretary Dianne Murray, archaeologist Ivor Noël Hume, landscape architect Donald Parker, master printer Willie Parker, mistress of protocol Kathleen Pickering, prints and maps curator Margaret Pritchard, secretary Sonnie Rose, vice- president Beatrix Rumford, Motor House manager James Ryan, secretary Patricia Schell, executive secretary Joyce Seaman, secretary Emily Seats, crafts program director Earl Soles, director of museum services Edward Spencer and his wife, secretary to the president Emily Spencer, domestic arts mistress Mary Stebbins, calligrapher Richard Stinely, vice-president F. Roger Thaler, carpenter Roy Underhill, landlady Peg Waite, architectural historian Mark Wenger, weaving mistress Marilyn Wetton, fife and drum director William White, secretary Mary Jean Wilson, actress Mary Wiseman, illustrator Vernon Wooten, travel marketing veteran George Wright, historian Shomer Zwelling.

Staff historians provided useful advice and read the text for accuracy in matters of "historical fact." (Obviously any remaining errors are mine.) John Hemphill II and Lou Powers brought the standards of their discipline to bear and I thank them for their candid comments and friendly help ante-factum.

People outside Colonial Williamsburg's official pale added substantial lore, especially two members of the Goodwin family, who showed great generosity of spirit: Rutherfoord's widow, Mary Randolph Mordecai Goodwin, and his thoughtful brother, Howard Goodwin. Bruton Parish was also a source of wonder, in the form of three persons: now retired rector, the Reverend Cotesworth Pinkney Lewis; former curate, the Right Reverend John T. Bentley; music director James S. Darling, who let me sing in his famous choir. Life tenant Dr. Janet Kimbrough and life resident Judge Robert T. Armistead provided valuable insights from special vantage points.

At the college of William and Mary, president Thomas A. Graves Jr., librarian Clifford Currie and manuscripts and rare books curator Margaret Cook opened their facilities. Scholar Thad Tate gave sound historical guidance. At the State Department, White House curator Clement Conger and deputy chief of protocol Timothy Towell provided expertise. Members of the cofounder's family graciously shared their views: Mrs. John D. Rockefeller 3rd, Laurance Rockefeller and longtime board member Abby O'Neill. Rockefeller Archive Center director Joseph Ernst provided useful documents.

I am also pleased to thank Abrams editor Sheila Franklin Lieber for her unwavering attention and thoughtful commitment, art director Samuel N. Antupit for his inspired design and good-humored patience and photographer Langdon Clay for his superb pictures. Without these three, the book simply would not be what it is. And it would never have gotten to the printer without the tireless layout work of Doris Leath.

Page numbers in *italics* indicate illustrations.

Houses are listed under the last rather than first name of the identifying owner or family.

Williamsburg (*see also* more specific topics): Act establishing, 41–3; aerial view in 1927, 146, *147*; backwater, time as, 28, 113–21, 141; Colonial times, during, 41–51, 65–96, 98; corporations and foundations, 31–2, 153, 203; early Virginia settlements prefiguring, 19–23; Graham drawing, *118–19, 119*; legislature moved from Jamestown to, 25, 38, 41, 45; legislature moved to Richmond from, 28, 108, 113; Middle Plantation, 23, 25, 32, 37, 40; modern management and development of, 191–211; museums, *see* museums and collections; naming of, 25; planning, design, and layout of, 41–7, 49–51; prosperity in 18th century, 72, 83; public buildings, first construction of, 49–63; public records burnt, 29–31, 204; purchase of, 142–50; restoration of, *see* restoration project; Revolution in, 26–8, 96–109; seal of, *158, 158–63*; secret restoration plan, period of, 141–50; town officials, negotiations with, 149–50
Williamsburg style, influence of, 179
Wilson, Douglas, 241
Wilson, Richard, 101
windmill, 13, *207, 217,* 226, 294
winters of 1983 and 1998, 210
Winthrop Rockefeller Archaeology Museum, 297
Wiseman, Mary, 291, *291*
Wolstenholme Towne, 22, 297
women in Colonial times, 22, 89, 207
Wood, Garland, *272*
Woods, Col. Arthur, 133, 153, 163, 165, 194
woodworking, *216, 270,* 271, *272, 273*
Wren, Sir Christopher, and Wren Building, 41, 45, 51, *52, 53,* 134,

135, 148, 149, 164, *168, 169,* 176–8, 234
Wythe, George, 81, 99, 108, 113, 114, 144, 148, 239, 252, 254, 289, 300
Wythe House and garden, 9, *11,* 13, *80,* 81, *81,* 91, *92, 93, 108,* 135, *140,* 141–3, *142, 143, 162,* 196, *202,* 203, 226, *287,* 294

Y

York County Project, 203–4
Yorktown: Battle of, 108, *108*; historical site, 170

Z

Zoffany, John, 16
zoning codes, 43, 173, 175
Zwelling, Shomer, 113